Nasty Girls, Thugs, and Humans Like Us

Social Relations between Severely Disabled and Nondisabled Students in High School

by

Carola Murray-Seegert, Ph.D.

The Frankfurt American High School
Frankfurt, Federal Republic of Germany

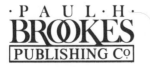

·P·A·U·L·H·
BROOKES
PUBLISHING CO.

Baltimore • London • Toronto • Sydney

205757

Paul H. Brookes Publishing Co.
P.O. Box 10624
Baltimore, Maryland 21285-0624

Typeset by Brushwood Graphics, Inc., Baltimore, Maryland.
Manufactured in the United States of America by
Thomson-Shore, Inc., Dexter, Michigan.

This work was partially supported by U.S. Office of Education Contract
No. 300-82-0365 to San Francisco State University. The content, however, does not necessarily reflect the position or policy of the USOE, and
no official endorsement of these materials is implied.

Library of Congress Cataloging-in-Publication Data

Murray-Seegert, Carola, 1947–
Nasty girls, thugs, and humans like us : Social relations between severely
disabled and nondisabled students in high school / by Carola Murray-
Seegert.
    p.   cm.
  Bibliography: p.
  Includes index.
  ISBN 1-55766-024-7
    1. Handicapped youth—Education (Secondary)—United
States. 2. Mainstreaming in education—United States. 3. High
school students—United States. 4. Interpersonal relations. I. Title.
LC4031.M87 1989
371.9′0973—dc19
                               89-737
                               CIP

contents

foreword

We are a nation of plumbers. As a people, we Americans tend to approach life as if it were a complicated hydraulic structure that constantly springs leaks all over the place which must be fixed. Seldom do we question the adequacy, let alone the function, of the structure itself. Our tendency is rather to wage war on it. We have war on poverty, war on drugs, war on crime, war on AIDS, etc., etc. We win pitched battles in these various wars, but we always find ourselves losing the wars themselves.

As we mature as a nation, we increasingly find that there are people in our various fields of endeavor who are not so inclined to wage war on our problems, to fix the various leaks that spring up across our creaking structure, but who would rather suggest a different course of action. Often, such people are "internationalist" in their perspective. They have been around a bit, and have examined our social "problems" from the perspectives of both insider and outsider. Carola Murray-Seegert is without question one of these people.

As a young doctoral candidate, Carola could have identified any number of problems (leaks) in the process of integrating students with severe intellectual disabilities into a public high school and designed an appropriate intervention to solve the problem. A carefully controlled study of the remedy in action would have made a perfectly acceptable dissertation, and our base of scientific knowledge of the evolution of social processes would have been enhanced. But she chose, rather forcefully at that, not to attack a problem, but rather to seek a better understanding of the structure itself—to ask, "What causes these leaks?"

There may be a trend emerging in special education toward studies of this type. If so, it is a very encouraging sign, for contemporary educational (and psychological) theory has generated little to get excited about in recent years. My colleagues and I have argued elsewhere (Sailor, Goetz, Anderson, Hunt, & Gee, 1988) that the prevalent behavioral paradigm in special education has pretty much played itself out. Many phenomena that we observe in education research seem to require a more complex paradigm, one that provides a more extensive framework of motivation than can be encompassed by simple reinforcement principles. Such statements, however, do not sit well with educational behaviorists. As did psychoanalysis in the 1950s, current behavioral theory purports to encompass all observable phenomena in education and thus to explain everything (e.g., Cuvo, 1989). It may be that the last vestiges of a dying paradigm are its claims to encompass (postdict) all phenomena in the field that it formerly guided.

New methodologies do not win acceptance in established disciplines without resistance. For instance, reviews of recent books on "qualitative" research methods, such as the development of ethnographic models, have conveyed a tone of benign indifference. Carola's own efforts to use a methodology more common to anthropologists than to educators encountered some obstacles in the beginning. One university advisor was heard to exclaim, "There has to be more to a dissertation study than standing around a schoolyard watching the kids go by!"

Certainly, as readers of this book will soon discover, there is much more than that to Carola's study. Properly done ethnographic studies, such as this one, are a blend of science and art. Observations are conducted in a rigorous manner with interpretative processes woven into the method rather than growing out of it. The richness of detail conveyed in this sort of study is unmatched in any other kind of educational research. And that richness, growing out of a highly creative yet equally systematic observational approach, is what makes a study of this type so valuable.

Carola's study, as is usually the case in ethnographic research, is hypothesis-generating rather than hypothesis-testing. At a time when current theory seems bereft of fruitful hypotheses, ethnographic studies offer the challenge of new interpretations. What current paradigm would, for example, have predicted that nondisabled high school students would experience positive academic and social outcomes as a result of having students with severe intellectual disabilities introduced into their social milieux? Carola's study suggests that such a hypothesis is worthy of empirical investigation. If substantiated, such a finding would do much to dispel resistance to special education integration efforts at the secondary level that is based on the fear that these efforts would compete with desired outcomes for regular students.

Our society places an enormous burden of expectation on our high schools. As we struggle to become an egalitarian and pluralistic society, we rely on the high school as a foundation of support. When this evolutionary process falters, as in our present time, the educational system is blamed, and calls for "reform" are in the air. But how can we reform something we understand so little?

Polls of the attitudes of college students are suggestive of the re-emergence of values that are reminiscent of the 1950s. Students are more interested in consumer goods than in social justice and equality. Racist values seem to be reappearing after decades of progress in civil rights. Staggering numbers of high school students never complete the requirements for a diploma. In some high schools in California, considered by many our most progressive state, fewer than 50% of entering ninth graders graduate. Drug abuse is everywhere on high school campuses, and even athletes, so revered by younger children, are caught up in substance abuse problems.

Does Carola's study have anything to say about all this? The infusion of students with severe disabilities into an inner-city high school has at least the potential to reveal something of how a particular kind of community, one whose members are at a particularly intense period in their development, adjust to change. On reading Carola's study, one is struck by the patterns of social organization that characterize the school.

Social enclaves are everywhere in the school, organized seemingly around language groups rather than social identity, and the psychological battles for turf are fascinating. Where do people with little or no linguistic ability and severe intellectual disability fit into such a system? Above all, how does the system react and what new patterns emerge over time as this unusual new group insinuates itself into life on campus? Carola's observations on the processes shed much light on the nature of social integration and acceptance as it occurs in a high school, and for this reason her study has implications far beyond the boundaries of special education. The richness of the hypotheses that have emerged from this significant study may contribute much in the long run to the development of some much-needed new theory in education. Time and further research will tell, but I feel that this book will stand as a classic of its genre.

Wayne Sailor, Ph.D.
Professor of Teacher Education
Director, California Research Institute
San Francisco State University

REFERENCES

Cuvo, A.J. (1989). [Review of *Generalization and maintenance: Life-style changes in applied settings*]. *The Journal of The Association for Persons with Severe Handicaps, 13*(4), 275–278.

Sailor, W., Goetz, L., Anderson, J., Hunt, P., & Gee, K. (1988). Research on community intensive instruction as a model for building functional, generalized skills. In R. Horner, G. Dunlap, & R. Koegel (Eds.), *Generalization and maintenance: Life-style changes in applied settings* (pp. 67–98). Baltimore: Paul H. Brookes Publishing Co.

preface

PURPOSE

I am a special education teacher who has also studied anthropology. During the 1984–1985 school year, in order to find out how integration (or "mainstreaming") for students with disabilities was working, I acted as a classroom volunteer in an urban high school while unobtrusively collecting data for an ethnographic study of student social relations. Among the young people I got to know during this period were self-described "Nasty Girls," "Thugs," and "Humans Like Us": teenagers who had become involved in a special education program designed to encourage interactions between disabled and nondisabled students.

For reasons having to do with the history of mental retardation, medical and psychological theories dominate current thought on disability, shaping both our professional vocabulary and the goals of our interventions. Because of this heritage, the special education and rehabilitation literature tends to focus on problems within the individual child—encouraging teachers and therapists to "diagnose" difficulties and "prescribe" solutions—while largely ignoring the ways in which sociocultural elements of the child's environment may *make* an impairment into a handicap.

Students of educational research know that our theoretical foundations also influence our choice of research questions (and therefore, the methods we use to find our answers). To paraphrase Ray McDermott's sardonic comments (McDermott & Hood, 1981), when observing groups of students with disabilities, medically oriented researchers typically ask, "Who's sick here?," educational psychologists ask, "Who's deviating from the norm here?," while ethnographers ask, "What's going on here?"

Because I was curious about the ways a school's social environment might contribute to differences in human behavior, and because my studies in anthropology and sociolinguistics had made me aware of the alternative perspective on schooling presented by classroom ethnographers (researchers predominantly trained in cultural anthropology or sociology), I designed the study on which this book is based. In order to supplement the existing literature, I wanted to look at a special education program to find out "what was going on" there.

AUDIENCE

I wrote *Nasty Girls, Thugs, and Humans Like Us* for present and future teachers, family members, and friends of people with severe handicaps who would like to understand what happens when teenagers with disabilities attend a regular high school. While aiming to provide fellow "insiders" with detailed information on the social outcomes of one school's integration program, I have also tried to make special education's goals and concerns intelligible to those "outsiders" concerned with school reform in general.

SCOPE

In this book, I describe what it is like to be a participant-observer in an inner-city high school. I document the ways in which this school's integration program affected student relations and teacher practices, and report the results of an ecological analysis of the school's social system. Finally, I relate these findings to the broader themes of quality education, student diversity, and social inequality.

The first four chapters orient the reader by providing a historical and theoretical perspective on the special education efforts at Explorer High School. Chapters 5–8 deal with the school's social and physical environment, focusing on contacts between disabled and nondisabled students and the ways in which students understood those contacts. In the final five chapters (9–13), I analyze Explorer's social ecology, identify puzzling results, and raise questions related to future research and educational practice.

acknowledgments

I would like to express my appreciation to the many individuals who contributed to the development of this book. I am most grateful to the staff and students of the San Francisco Unified School District with whom I worked at "Explorer" High School. Deep gratitude also goes to my former colleagues at the California Research Institute on the Integration of Students with Severe Disabilities, especially Susan Porter Beckstead, Ann Halvorsen, and Chesca Piuma, whose work with Project REACH provided the impetus for the study on which this book is based.

I also owe a great deal to the faculty at San Francisco State University and the University of California-Berkeley whose ideas guided this study: Wayne Sailor, for his unfailing support and good humor; James Stone, for encouraging me to persist when the going was rough; and John Ogbu, who taught me how to do ethnography. I would also like to thank Robert Gaylord-Ross, who introduced me to my first *micro*ethnographer; Douglas Ross, who guided me through the sociolinguistic literature on schooling; and Tony Stigliano, whose inspired discussion of the philosophy of science first sparked my interest in nonexperimental research.

I'd also like to express my sincere appreciation to the people who helped me turn a somewhat dry dissertation into the present book: Vince Ercolano for his skillful editing, Bob Finders and Laura Peterson for their down-to-earth comments on my manuscript, and Sue Rockwell and Patricia Fleming for helping me maintain my sanity while I struggled to write *Nasty Girls* and teach school at the same time. Finally, my warmest thanks to Jochen Seegert for his emotional—and culinary—support.

To the loves of my life—
Arlene, Biff, Vera, and Jochen

Nasty Girls, Thugs, and Humans Like Us

chapter 1

Finding a
High School
to Work With

'GRASS, 'LUDES, OR BLOW?'

It was a brilliant October morning in San Francisco. As I walked out the door of Explorer High School,[1] the dazzling sunlight reflecting on the white walls of the building made the graffiti-covered corridors inside seem even gloomier. Shading my eyes, and thinking about the meeting I had just concluded with the principal, I didn't even notice the young man standing on the school's front steps until I heard his murmured offer of "grass, 'ludes, or blow?" (marijuana, Quaaludes, or cocaine).

I had lived near Explorer High School for 2 years while working on my doctorate in special education in a combined program at San Francisco State University and the University of California-Berkeley. I knew the school and the adjoining park as areas to be wary of, particularly at night when gangs hung out there and deals were done. But now it was broad daylight, and I was clearly an adult on official business, dressed (or so I had hoped that morning as I put on my only suit and exchanged my usual backpack for a briefcase) to broadcast my status as a member of a university research project. What *have* we gotten ourselves into, I thought, starting an integration program for severely disabled teenagers in a place like this?

I had grown up on Chicago's South Side, had tutored in the Lawndale slums while an undergraduate at Northwestern, and had worked in an elementary school near the notorious Cabrini-Green Housing Projects as a

---

[1]Not its real name. All faculty, staff, and students at the high school who are mentioned in this book have also been assigned fictitious names.

1

member of the Chicago Urban Teacher Corps, so my assessment of Explorer wasn't that of a sheltered suburbanite recoiling from her first contact with inner-city reality. However, I had previously wondered if Explorer posed too great a challenge to our project; the drug dealer on the school's front steps only served to strengthen my doubts.

Many people would regard autistic, deaf-blind, multiply handicapped, or mentally retarded adolescents as unlikely candidates for participation in typical teenage social groups; a school such as Explorer High, serving a transient, multilingual, mostly poor population, and located in a high-crime area, might seem an equally unlikely setting in which to try out a program intended to promote social acceptance for people with disabilities. But Project REACH (Regular Education for All Children with Handicaps) had successfully established model classrooms in elementary and middle schools during its past 2 years in the San Francisco Unified School District; now we would see whether "Thugs," "Nasty Girls," "New Wavers," "Rappers," and "Popular People"—students at Explorer—could be encouraged to make friends with disabled adolescents.

The previous spring, when we were looking for a high school to work with, my colleagues argued that we had to adapt to school district reality— the city's better high schools claimed to have no room for new classes; one of the two schools that *did* have space was located on a windy hill, difficult for students in wheelchairs to negotiate and comparatively far from the shops and other small businesses our teachers needed for their community-based lessons.

Then, too, a district administrator had confided that a group of severely disabled kids, newly transferred from a special school to Explorer, had not been well-accepted there. Of the high schools available to us, she argued, Explorer was having more problems, and "really needed help" with integration. We were hooked.

During the 1980–1981 school year, San Francisco Unified School District (SFUSD) had embarked on an ambitious program to improve its services to students with disabilities. In order to comply with the Education for All Handicapped Children Act and Section 504 of the Rehabilitation Act, California enacted nine bills in 1980 that were designed to restructure special education services within the state's schools. Under the provisions of these bills (known collectively as the California Master Plan for Special Education), each district was required to develop a local plan that would lead to revised pupil assessment, instruction, and assignment procedures.

An important feature of San Francisco's local plan was the district's decision to *close all segregated special education schools* (those only serving students with disabilities) and place their students in regular public schools. The district, in cooperation with San Francisco State University, received a 3-year federal grant to develop a model program for the integration of those students believed to be most difficult to accommodate in regular schools: students with severe disabilities. This grant funded Project REACH (USOE Contract No. 300-80-0745). I was hired as one of the project's two site coordinators whose particular responsibility was to help classroom teachers organize buddy systems, tutoring programs, and lessons that would involve nondisabled students with their peers who had severe disabilities.

Project REACH began with political "systems-change" efforts directed at the school board, upper-level SFUSD administrators, and school-site administrators (Piuma, Halvorsen, Beckstead, Murray, & Sailor, 1983). These efforts were designed to create support for integration among powerful district personnel, and thus lay a foundation for Project REACH's school-site activities.

Despite support from the district, we had a hard time recruiting children for the project at first. Parents who had been satisfied with San Francisco's special schools were wary of the integration experiment, and so our first classroom opened with one kindergarten-aged deaf-blind student. Two years later, six REACH-sponsored classrooms were serving 60 children in preschools and elementary and middle schools, and a parent support group was thriving (Halvorsen, 1983). During the 1982–1983 school year, the third year of our grant, we planned to involve a high school in project activities. This turned out to be Explorer High.

'SHOOTING A GUN MIGHT NOT QUITE BE A SOCIAL SKILL'

Explorer was a troubled inner-city school serving approximately 2,100 students from San Francisco's rougher neighborhoods. Academically, Explorer was one of the worst of the district's 17 high schools. According to their California Assessment Program scores, Explorer seniors ranked 15th in the district in reading, 13th in written expression, 14th in spelling, and 10th in mathematics (Alioto, 1985). Seventy-eight percent of Explorer's students were eligible to receive extra services paid for by federal "Chapter I" funds because they either spoke limited English or were "Educationally Disadvantaged Youth" who had scored below the 50th percentile on the nationwide Comprehensive Test of Basic Skills (CTBS).

Student transiency was another major problem. In 1984–1985, the year I conducted the research on which this book is based, the total school population had a 50% turnover—a figure identified by a site administrator as San Francisco's highest transiency rate. Only about half of all entering freshmen ever graduated from Explorer, a fact that made it difficult for teachers to maintain subject-matter continuity. The rapid turnover also disrupted student social relations.

Order and discipline were precariously maintained with the help of seven security guards who constantly patrolled the halls. Teachers told me that fewer violent incidents occurred now than in the 1970s, when fights between rival gangs were common and classroom doors were kept locked to protect teachers and students during lessons. However, students still described the school as a rowdy place in comparison to other district secondary schools.

I often heard students joking about Explorer's reputation, as in the following exchange which occurred during an honors English class:

Teacher: People have a lot of things that they do for leisure, including stuff that's social. You guys know Explorer High School. What kinds of skills do you have to have to survive socially?
Student: Know how to fight! (the class laughs)
Teacher: That's a social skill!
Student: How to use clubs!
Teacher: Know how to defend yourself?
Student: How to shoot a gun.
Student: Be assertive!
Teacher: Shooting a gun might not quite be a *social* skill, I don't know . . . (class laughs)
Student: Well, a sense of humor would help.

'DUMP AND HOPE'

Although one self-contained class of students classified as "Trainable Mentally Handicapped" had been at EHS for a year when Project REACH arrived, there was little friendly contact between these young people and the regular student body. From what we had heard about Explorer, it sounded like what we called a "dump and hope" situation: someone had *dumped* the disabled students and an unmotivated teacher there, and then *hoped* that things would work out of their own accord.

Our initial meeting with Mr. Tetrowski, the class's special education teacher, confirmed our initial impression. He said the district had transferred him against his will from another high school where he had taught students who were mildly retarded. He felt unprepared to teach the students with more severe disabilities, and doubted they could ever make friends with nondisabled peers. Mr. Tetrowski also described his difficulties in promoting contact between students: although he had enrolled 12 nondisabled volunteers through the school's Internal Work Experience (IWE) program, there were "problems with kids in the hall making fun of kids coming in to work in the room."

During the next weeks, REACH staff spent time in the high school in order to figure out what was making integration so difficult. We identified three basic problems with the classroom: the curriculum, classroom materials, and staff attitudes were inappropriate for teenaged students.

Mr. T's "curriculum"—a series of unplanned busy-work activities—was neither age-appropriate nor functional. He had these teenagers watch Sesame Street daily (a television was permanently on loan to the classroom); although many had basic academic skills, they spent much of their time tracing mazes or coloring ditto sheets, and Mr. T.'s fine-sounding "mobility training program" actually involved going for walks around the block.

Classroom materials designed for young children, which stigmatize teenagers with disabilities by causing peers to view them as more incompetent than they really are (Bates, Morrow, Pancsofar, & Sedlak, 1984), were commonly used. As decoration, an "ABC Train" in the form of pastel-colored railway cars carrying letters of the alphabet ran along the walls. The students did their work with crayons, and the nondisabled student volunteers were instructed to read aloud to the class from Little Golden Books such as *Corduroy the Bear*.

Worst of all, Mr. Tetrowski and other staff (such as the school's speech therapist) seemed deliberately to convey their negative evaluations of the students' capabilities to the nondisabled kids. I recorded an instance of this in the journal I was keeping at the time:

> Today, for the first time, representatives of the Leadership Class (a group made up of all the student club and class officers) visited Mr. Tetrowski's room. Their goal was to involve his students in school social activities by presenting information on club meetings and the upcoming homecoming dance. I left the room briefly and came back in to see "introductions" going on. Mr. T. and the speech therapist were prompting George and May Li (who were shyly covering their faces) to speak, saying, "Tell them your name or go stand in the corner!" After the visit was over, the speech therapist followed us out in the hall and, in front of the Leadership kids, said, "I have TESTED those students, and perhaps you are unaware that you are dealing with the lowest comprehension level in these students—the BOTTOM of the barrel. Asking them to understand announcements or formulate questions is out of the question!" Since I had heard—and tape recorded—long, playful, complex conversations among the disabled kids, I knew her remarks were off the wall, but I didn't feel I should argue with her in front of the high schoolers. I thanked her for her "interesting" comments and went back to the Leadership classroom, where we had a moment to talk about what had happened.

It really did seem, as the district administrator had said, that help *was* needed if integration were to be successful at Explorer. The REACH staff felt that, as long as teenaged students with disabilities were treated like large kindergarteners, problems like teasing in the halls would continue. Therefore, we worked with the classroom teacher to develop five integration goals that were then sent as a memo to the head of the school's special education department:

1. To convey accurate *information* about the functioning of disabled students at Explorer High
2. To encourage positive, accepting *attitudes* toward disabled students

3. To increase *interactions* between nonhandicapped and severely disabled students in school and in the community
4. To provide *training* for general education students and staff who are interested in working with disabled students
5. To convey accurate information about *curriculum and career objectives* for severely disabled students

We met with teachers identified by the department head as key members of the faculty, and then made plans: we would contact student leaders, ask them for advice about the best way to integrate disabled students into school activities, and involve these leaders themselves in integration efforts in the hope that their example would influence others.

REACH also worked with the special education teacher in an effort to introduce classroom practices that would promote integration. We had already collaborated with district special education administrators to develop a detailed job description that spelled out the teacher's responsibility to encourage peer social interaction through curriculum development, staff inservice training, and the promotion of a positive image for the disabled students (SFUSD, 1981a). REACH made sure that Mr. T. received a copy of this job description, then provided funds to purchase classroom materials that would project an age-appropriate image for the students, and accompanied the teacher on shopping trips to look for leisure activity materials (such as hand-held electronic games) that would appeal to both severely disabled and nondisabled students.

During that year, efforts to promote integration developed in five general ways:

1. Involvement of IWE students as classroom helpers
2. Involvement of severely disabled students in school activities such as dances, festivals, and food sales
3. Informational presentations by REACH and special education staff to classes and club groups
4. Visits to the special education class by members of school clubs
5. Modifications of the special education class environment

At the end of the first semester, Mr. Tetrowski succeeded in transferring back to his former position. He was replaced by Mrs. Anderson, who was committed to the integration program's goals and who had been trained to work with students who had severe disabilities.

At the end of the 1982–1983 school year, the REACH project's school involvement and federal funding ended. During 1983–1984, however, the integration program continued with support from SFUSD, and two new self-contained special education classes for students with severe disabilities were opened.

chapter 2

Understanding
a Paradox

In the fall of 1984 I was back at Explorer, this time to do a follow-up study of the social relations that were an outcome of the school's integration efforts. This became the research on which this book is based. By now, I knew that Explorer presented a paradox: it was a troubled urban school where, against the odds, good things were happening between nondisabled teenagers and students with severe disabilities. I wanted to document what was going on there, and why. By spending a year in this high school, I hoped to obtain *an insider's understanding of one integration program, the ways teachers promoted intergroup acceptance, and the nature of the social relations among teenagers that resulted.*

After overcoming the initial opposition of the more conservative members of the professorial fraternity, my dissertation committee and I had decided on an unconventional approach to this research problem: instead of the traditional *experimental* study that the Berkeley committee had wanted, I would use ecological theory (Bronfenbrenner, 1979; Ogbu, 1981) and ethnographic methods (Bogdan & Biklen, 1982; Goetz & LeCompte, 1984; Spradley, 1979, 1980) to create a *qualitative* description of the individuals and social forces involved in Explorer's integration program.

With support from the federally funded California Research Institute on the Integration of Students with Severe Disabilities (Contract No. 300-82-0365) at San Francisco State University, I planned to spend the school year as a classroom volunteer, unobtrusively observing and interviewing students and staff in order to document their perspectives on integration.

'ARE YOU A STUDENT OR A LADY?'

In order to encourage the teenagers to behave as naturally as possible, I resolved to abandon the professional trappings that I had previously assumed in dealing with teachers and administrators. I preferred, when explaining my presence in the school, to emphasize my student status and to give a vague description of my goals. For example:

> A kid stops me on the stairs to ask, "Miss . . . Miss . . . are you a student or a lady?" I answer, "I'm a student . . . at STATE! I'm here to learn about how handicapped kids get along in high school." He says he thinks it's a good thing: "There goes one of 'em. He's in my weight training class. He be jokin' around with everybody."

I enrolled in the San Francisco School Volunteers (a program designed to enrich school programs and assist teachers through participation by community members) at the suggestion of one of the school's administrators, and thus obtained both insurance coverage and the legal status I needed to work directly with disabled students. At the same time I acquired a role that allowed me to answer questions about what I was doing without giving too much away. For example, when a school cafeteria worker (who had seen me sitting in apparent idleness with a group of disabled and nondisabled students) asked, "How much do you get paid for doing *this*?," I was able to reply, "I don't get paid, I'm a volunteer, helping Mrs. Anderson's class."

Like other volunteers at Explorer, I acted as a teacher aide, accompanying students around the school, preparing teaching materials, or assisting as necessary when spills or accidents occurred. I was careful, however, to avoid being seen as an authority figure. I therefore refused, when a teacher asked me if I would train a nondisabled student, to "take data" as part of a peer tutoring activity, and when an English teacher asked if I would present disability awareness activities (Murray & Beckstead, 1983) in her class, I instead showed her how to conduct these simulation experiences herself. In these ways, I assisted the teachers while maintaining a nonauthoritative stance in relation to student behavior.

At first, my nonprofessional status made me feel terribly vulnerable. The students were so numerous and so *large*—I felt quite intimidated when they loomed over me, crowding the halls between periods. Now that I had left my briefcase and "dress for success" suit at home, I felt like a nonentity. Worst of all, because I wanted to observe the way these teenagers "really were," I could no longer use teacherly tricks to control their behavioral extremes. For example:

> I pass the basketball courts, walking along the side of the school by the park, and hear a voice from the courts: "Hey freak! Freak! Hey bitch, you walkin' on MY turf, you better turn around!" I don't turn or challenge him, however, but keep walking. I am wearing jeans for the first time, and a pink-and-black striped t-shirt, and I suppose that I don't look like a teacher today.

My decision to look like a college student had the advantage of allowing more natural communication with the high schoolers, but I felt that I lost a certain amount of protection that the higher-status image provided.

Just as clothes seemed to give members of the high school clues about my role and status, so did my demeanor. During my first few weeks in the school, I identified places where students "hung out," and I began trying to make observations in order to create an ecological inventory of these areas. I soon came to realize that a person who is hanging out in a high school is not treated the same way as someone moving purposefully through the halls, and is at once more vulnerable to sanctions by authorities and to intrusive attentions by peers. The following incident gave me additional insight into the vulnerability associated with losing one's "professional armor":

> When I first came into school this morning, I was standing in the main hall outside the principal's office, waiting for one of the teachers and watching some kids hanging out in the hall (even though school rules forbid hanging out, everyone seems to do it—sometimes dancing or listening to their Walkmen right in front of the office). A tall guy who was standing there saw me and began to flirt with me, and since I'm downplaying my professional image I answered like a kid. When he said, "Is all that hair yours? . . . C'n I get some?" I just said, "None of your business" and walked away. Then he called after me loudly enough for a passing teacher to hear, "C'n I get in your pants?" I kept walking, embarrassed as hell but also wondering if this was a sign that I was fitting into the "native population." The teacher confronted him: "Do you go to school here? Do you have a hall pass?" The guy ran away.

QUANTITATIVE OR QUALITATIVE RESEARCH?

Broadly speaking, researchers have two ways of trying to understand what goes on in schools: *quantitative* and *qualitative* approaches. Quantitative methods depend on experimental manipulation of social situations. The researcher develops hypotheses or hunches about educational procedures (for example, "Children who have viewed a film about disabilities will interact with disabled peers for longer periods of time than those who haven't viewed such a film"), defines the phenomena she's interested in (for example, "Interaction includes verbal, gestural, and/or visual contact between two individuals"), measures the occurrence of these phenomena in contrasting groups (children who were shown the disability film versus children who viewed another film), and thereby confirms or denies the experimental hypothesis.

Quantitative methods, then, are best used in situations which the researcher already knows a lot about, and are most accurate when used to study behavior that can be reliably counted or tested over a short period.

Qualitative researchers operate differently. Their descriptive methods, originally developed by anthropologists and sociologists (e.g., Edgerton, 1984b; Murray, Anderson, Bersani, & Mesaros, 1986; Stainback & Stainback, 1984) are designed to be used in unfamiliar settings or where the phenomena of interest are poorly understood. Instead of *starting* with a hypothesis they wish to test, qualitative researchers aim to immerse themselves in a social setting (such as a school), and after long-term participation and observation, to describe the people there, their ways of behaving, and the conscious and unconscious rules that make them act as they do. Through such groundbreaking work, qualitative researchers also develop hypotheses that will serve as the bases of further investigation. They collect historical documents, obtain demographic data, conduct interviews, "hang out" to observe (and sometimes take part in) student social activities, and join in assemblies, sports events, graduation ceremonies, and other rituals.

Because a central goal of qualitative study is to "understand another way of life from the native point of view" (Spradley, 1980, p. 3), and then to evoke that way of life in written form, researchers combine participation *in* and observation *of* cultural scenes; the term *participant observation* reflects the dual roles required in this kind of work.

Because school integration for severely disabled adolescents is so new, the teenage social relations that result are hard to analyze with standard questionnaires or surveys. Sociograms and standardized attitude tests are research tools that reveal "best friend" preferences, but not much more. Questions such as *"Who* are the students involved?," *"Why* do they get involved?," and *"What do they really think* about their relations with disabled fellow students?" demand long-term study if the researcher is to get beyond the superficial responses that are often the only outcome of "quick and dirty" experimental techniques. I therefore tried to fade into the background at Explorer, in order to see how teenagers acted towards disabled fellow students on a daily basis. (The research methods and design for this investigation are reported in more detail in the Appendix.)

Although being a nonprofessional "participant" was uncomfortable, especially until I made friends among the Explorer students, this discomfort was essential to doing a qualitative participant-observation study: I had to *experience* being a new member of a big high school community in order to understand the students and the ways their social behavior was adapted to suit that setting. If I felt uneasy, then that was probably what a new kid (disabled or nondisabled) would feel too, until he or she had friends. If I could put myself in their places, I would, in the end, gain valuable information about the realities of daily life at Explorer High School.

I wasn't *really* at ease until about the third month of school, by which time I had made about 30 acquaintances (students I knew well enough to exchange greetings with in passing), and had developed closer relations with six or seven others. By then, I had begun to figure out where to go and how to act so as to avoid trouble, learning, as anthropologists say, "the rules or expectations that others use to provide a framework of mutual intelligibility" (Bateson, 1984, p. 164). Just like an anthropologist studying a distant culture, I continued to make mistakes—sometimes behaving like a "foreigner" or "outsider." Teenagers might offer me advice or even act to protect me when I made mistakes that violated informal social rules. For example:

I station myself on the front steps, where I've noticed that a group of black kids gather for lunch. I eavesdrop on this exchange between two girls: "I'm n'a be flunkin' OUT!" "Un UH! I'm not gonna let MY momma send me to Juvie!" As I'm wondering whether flunking out would be a violation of a Juvenile Court probationary agreement, Ronny (a student who has mild cerebral palsy), comes out and tries to pick up one of the girls: "Hey baby, how ya doin'?" She says "Fine, how 'bout you?" "Wanta go out t' lunch?" he asks, but she brushes him off with "Not today" and he goes on down the steps and begins to engage in mock-fighting with some other kids. Ronny's not in my study because he's not "severely disabled" enough, but I'm writing all this down anyway, trying not to be too obvious about it. Just then a group of boys gathers near me, and they start talking—too loudly, I think—about heroin. One of them pulls out a newspaper clipping and starts to read about a gun battle between the Oakland police and some drug dealers. I have the feeling that they think I may be a narc, and that this loud talk is bravado—they're showing off for me! I'm wondering whether I will look even *more* suspicious if I put my note pad away when Harold, one of Mrs. Anderson's peer tutors, comes over to talk to me: "How's school? You comin' to the class again today?" Like the other boys he has been hanging out with on the steps, Harold is dressed in "Thug" style: corn rows, several gold necklaces, red and blue Fila track suit, and fat high-topped white leather sneakers. I'm grateful to him for coming over, showing the others that I'm okay. I've noticed him being very "big brotherly" toward the severely disabled kids in Mrs. Anderson's class, and now I feel like he's protecting me, too.

I differed from the students that I became closest to in two important aspects: age and ethnicity. I was in my 30s and from an Irish family, whereas the teenagers I got to know best were black. Nevertheless, they slowly began to trust me, perhaps because I acted as a willing and noncritical audience for their personal stories, entertained them in my home (within walking distance of the school), supplied them with snacks and sodas, and sometimes drove them around the city. They, in turn, invited me to hang out with them, go clothes-shopping, and even (at the end of the year) participate in forbidden activities such as drinking alcohol in school.

WHY ARE SOCIAL RELATIONS SO IMPORTANT?

I remember when I used to think that my students' social relations were a low priority, considering all the *other* things these young people needed to learn. In 1978 I was working in Australia, teaching the multiply handicapped deaf residents of a 900-bed "home" for mentally retarded persons, when I got my clutches on the first methods text *I* had ever seen that dealt with students like mine: *Systematic Instruction of the Moderately and Severely Handicapped*, edited by Martha Snell (1978). This was (and is) a marvelous resource, and I eagerly skimmed through it, marking the chapters on communication, self-help, and mobility skills that would be immediately useful. I clearly remember skipping the chapter on social skills, thinking "That's like icing on the cake—nice but not essential." Since then, having worked in integrated, community settings, I've changed my mind about the importance of social relations in education.

The Capacity for Peer Relations

It comforts me to realize that I am not the only person in our field to have neglected the social area! A review of the special education literature shows that peer social relations have been studied *much less frequently* among children and youth with disabilities than among typical children. This is probably because of the assumptions inherent in the medical and psychological paradigms that have dominated research in disability, encouraging us to focus either on the delineation of disabled individuals' differences and defects, or on the development of treatments designed to make such individuals as "normal" as possible.

Our field's traditional emphasis on the *intra*personal aspects of disability is accompanied by a lack of inquiry into the *inter*personal aspects of disability. And, in general, the more severe the disability experienced (especially if mental retardation is involved), the less likely it is that interpersonal behavior will be described. One reason for this neglect is that people who experience mental retardation are often (falsely) assumed to be incapable of participating in social relations (Arkell, 1979). Actually, Arkell's participant-observation study documents in great detail the strategies (verbal and nonverbal) that children with profound retardation use to initiate, maintain, and terminate interactions with others—strategies that she observed to be frequently misinterpreted or discouraged by the staff of the institution where the children whom she studied lived.

The work of Robert Edgerton and the Socio-Behavioral Group at the University of California-Los Angeles provides another striking exception in this neglected research area (e.g., Edgerton, 1984a; Kaufman, 1988; Platt, 1984; Sabsay & Platt, 1985; Zetlin, 1986). During the 1960s, they began a longitudinal qualitative study of mildly and moderately retarded adults who had been moved from closed institutions into homes in the community (Edgerton, 1967; Edgerton & Bercovici, 1976; Edgerton, Bollinger, & Herr, 1984). One of their most striking findings (Edgerton has continued follow-up studies for more than 20 years) is that *the success of this move depends largely on whether these disabled persons are able to find nondisabled friends or "benefactors"* who will help them to blend into their new communities (Edgerton, 1967).

Not only do even the most severely disabled individuals have the capacity to develop peer relations, but these relations make the difference between surviving in the community and returning to closed institutions. There is no better argument for encouraging this capacity as early as possible, through school programs as well as family efforts.

Peer Relations in Integrated Schools

Unfortunately, few researchers report in such detail on the *quality* of social relations experienced by severely disabled individuals. For example, in a large-scale study involving 14 school districts in nine states, Brinker observed 245 severely mentally retarded students (ages 3–22) in both integrated and segregated social groups (1985). His findings affirm the benefits of integrated settings: disabled students were involved in *more* social interaction there, and the quality of these interactions was better. Brinker found that negative interactions seldom occurred, positive interactions occurred more frequently in integrated than in segregated schools, and that the majority of social interactions observed had neutral affect (1982, 1985). These were encouraging findings, but unfortunately the scope of this study was so large that Brinker had to settle for a highly simplified rating system that compressed his quality data to the point of meaninglessness. "Positive, negative, or neutral" are convenient analytic descriptors, but these bare terms tell far too little about the nature of the interactions that occurred in these classrooms.

Another relevant piece of research was an observational study of 43 children and adolescents with severe disabilities (students in three elementary and two intermediate schools) by Voeltz and Brennan (1983). Pairs of children (one each disabled and nondisabled peers) were compared with teacher-disabled child pairs in order to determine qualitative differences between the two types of social relations. In addition to being observed while engaged in interactions with disabled peers, nondisabled students were asked three questions (reason for liking, favorite joint activity, and how they felt when with the other) with respect to their disabled friends, best friends, and family caregivers. About a third of the students noted that they liked both their best friends and disabled friends for reasons of sociability. A small percentage (8%) liked their disabled friend because they played a nurturing role for that person. When identifying a favorite activity, children were more likely to pick a "helping" activity for both their family caregiver and disabled friend in comparison to their best friend, although the most frequently chosen activity across all three persons was a joint activity of some sort (i.e. cooperative play or going shopping). When asked to describe their feelings in the presence of the other person, 17% of the students described some degree of increased self-esteem when with their disabled friend; this was almost never mentioned with respect to a best friend or family caregiver (3% and 4% respectively). The investigators concluded that the peer relations they observed were clearly of benefit to both student groups—the nondisabled children perceived value in their interactions, and the interactions provided the disabled children with social (and perhaps learning) opportunities not otherwise available to them. Voeltz and Brennan (like Brinker, 1982, 1985) found that most dyadic interactions (those involving two persons) were neutral in affect, with no significant difference between peer-peer or teacher-child relations.

A study of social skills training, conducted as part of a high school vocational program (Breen, Haring, Pitts-Conway, & Gaylord-Ross, 1985), also reports briefly on the quality of the intergroup social relations achieved through training, measured in terms of the social responses of coworkers with whom autistic teenagers interacted during coffee breaks. Of 26 interactions initiated by the four young men, seven were classified as active willingness interactions, 16 as passive willingness interactions, and three as active avoidance interactions, depending on the coworker's response to the initiation. The largest proportion of the interactions therefore had a *neutral, polite quality*, paralleling the observations of Brinker (1985) and Voeltz & Brennan (1983). The authors conclude that the bids by the students were successful in that few avoidance reactions occurred, and that the bids "did lead to meaningful social responses of different types by the coworkers, i.e., interactions occurred" (p. 49).

Beyond 'Positive, Negative, or Neutral'

When reading the research literature, I often think: Is this the best that disabled people can hope for—to be treated "neutrally"? I know I couldn't bear it if *my own* social relations were typified by "polite acceptance" and nothing more—or less! Because of my experiences with the REACH project, I suspected that disabled students like ours experienced a *far richer array of relations* than had been reported, that *unexpected influences* might perhaps be shaping the character of these relations, and that integration program outcomes included *effects on their participants* that could not simply be described as "positive, negative, or neutral."

During the year at Explorer I planned to hang around until the kids got used to me, watch and listen to what went on between them, record their thoughts in their own words, and then try to be as objective and critical as possible when I analyzed and described what I had observed. In this way, I hoped that *my* social relations within the high school would provide answers to my questions about the outcomes of one school's integration program—an understanding that would allow me to go beyond the surface in describing these outcomes.

chapter 3

The Origins
of Integration
in U.S. Schools

Harold, a black senior, and Lin, a freshman from
Laos, join me at a table where I've been writing a note to Lin's homeroom
teacher. Harold is talking about the food served at the prom when Lin interrupts . . .

Harold:	. . . They had these big old steaks and they weren't done . . .
Lin:	(inviting Harold to shake his hand) Frien' . . . frien.'
Harold:	(shakes his head negatively) Un-unh.
Lin:	(insisting) Frien' . . . frien'!
Carola:	(thinking Harold hasn't understood) He says "Friend."
Harold:	Un-unh, Lin. I'm gonna do what *you* did to me when *I* did that. This is what YOU did! (Harold puts his head down on his folded arms, hides his eyes, then peeks at Lin. Lin laughs, makes a circle with his fore-finger near his head, looks at me with complicity, then points to Harold.)
Harold:	Un-unh, Lin, YOU! (He imitates the finger-circling gesture, but points to Lin.)

The two boys laugh, looking at each other. As they continue to mess
around, I briefly record what goes on, gazing now and then at my appoint-
ment book as I pretend to consider my weekly plans. Later, when I'm rewriting the day's notes, I add codes for the shared gaze, gesture, and laughter
that mark the boys' mutual feelings. The "balance of power" between these
two students—an important measure of quality in the ecological model of
interpersonal relations that I'm using in my research—seems remarkably

15

even; I remind myself to check this characteristic across the rest of the two boys' interactions.

The playful conversation between Lin and Harold is interesting, not only because these boys had a friendship that bridged differences in language and ethnicity, but also because their relationship exemplified the results of a rather dramatic development in public education in the United States: the integration of students with severe disabilities into age-appropriate regular schools.

Lin was a teenager with Down syndrome, moderate mental retardation, and impaired vision. He and his family were refugees who had recently arrived in the United States from Indochina. Harold was a Thug, a young man who came from a low-income family, whose academic achievement and attendance were poor, and who played a tough-guy role in the student social system.

Lin was *not* (as had once been usual) assigned to a separate "development center for the handicapped" (DCH) when he arrived in San Francisco. Instead, he enrolled in a regular high school where he took physical education and building maintenance in mainstream classes with nondisabled students, and received vocational training and domestic skill instruction in special education classes with disabled peers. Lin had developed a range of social relations with his fellow students. Harold, who was nondisabled, was one of his friends.

In the recent past, when young people with severe disabilities were routinely segregated in separate schools or residential institutions, it would have been much less likely that Lin and Harold would have had the chance to develop such a relationship. But when SFUSD became one of the first school districts in the United States to phase out *all* "special" schools, friendships like that of Lin and Harold became more possible.

Early mainstreaming efforts in U.S. schools had addressed the needs of students whose disabilities were less severe than Lin's—children with learning disabilities, hearing or visual impairments, or mild mental retardation. Not until the late 1970s, when unserved children and those with the most severe handicaps began to be targeted for federal education spending (under Public Law 94-142, the Education for All Handicapped Children Act) did people like Lin begin to be included in plans for integration or education in the "least restrictive environment."

Advocates argue that the ultimate goal of school integration is full participation in society by all citizens with disabilities. Programs like the one at Explorer aim to promote this goal in two ways: first, by providing better learning opportunities than segregated settings, and second, by creating environments in which positive interactions between disabled and nondisabled students can be encouraged. Through mutual learning and the development of positive peer relations, advocates believe that school-based efforts can promote broad social acceptance for people with severe disabilities.

Because I now live in Germany, where I teach students with severe disabilities who are integrated into a U.S. Department of Defense high school, I often find myself in conversations with European parents and professionals in which I'm asked about the *origins* of the mainstreaming programs in the United States. When I contrast the German situation with that of the United States (unlike neighboring European countries, the Federal Republic has strongly resisted the movement to integrate disabled students in school), it becomes clear to me that efforts in the United States have been shaped by unique historical, legislative, and pedagogical influences which have helped create a particular cultural response to disability.

CULTURE CHANGE

Culture is a broad term that refers to the knowledge we humans transmit from generation to generation. Anthropologists explain that this knowledge allows us both to create *and* to understand social behavior (Spradley & McCurdy, 1972). Our culture has *material* elements such as tools, clothing, and shelter, and it has *nonmaterial* elements such as beliefs, traditions, and rituals. New material elements—new inventions, for example—promote the most dramatic, rapid cultural change.

Considered from the broad cultural perspective, the U.S. integration movement and the student interactions that interested me at Explorer could be viewed as elements in a process of cultural change, set in motion by a new element of the material culture. This was an advance in medical technology that irrevocably altered the demographics of disability: the invention of penicillin.

Before the early 1950s, when powerful antibiotics first became available for public use, few people with severe disabilities survived early childhood. Penicillin successfully controlled the respiratory disorders to which such children were particularly susceptible. The new antibiotics that became publicly available after World War II made possible a quantum leap in the quality of surgical treatments, which became much safer once infection could be reliably controlled. As a result of that technological advance, the severely disabled population began to increase, with a concomitant increase in the need for social services designed to meet the needs of these children and their families (Scheerenberger, 1983).

In the 1950s, institutionalization was the most common service option available to families that were unable to manage 24-hour-a-day home care for individuals with severe disabilities. Access to public education was largely unavailable. Parent organizations, such as the National Association for Retarded Citizens (now known as the Association for Retarded Citizens of the United States, or ARC-US), whose membership increased dramatically after 1950, led the movement to provide alternative, community-based education and habilitation services to young people with mental retardation who lived at home (Scheerenberger, 1983).

Beginning in the 1960s, guided by the example of the Civil Rights Movement among blacks, disabled persons and their advocates argued that they were an "unexpected minority," experiencing the same discrimination in school, community, and the work place that had been documented for racial and ethnic groups (Gleidman & Roth, 1980). Parents led the fight for legislation to establish the right of *all* young people, regardless of the severity of their handicapping conditions, to educational equality (a process summarized well in Gartner & Lipsky, 1987). Deinstitutionalization was actually realized as a national goal in the 1970s, as increasing numbers of persons with severe disabilities became visible in their home communities (Scheerenberger, 1983).

Current ethnographic field reports repeatedly document the speed with which the material culture changes when new technology is introduced. The beliefs and traditions that make up the nonmaterial culture, however, *resist* rapid change—a phenomenon referred to as *cultural inertia* (Landis, 1980). Altering the way one thinks and behaves is hard work, demanding flexibility and strong motivation. It is clear that, since the 1950s, American material culture has changed rapidly in respect to disability (this change encompasses not only medical improvements, but also technological advances that offer greater mobility, communication, and learning possibilities). However, attitudes and beliefs about disability have changed much more slowly.

For example, architectural barriers (including aspects of the design of public transport systems) still widely limit disabled persons' freedom of movement in many U.S. communities (DeJong & Lifchez, 1983). Attitudinal barriers still prevent access to social and educational opportunities (Bowe, 1978; Donaldson, 1980; Gartner & Lipsky, 1987). Inaccessible environments and restrictive attitudes combine in the work place, creating occupational barriers that are particularly resistant to change. Not surprisingly, in 1984, 70.6% of all nondisabled employable Americans had jobs, while only 27.4% of individuals with disabilities who were considered able to work were employed. Furthermore, U.S. citizens with disabilities are still more than twice as likely as citizens without disabilities to have incomes below the federal poverty line (Frey, 1984).

Although, when viewed from abroad, the United States appears to have undergone a positive and dramatic culture change in response to disability, problems continue to exist.

ARGUMENTS FOR INTEGRATION

The persistence of cultural and economic disadvantages has fueled almost three decades of effort by parents, disabled individuals, and professionals working to end the social inequality experienced by people with disabilities. When Mrs. Miller, a special education teacher at Explorer, showed slide photographs of her students as part of a "disability education" presentation to an English class, her words summarized the essence of the integration advocates' arguments:

> This is Patrick. Patrick is a student who has Down syndrome. That used to be called "mongoloid" and it's no longer called that because very bad connotations were associated with that label. People with mongolism were thought to be hopeless—they couldn't do anything. *Patrick is very capable.* He uses sign language to communicate and he can do it very well. He can say "I want," and then he can say a variety of things he wants to do—play a game or have something to eat or have something to drink, and he's actually a good cleaner. In this picture he's wiping up the counter at the church.
>
> Most of the students in my class have been disabled since they were born. It's not a disability that they got later in life—it's a disability they were BORN with, so from the time that they were born they have been learning to live with it and to compensate for it. *They just need assistance in some of the basic skills that you learned at a different age,* and so Patrick is wiping the counters not only as a job skill—it might *provide him a job some day*—but also a skill he can use to *help in his home.*
>
> Patrick is 18 years old and has been in public school for—this is his 4th year now. Before that time he was in a development center, and his skills were mostly recreational. If you're concentrating mostly on recreational skills, then you're missing out on a lot of community skills—job skills, social, leisure skills, and mobility skills. And Patrick DID miss out on that community skill training. He might have learned those things at a younger age had he been in a public school program.
>
> That's my plug for regular PUBLIC schools and that's why we want our students to be involved in education from the time that they're born *just like anybody else is.* Unfortunately, the history of education for disabled people has been somewhat segregated—that is, they have been put into special schools for handicapped people or sometimes not even GOING to school—staying at home. They need to learn also, and *they need to learn with other students who have regular skills* and regular academic programs so that they can learn what IS regular. What IS normal? What do I have to do to live on my own? When you're just surrounded by people who just have disabilities, you may pick up more habits that are more dependent on people—because people are doing more FOR you when you're in that kind of environment. But *when you're with people who are doing things themselves, you tend to want to do things for yourself also.*
>
> I would love it if I got up in the morning and somebody brushed my teeth and somebody combed my hair and if they cooked me breakfast and everything else. But if I'm with other people who AREN'T disabled and who are doing those things for themselves, then I want to do those things for myself. It gives me a sense of pride, it gives me a sense of independence and freedom, that you don't HAVE if people are doing things for you. It also gives you CHOICES about what you are going to make for breakfast, what you're going to wear, that you might not have if somebody else was doing those things for you!

Mrs. Miller's presentation clearly put across three messages: 1) kids with disabilities have the right to go to regular schools, just like anybody else,

2) they have needs and expectations like those of nondisabled kids their age, and 3) they are capable of learning.

The formal arguments that provide the foundations for the school-based efforts Mrs. Miller described are of three types: *social/ethical*, *legal/legislative*, and *psychological/educational* (Bricker, 1978).

Social/Ethical Arguments

Social/ethical arguments for school integration focus on the need to recognize the *human rights* of persons with severe disabilities. According to a statement by The International League of Societies for Persons with Mental Handicap, adopted by the United Nations, "The mentally retarded person has the same basic rights as other citizens of the same country and same age" (United Nations, 1971). Social/ethical arguments promote deinstitutionalization and the establishment of community-based education, habilitation, and residential services as ways of rectifying the exclusion from society that persons with severe disabilities have long experienced. A service delivery model from Scandinavia, guided by the principle of normalization, offers one means of implementing these standards.

When Bendt Nirje and N.E. Bank-Mikkelson, influential policy-makers from Scandinavia, were invited to the United States to visit institutions and speak to parents' groups in the late 1960s, they observed that "not even cattle in Denmark are kept as the U.S. keeps retarded people" (Wolfensberger, 1985). Sweden and Denmark, which had begun to redesign their disability services in the late 1950s, had originated a service model that was designed to emphasize the ethical treatment and social rights of persons with disabilities.

Normalized services differed from conventional services in that they aimed to duplicate as closely as possible the characteristics of life in ordinary society. This would allow the disabled person to undergo the same life-cycle changes experienced by more typically developing people, and would thereby help each individual become as independent as possible in the mainstream of society (Nirje, 1969).

Present-day school integration programs, with their emphasis on *age-appropriateness* and *education in the least restrictive environment*, reflect the concern with "appropriate life cycle" associated with Nirje's expression of the normalization principle.

In the United States, advocates such as Gunnar Dybwad and Wolf Wolfensberger recognized that the normalization principle offered an excellent foundation for the reorganization of residential *and* educational services, and that in fact, the principle could be viewed as signaling a "paradigm shift" (Kuhn, 1962) in the field of mental retardation services (Wolfensberger, 1972, 1985). Whereas such services had previously been conceived in terms of a "medical model," in which caretaking or protection were the goals, the normalization principle signaled the emergence of a "socio-political model" in which obtaining equal rights and societal access was central. Whereas in the medical model the problems of disability had been primarily attributed to the individual's *deviance from a normative medical or developmental standard,* the new paradigm directed service providers to give increased attention to the *environmental and attitudinal factors* that were limiting the development of people with disabilities (Gleidman & Roth, 1980).

Legal/Legislative Arguments

Legal/legislative arguments originated in the proposition that young people with disabilities should enjoy the same *civil rights* possessed by other citizens, including the right to a free and appropriate education.

Federal legislation in support of community-based programs for students with disabilities began to be introduced in the early 1960s in response to President John F. Kennedy's interest (an interest almost certainly inspired by his experiences with a sister who was mentally retarded). Congress responded positively to Kennedy's initiatives, eventually passing 116 acts over 20 years that supported persons with disabilities and their families in the areas of health, employment, housing, civil rights, transportation, and social services (Scheerenberger, 1983; U.S. Department of Education, 1980).

While legislation (and associated funding) helped expand teacher training programs and special education services, it did not necessarily lead to the equal provision of services to *all* students with disabilities. Until the mid-1970s, local school districts were able to "excuse" any individual from school attendance if that individual was perceived as "too handicapped" to profit from available programs. State residential facilities were sometimes the only service option that parents could find for children with severe disabilities (Sailor & Guess, 1983). The federal courts began to turn their attention to this problem in the early 1970s. The "right-to-education" concept, first articulated in reference to the rights of black children in the decision of *Brown v. Board of Education* (1954), provided the legal precedent. In two landmark decisions, *Pennsylvania Association for Retarded Children v. Commonwealth of Pennsylvania* (1972), and *Mills v. Board of Education* (1972), the right to a free and appropriate education was also extended to children with disabilities, regardless of the severity of their impairments. Following these decisions, two important pieces of federal legislation, the Rehabilitation Act of 1973 (PL 93-112) and the Education for All Handicapped Children Act of 1975 (PL 94-142), were enacted. These acts gave additional affirmation to the court decisions and identified the financial and procedural means by which they should be implemented.

The practice of educating students with severe disabilities in regular public schools originated in a principle central to these legislative developments pertaining to the concept of appropriateness: the principle of education in the *least restrictive environment* (LRE). The application of the LRE principle to the assessment of educational appropriateness was first ordered in the Pennsylvania decision and supported in the Rehabilitation Act and PL 94-142. The LRE principle as stated in PL 94-142 required each state to establish "procedures to assure that, to the maximum extent appropriate, handicapped children, including children in private or public institutions, are educated with children who are not handicapped" (20 U.S. Code, Sect. 1412 [5] [B] [1975]).

The history of the development of PL 94-142 shows that Congress based the incorporation of the LRE principle's "integration imperative" on three judgments: 1) integration provided opportunities for disabled children to learn through modeling, 2) integration prepared disabled children for life in the community by allowing disabled and nondisabled children to form personal relationships, and 3) integration ensured that children with disabilities received educational services equal to those provided to nondisabled peers (Gilhool & Stutman, 1978).

Although the states have differed in their interpretation of PL 94-142's integration imperative (with the result being litigation initiated by parents and other integration advocates), California and other states with active disability lobbies have committed themselves to an interpretation of the law that has resulted in widespread desegregation from kindergarten through secondary school, and have moved large numbers of students from special schools to regular education sites.

Psychological/Educational Arguments

Arguments from the psychological/educational viewpoint emphasize the potential benefits to disabled young people of observing and *learning* from the age-appropriate behavior of nondisabled peers. While separate schooling was first questioned in relation to students with mild disabilities (Dunn, 1968), students with severe disabilities were later included in the arguments for integration. The benefit to peers without disabilities is also argued. This argument is most effective when guided by a pragmatic concept: the *Criterion of Ultimate Functioning* (Brown, Nietupski, & Hamre-Nietupski, 1976). In essence, this means that the quality of educational services should be evaluated in terms of *the degree to which they prepare a student for his or her future*. While most young people with severe disabilities were once expected to spend their lives in institutions or other protected settings, the growing normalization movement and the increase in federal support for community-based programs means that educational services should begin to prepare disabled students for another kind of future: *life in the community*. Brown et al. (1976) reason:

> If severely handicapped adult citizens are to function effectively in heterogenous community environments, both handicapped and nonhandicapped citizens will require longitudinal and comprehensive exposure to one another. Such exposure

will enhance the probability that skills, attitudes, and values so necessary for tolerance, understanding, and absorption will be realized. (pp. 8–9)

School integration and age-appropriate educational practices are identified by Brown et al. (1976) as essential to the general effort to promote the eventual "absorption" of disabled persons into the mainstream of community life.

The 1975 enactment of PL 94-142 enabled special educators to begin to gain practical knowledge of both the problems and advantages of attendance in regular schools by students with severe disabilities. Beginning with the publication of a landmark work, *Educational Programming for the Severely and Profoundly Handicapped* (Sontag, Smith, & Certo, 1977), textbooks began to report research-verified techniques for adapting special education methods to the new needs of students in integrated community environments (e.g., Certo, Haring, & York, 1984; Sailor & Guess, 1983; Sailor, Wilcox, & Brown, 1980; Snell, 1978; Stainback & Stainback, 1985; Wilcox & Bellamy, 1982). These texts made it clear that students with severe disabilities attending age-appropriate regular schools could expect *social benefits* from interactions with nondisabled peers that would not be available were the disabled students assigned to segregated special schools.

In particular, it was argued that social benefits to students with disabilities would accrue through four important types of interactions: *proximal, helping, service,* and *reciprocal* (Brown et al., 1983; Hamre-Nietupski et al., 1978; Schutz, Williams, Iverson, & Duncan, 1984; Stainback & Stainback, 1985).

It was also argued that people without disabilities were able to benefit from associating with persons who had severe disabilities. Young people who had participated in early integration programs had evaluated their experiences positively, reporting personal benefits such as an enhanced understanding of personal differences (Voeltz & Brennan, 1983). It was further argued that long-term contact with disabled peers would benefit nondisabled young people by giving them realistic preparation for parenthood (should they be parents of a disabled child), and also prepare them for professional roles in which they could be expected to interact in community settings with disabled fellow citizens:

> The best way for physicians, secretaries, group home managers, waiters, architects, nurses, teachers of nonhandicapped students, school board members, legislators, and others to develop the skills and attitudes necessary to function effectively with and for severely handicapped persons is to grow up and go to school with them. . . . Why do pediatricians still encourage parents to send their children to lives of waste and degradation in the wards of institutions[?]: If they had grown up with severely handicapped peers, it is extremely doubtful that they would act in such negative, feudal, and rejecting ways. (Brown et al., 1983, pp. 20–21)

Harold and Lin, whom I introduced at the beginning of this chapter, had a relationship that had begun with initial hesitation, but which, through mutual involvement in "peer tutoring" (Harold had worked with Lin in a building maintenance class), had become affectionate and playful. In an interview at the end of the year, Harold explained to me that he hadn't gone to school with disabled people before, and when a guidance counselor suggested that he enroll in Explorer's Internal Work Experience (IWE) program and act as a tutor for the students in Mrs. Anderson's class, he had hesitated.

Carola: I know you've told me this before, but run it down for me again how you got started comin' into Mrs. Anderson's class. Did you ever work in any other handicapped classes before?

Harold: Not really. It was just that I think I c'n DO it. So I just gave it a try!

Carola: Uh-huh.

Harold: So . . . and then, my counselor asked me if I wanted IWE and I asked him what that was and he said it was with the handicapped . . .

Carola: Umm-hm.

Harold: . . . And at first I said, "Well, I don't know," and then I thought it over and I just said, "Yeah, I guess I'll go ahead."

Carola: Did you go up and check it out or anything?

Harold: (shakes head) Mm-mm.

Carola: You just thought it over in your head.

Harold: I just went on WITH it.

Carola: Yeah, okay, so anyway you got started like that. You thought it over and then you went in and saw how it went, huh?

Harold: And then I went in.

Carola: Mmhm. Are there any kids in that class that you spend MORE time with than others?

Harold: Maybe . . . Lin . . . or . . . maybe just Lin.

Carola: So you see Lin a lot?

Harold: Yeah, I used to spend a LOT of time with him, 'cuz I had to go sweeping—teaching him how to sweep?

Carola: Uh-huh?

Harold: So that's probably who I spent more time with from the beginning.

Carola: I remember—that was in the fall you used to do that. And now he's on the janitor crew—I guess you must have taught him . . .

Harold: You know, how to stay close to the walls, and stuff?

Carola: Yeah?

Harold: How to watch the trash and put it into little piles . . .

Carola: Did anybody teach YOU how to teach HIM? Or did you just kind of play it by ear?

Harold: Well I already KNEW how to sweep, from working at the Nabe (the Potrero Hill Neighborhood Center) and . . . well, and years before that I used to do janitorial work and you know chop WEEDS and stuff so that automatically teaches you how to sweep! So that's how I learned myself.

Carola: Um-hm . . .

Harold: Of course THEY taught us how to sweep.

Carola: Mrs. A?

Harold: Uh-huh, and the janitor, he told me how he wanted it done. But you know really he TAKE too long . . .

Carola: Lin?

Harold: Naw, the janitor. You know, he go up and then he come down, and he go up, down, up, down. I just go up ONCE.

Carola: So you had a better system, and you just thought, "I'll do it," 'cause I mean it seems to work—Lin really gets every little BIT!

Harold: You know, I'll push one side up to a certain extent and then I'll go back and then I'll do the other side, and then I'll put it all together close to the wall? And then I'll go down AGAIN.

Carola: Mmhm?

Harold: Like that, so you won't have to BACKTRACK.

Carola: Mmhm. Did anybody, you know—was there any particular problem teaching Lin? Did Mrs. A show you any particular way to work with him? Or did you just figure it out?

Harold: No, I just figured it out. It's just that he—he couldn't keep—he didn't watch the floor, he just wanted to PUSH. And you know, I told him he had to watch the floor, and keep his eyes in FRONT of him so he won't be sweepin' the PEOPLE, right?

Carola: (laughs) Right!

Harold: And, you know, keep the broom to the wall, 'cuz there'd be trash to the wall, so just stay close to the wall, and then he just learned from that.

Carola: Uh-huh. Compared to the other guys that he works with in that building maintenance class—I have the feeling that he actually, you know, like every time I see HIM he's WORKING. And I see some of the other guys in the class and they're kind of, you know, standing around . . .

Harold: He used to get the whole downstairs floor in one period!

Carola: Wow!

Harold: And try to go up to the second floor . . .

Carola: Wow, uh-huh?

Harold: Lin used to try to—see, the janitor just told us just to try to get the trash from the FLOOR, and you know Lin he'd try to—if he see trash on the steps he'd try to go get THAT. I'd say, "Lin, not the trash on the STEPS, just on the floor."

Carola: Uh-huh.

Harold: But probably now, he's still trying to get the trash on the steps, you know.

Carola: But it seems that he does a nice thorough job, anyway, and I know that he enjoys doing it. So it was really good that you taught him how to do it.

Harold: He can do it by hisself now.

Carola: He's a GOOD sweeper, as far as I can see, huh?

Harold: What could I say?

Carola: What COULD you say—I mean, really!

Harold: I taught him!

Carola: Yeah! (After talking for a while longer, I changed the subject) . . . 'Spose when you talk to your parents about what you're doing in school—like when you told your mother about what you're doing—what do they say?

Harold: They say they're SURPRISED . . . Jus'—I tell 'em like I tell you—I help 'em read, write, and you know, wash dishes, wash clothes, sweep . . .

Carola: And do they ever say, "Why?"

Harold: Why do I help 'em do that? 'Cuz, they 'sposed to know it, just like anybody else. They 'sposed to know at least half of the stuff.

Carola: Why, do you think? What good's it gonna do 'em?

Harold: 'Cuz . . . 'cuz one day they brain might jus' get 'em t' ACT right! You know, it might just come TOGETHER and then they'll know everything—you know it just might come together like one of US— a regular person.

Carola: Uh-huh, they might just function like anybody else.

Harold: Yeah.

Carola: Something like that . . . Well, anyway, when you're talking to your mom or dad they go, "Oh, I'm surprised!" How come they're surprised?

Harold: 'Cause they didn't think I would be doing anything LIKE that.

Carola: Huh! How come?

Harold: They didn't think I'd have the patience.

Carola: Really? 'Cuz they don't see that side of you?

Harold: Yeah. They know I've got a little patience, but not as much as being with handicapped people.

Carola: Anything else they're surprised at?

Harold: The way—you know—how I teach 'em.

Social/ethical, legal/legislative, and psychological/educational arguments that are used to justify integration in the United States carry a common message: Segregating individuals who are disabled deprives them of their rights and denies them opportunities to achieve personal independence through learning and living in community settings. It is clear from Harold's proud description of the sweeping lessons, and from his report of his parents' reaction to his work with Lin, that he too gained something valuable from the Explorer integration program. And indeed, advocates stress the two-way benefits of integration. Arguments for integration in U.S. schools stress the ways in which *both* disabled and nondisabled individuals need to get to know each other if the normalized community environments promoted by activists, parents, and advocates, and supported by federal legislation, are to become more than rhetoric. School integration is a *critical element* in the effort to promote mutual learning like that experienced by Harold and Lin.

chapter 4

What Can
We Expect from
Integration?

PROMOTING INTERACTION

When you read the social science literature on the outcomes of the U.S. Civil Rights Movement, a concern with social interaction paralleling that in the special education literature becomes apparent. Reports on racial integration in schools also distinguish between *desegregation*—bringing disparate racial groups into proximity—and *integration*—promoting positive contact between the different groups (Pettigrew, Useem, Normand, & Smith, 1973; Schofield & Sagar, 1979). In this sense, a school might be said to be desegregated if the ratio of minority-group to majority-group students in its student body reflects the ratio of such individuals in the entire school system. But, the same school would not necessarily be integrated (Kirp, 1982; Schofield, 1982).

Because people with severe disabilities experience significant cognitive impairment typically accompanied by limited communication skills and atypical behaviors, "dump and hope" programs that merely establish physical proximity between disabled and nondisabled students are unlikely to promote positive social relations (Guralnick, 1980; Porter, Ramsey, Tremblay, Iaccobo, & Crawley, 1978; Stainback & Stainback, 1981). Researchers in the United States believe instead that a critical factor in accomplishing integration is the promotion of positive social interaction through *systematic intervention* (Bricker, 1978; Fredericks et al., 1978; Sailor & Guess, 1983; Snyder, Apolloni, & Cooke, 1977; Stainback & Stainback, 1982; Wilcox & Bellamy, 1982).

Problems in Social Skill Development

Individuals with severe disabilities often fail to initiate, maintain, or terminate interactions in ways perceived as socially acceptable. Lacking appropriate social skills, they may use behaviors others perceive as frightening or unpleasant to communicate messages such as "I'm tired of doing this," or "Pay attention to me" (Schuler & Goetz, 1981). Monica, a senior who tutored Mrs. Miller's students, described her first impressions of them, and guessed at the effect that their behaviors could have on others:

Carola: Did you know any disabled people yourself before you got into this?

Monica: Um, no.

Carola: No, this was your first time? So, did you notice any changes in your feelings, like from when you first started until now? Any changes, I mean, in your feelings towards the students in this class?

Monica: No, I just, my—at first—you know at FIRST when I just got into the class it was like, you know, it looks kind of TOUGH, you know, the way how they ACT, and . . .

Carola: Yeah.

Monica: You know, when they get into THEIR bad moods, that they should . . . But, you know, as I WORKED with them, and you know, HELPED them, I understood—I liked them more, because it gives me something to do and then, you know, it's probably something I would do for a living maybe, you never know . . .

Carola: Uh-huh?

Monica: But it is, you know, it's fun. Just, you know, just to be out there knowing that YOU'RE helping someone. It makes ME feel good.

Carola: Uh-huh! I know, when I think of—if somebody was interviewing ME and they asked me why did I go into special ed—I probably would say the same thing. I think it just made me feel good to know, for sure, that I was helping somebody.

Monica: At first, I had wanted to do this in 9th, 10th, 11th grade, but I thought, "Oh! These students are TERRIBLE!" Then when you get to know them they're real sweet.

Carola: Really? That's interesting, Monica.

Monica: 'Cuz I would walk in the hall and I would see them at their temper, and it would be like . . .

Carola: Yeah?

Monica: . . . Uh-oh, they none of them don't like—uh-oh, must be one of their off days.

Carola: See them in a temper tantrum or whatever?

Monica: Yeah, and throwing things and everything, and that SCARED me!

Carola: It IS scary, you're RIGHT! So, you had thought about doing this in 9th, 10th, and 11th grade but then—then you said "Ooooh! . . . "

Monica: Yeah.

Carola: . . . It looked too weird!

Monica: You know—"Oooh! They might HURT me." And one day, um, I was just sitting there, and all of a sudden Tricia's shoe hits me in the MOUTH! Were YOU there?

Carola: No, but it happened to me once.

Monica: Oh! She just—BOOM—right into my mouth and I was like "Uuuuh!" I didn't get mad or anything, 'cause SHE didn't know . . .

Carola: . . . You knew her already?

Monica: I wanted to cry, though.

Carola: Oooooh! (We both laugh). Let's see . . . I was wondering, like suppose . . . 'spose some new freshman came to this school next year, you know, they walk in and they've never seen kids—kids so severely handicapped as Mrs. Miller's kids before. They might be kind of surprised to see them, huh?

Monica: Oh, they'd be scared. Because, like one girl—oh, I don't know, she probably knew that they're handicapped and everything—Lucy just came up to her and was going to give her a big old hug, and she just PUSHED Luce and I really got MAD! And I said, "You know, she's not going to hurt you!" But she still backed off, but she backed off with a smile, you know.

Carola: Uh-huh.

Monica: I said, "Oh, she won't hurt you! That means that she LIKES you!"

Carola: Uh-huh?

Monica: And so she understood, you know, that . . .

Carola: She understood what you explained.

Monica: Yeah! That Luce wasn't trying to hurt her or anything. 'Cause Luce, you know, she's a real loving person, and she likes to give hugs and everything!

Carola: Yeah . . . but she's big, and someone who didn't know her . . .

Monica: Right! Yeah, they just . . .

Carola: Mightn't understand . . .

Monica: Yeah, they might not understand, so, I had TOLD her and she understood, but she backed off with a smile. But she understood!

In the United States, programs designed to promote social acceptance for young people like Lucy usually take one of three forms: efforts to develop social skills in individuals with severe disabilities, efforts to change negative attitudes in individuals without disabilities, and efforts to facilitate direct social interactions between disabled and nondisabled youth.

Teaching Age-Appropriate Social Skills

Early research conducted with young disabled children demonstrated some success in teaching appropriate social behaviors through behavior analytic techniques involving nondisabled peers as social skill models or as agents to reinforce disabled children's social efforts (e.g., Allen, Hart, Buell, Harris, & Wolf, 1964; Apolloni, Cooke, & Cooke, 1977; Ragland, Kerr, & Strain, 1978). Unfortunately, enduring results that generalized from the experimental situation to real life were difficult to obtain with severely disabled students (Strain & Fox, 1981).

More recently, research conducted with adolescents has refined the same behavioral technology (e.g., Gaylord-Ross, 1981) in order to encourage young people to use their new social skills with a variety of individuals and across multiple community environments. In one study, for example, three autistic young men were taught by "peer tutors" to initiate, maintain, and terminate object-centered social interactions (listening to a Walkman or offering chewing gum, for example) during leisure time in their integrated high school (Gaylord-Ross, Haring, Breen, & Pitts-Conway, 1984). After training, the subjects had generalized the social skills across persons, and they were more frequently the objects of social initiations by nondisabled persons. In a replication of this study (Breen, Haring, Pitts-Conway, & Gaylord-Ross, 1985; see discussion, Chapter 2, p. 14, the present volume), similar methods were successfully used to teach the same three autistic adolescents (and one additional student from the same high school class) to participate in social interactions with coworkers during coffee breaks at their off-campus job sites (Breen et al., 1985). Nondisabled schoolmates taught these boys a social skill chain that involved greeting a familiar coworker, offering a cup of coffee, and elaborating the conversational exchange when the coworker displayed willingness to continue the interaction.

Social skills, these studies show, *can* be taught, but severely disabled adolescents must learn to use these skills in multiple environments and with different persons. Furthermore, if individuals with disabilities are to maintain the skills they've learned, the attitudes and behavior of persons in their environments must also undergo enduring modifications (Stainback & Stainback, 1982).

Attitude Change

Negative and stereotypic attitudes toward persons with disabilities have a long history (Scheerenberger, 1983; Thomas, 1982). Even in recent times, people with disabilities have only rarely been perceived as individuals with distinct skills, interests, and personalities; instead, these people have been stereotyped as helpless, hopeless, ill, and asocial (Arkell, 1979; Donaldson, 1980; Wolfensberger, 1972). These stereotypes may well have originated in pan-cultural reactions to individuals who did not match social norms and who were therefore "stigmatized" (Berreman, 1981; Goffman, 1963).

The advent of federal legislation mandating school integration for disabled children made it imperative that advocates and professionals make concentrated efforts to dispel negative attitudes and stereotypes (Donaldson, 1980; Jones, 1984; Voeltz, 1980, 1981).

A typical "attitude change" program might incorporate: 1) audio-visual media emphasizing the capabilities of individuals with disabilities, 2) disabled guest speakers, 3) disability-simulation activities (allowing participants to try using a wheelchair, for example), and 4) discussion periods (e.g., Murray & Beckstead, 1983). For example, when the English department at Explorer incorporated information on disabilities into its curriculum, the special education teachers visited classes, showed slides of their students, and organized panel discussions by nondisabled peer tutors who were then available to participate in question-and-answer sessions. The following is an example:

Teacher: Doretha, would you explain what a peer tutor is?

Doretha: It's like a teachers' aide that help the kids if they need something.

Teacher: Uh-huh . . . . Could you talk a bit about the disabilities the students have and about what you do with them?

Doretha: Well, they're blind, deaf AND handicapped. You know, some people like Ray Charles . . . It may not seem like much to y'all, but pool, laundry, shopping are important for them to learn 'cuz lot of 'em don't know that stuff. It's hard but it's fun but it takes a lot of PATIENCE—A LOT. I din' have none before I joined!

Teacher: What takes patience?

Doretha: Well, for example, we're all in the bathroom, and Xuan, she takes 15 minutes. Or Tricia throws things, like one time she threw her shoe out the window. Sometimes, you know, the regular students don't understand, and it takes patience not going off on THEM. . . .

Teacher: In the film we saw, David had Down syndrome. Who can tell me what that is?

A Boy: One too many hormones.

Class: No! No! CHROMOSOMES!

Teacher: What makes people retarded?

Class: They're slow to learn but they CAN learn.

Doretha: I call 'em "handicap." They just got a little handicap, that's all. We all got a handicap. They try over and over and so they get the hang of it, and then we learn something too.

Teacher: What do you learn?

Silvia: Well, we learn useful stuff in case our chilren are handicapped.

Teacher: What else do you learn?

Silvia: You can learn to be patient. When I started I was scared. Doretha really helped me, too. I'd say I'm scared, she'd say, "No, it's fun."

Teacher: What were you scared of?

Silvia: Scared I'd do something wrong.

Doretha: Plus, some people're scared it'll rub OFF on 'em!

Silvia: Plus, the way I saw other people working with 'em—that helped too.

To be effective, efforts to change attitudes must incorporate a *behavior change* component—that is, nondisabled students should not only discuss disability, but also should be involved in regularly repeated interaction with disabled peers. As Silvia said, they should also have the chance to watch other teenagers who are involved in activity with disabled peers. This sort of modelling is one of the quickest ways to help students overcome initial discomfort.

Project REACH, the model development effort I worked for in San Francisco, combined these recommended practices with positive results: systems-change activities, "disability education" lessons and discussions in regular classes, a "special friends" program, peer tutoring, and a parent support group (Goetz, Piuma, Gaylord-Ross, Halvorsen, & Birns, 1983; Halvorsen, 1983;

Murray & Beckstead, 1983; Piuma et al., 1983). Of all these components, those that directly facilitated repeated interactions between students with and without disabilities seemed to offer the most effective means of modifying the avoidance associated with negative attitudes (Donaldson, 1980; Jones, 1984; Voeltz, 1980, 1981; Voeltz, Hemphill, et al., 1983).

Facilitating Direct Social Interactions

Planned interactions may involve class-time tutoring or involvement in free-time activities (Hamre-Nietupski & Nietupski, 1981; Hanline & Murray, 1984; Thomason & Arkell, 1980). For example, a program conducted in Hawaiian elementary schools combined informational presentations with planned interaction programs in which nondisabled students volunteered to act as "special friends" during leisure activities with severely disabled schoolmates. Evaluation studies compared the effects of three types of contact/interaction ("no contact" in nonintegrated schools, "low contact" in schools where disabled students attended regular schools without systematic intervention programs, and "high contact" in schools with the intervention programs). The nondisabled students' attitudes were assessed after high and low contact schools had experienced a year of integration, with the high contact group found to score higher in acceptance of disabled persons than the other two comparison groups. Girls were significantly more accepting than boys on all dimensions of acceptance measured (Voeltz, 1980, 1981).

Pioneering studies of interethnic and interracial relations demonstrated that a critical factor in the promotion of positive interaction is the *quality* of the contact situation (e.g., Allport, 1954; Amir, 1969, 1976; Sherif, Harvey, White, Hood, & Sherif, 1961). In order to lead to improved intergroup relations, the contact situation must provide *equal status* for both minority and majority group members, strong *institutional support* must be provided for positive relations, and members of both groups must have extensive opportunities to *work cooperatively* toward shared goals (Allport, 1954).

The early studies on intergroup relations have led to research on the effects of instructional structure (Johnson & Johnson, 1974, 1975) and classroom organization (Karweit & Hansell, 1983) on the quality of student interaction. These studies show that when instructional structure and classroom organization reflect Allport's (1954) principles, they can promote positive contact between diverse student groups, such as in the case of racially integrated schools (Schofield, 1982). Of particular interest to special educators are the studies by the Johnsons, an impressive body of evidence documenting the ways in which cooperative goal structuring (as opposed to competitive or laissez-faire conditions) lead to interpersonal interaction and attraction between young people in school settings (e.g., Johnson & Johnson, 1980).

Two studies that extend the Johnsons' research into the structure of intergroup social interactions include brief reports of observed social relations between disabled and nondisabled teenagers. One study (Johnson, Rynders, Johnson, Schmidt, & Haider, 1979) involved 30 high school students (18 nondisabled and 12 with moderate mental retardation and Down syndrome) who were randomly assigned to bowling teams that differed in terms of their goals. "Cooperative" teams were told to maximize the *group* bowling score to meet a set criterion by helping each other when necessary. "Individualistic" teams were made up of students who were told to maximize their *individual scores* to meet a set criterion by concentrating on their own performance.

"Laissez-faire" teams were given no instructions about their goals. Social interactions were measured by two dependent variables: frequency of positive, neutral, and negative interactions between the bowler and other students on his or her team, and frequency of team cheers (cheers for other members of one's own team).

Analysis of the data provides convincing evidence that the *structure of the contact situation* significantly affects the quality of intergroup social relations. Disabled students on the cooperative team participated in significantly more positive interactions with nondisabled peers than did members of the individualistic and laissez-faire teams (an average of 17 cheers per hour versus five and seven per hour respectively). Nondisabled students positively reinforced mentally retarded students considerably more often in the cooperative setting than in individualistic or laissez-faire settings (50% of the students' bowling turns were reinforced versus 22% and 38%, respectively). In addition, disabled members of the cooperative team received team cheers for their bowling turns much more often than did members of the individualistic and laissez-faire teams (58% versus 9% and 13% respectively).

The study by Johnson et al. (1979) was replicated by Rynders, Johnson, Johnson, and Schmidt (1980) with similar results. In addition, the replication study revealed that positive interactions between teammates that occurred under cooperative goal-structuring conditions were accompanied by higher sociometric ratings of disabled bowlers by nondisabled teammates.

Social Outcomes

The results of these studies of planned interactions raise important questions about the *kinds* of intergroup relations that such interactions promote. Although empirical evidence is lacking, some professionals have advised against putting nondisabled peers in the role of instructor or peer tutor because they suspect that the status inequality inherent in the teacher-student relationship mitigates against the possibility of friendly relations developing between disabled and nondisabled students (Meyer, Kennedy, Kishi, Pitts-Conway, & Sasso, 1985).

However, when a school already *has* an institutionalized means of organizing tutoring or teacher assistance (such as the Internal Work Experience program at Explorer), such a program can serve as a useful means of *initiating* contact between students—contact that can later lead to non-tutorial, friendly relations.

If care is taken when one structures the "contact situation," even tutoring can incorporate playful, social elements. The following example illustrates the variety of interactions that characterized a typical period in Mrs. Miller's class. The time is 10:40 A.M. Veronica (an IWE peer tutor) and Warren (a teacher aide) are goofing around together—insulting each other while they pick up the game pieces that have spilled on the floor. They and Mrs. M. are talking about clothes (Warren is very good-looking and wears gorgeous preppy clothes):

Warren:	How much d'you think these pants cost?
Veronica:	Five cents! (After things get cleaned up, Warren takes Lucy and Xuan over to a table at the side of the room for an auditory training program designed to prepare them for a formal hearing test, and Mrs. M. asks Veronica to take Tricia down to the home economics room to put Tricia's laundry into a washing machine there. As she passes me, Veronica tells me about a chance meeting with one of the disabled students).
Veronica:	I caught the bus with Lucy today. She kept saying, "Oooh! . . . aaah-mah!"
Carola:	What'd you say back?
Veronica:	I said, "If I knew what you were saying, I could have a conversation with you!" (Veronica goes to Tricia, who is blind, to begin the laundry sequence. Tricia hugs her, and Veronica says, "Gimme a kiss?" Tricia doesn't give her a kiss but Veronica tries her mirrored sunglasses on Tricia anyway. They head for the door but stop to get Tricia's cane.)
Veronica:	Wait, Trish, that's the wrong cane. C'mon, come open the door. (They go out to the home economics room. Ten minutes later, they come back. I see them in the hall and ask how it went.)
Veronica:	She did great. Now I'm trying to teach her to *say* when she needs to go to the rest room (Tricia usually just grabs her crotch), but she doesn't quite get it yet. (The other day, Veronica told me Tricia's "words were coming out clearer"—I must check "seeing progress" as a motivation for peers. Veronica and Tricia re-enter Mrs. Miller's room and Mrs. M asks Tricia what she'd like to do next with Veronica. Tricia begins to shake her head (I am reminded of the comment Tricia's former teacher made about how kids like Tricia, but Tricia likes adults). When Trish continues to refuse, Mrs. M changes tactics.)
Mrs. Miller:	Oh, I guess Tricia isn't ready. Maybe Xuan would like to play a game with you. (She explains her objective to Veronica.) Okay, Xuan is learning how to put the Battleship game away. One of the parts of that is putting the red and white pegs in separate holes . . . (more explanation I didn't get down). If you'll just sit by her and talk with her while she puts them away . . .

This observation demonstrates how teacher-structured tutoring can lead to informal, friendly social interaction between students both *in* and *outside* school (as in the chance meeting on a city bus reported by Veronica). When they combine structured interaction with individual training in social skills and attitude-change efforts, programs like the one at Explorer seem to offer an effective means of ending the social isolation and loneliness suffered by so many adolescents with disabilities.

WHAT DO WE KNOW ABOUT
SOCIAL RELATIONS IN ADOLESCENCE?

One way of ascertaining what sorts of relations teenagers typically engage in (and therefore, what we might expect in relations between disabled and nondisabled peers) is to review the literature on adolescent social relations. In psychological/developmental studies, adolescence is widely recognized as a critical stage for the individual, sometimes reported to involve dramatic upheaval (e.g., Freud, 1969), and sometimes more gradual change (Dusek & Flaherty, 1981; Mead, 1928; Offer, Marcus, & Offer, 1970). Because adolescence is the time when young people begin to experiment with new styles of social and sexual behavior, start to develop a fuller idea of self, and embark on the evolution of vocational plans (White & Spiesman, 1968; Zetlin & Turner, 1985), some of the developmental changes typical of adolescence relate directly to integration questions.

Research emphasizes *the particular importance of peer social relations* in adolescence (Douvan & Adelson, 1966; White & Spiesman, 1968; Zetlin & Turner, 1985). These special relations serve a highly positive developmental function by allowing the young person to learn and practice social behaviors forbidden to the parent-child or teacher-student relationships (Fine, 1980; Hartup, 1978; Lewis & Rosenblum, 1975).

Disabled adolescents experience the same need for increased independence and freedom to experiment felt by their nondisabled age-mates, although handicapping conditions can make the realization of these needs more difficult. This, in turn, can lead to prolonged dependence on parents, limited access to nondisabled peer models, and restricted possibilities in both the social and vocational spheres (Abramson, Ash, & Nash, 1979; Thomas, 1982; Zetlin & Turner, 1985).

Adolescence is also a key stage in the understanding of social relations because of the way in which the development of identity at this age allows the formation of more intimate and independent friendships than those experienced by younger children (Erikson, 1950). Researchers who assume a close connection between cognitive development and social behavior theorize that more complex peer relations become possible in adolescence because at this stage the individual gains the capacity for abstract moral thought and therefore the cognitive capacity for loyalty and altruism (Kohlberg, 1969; Piaget, 1932).

The ways in which young people describe their social relations vary with age—younger children emphasize propinquity and common interests, and older children mention mutual acceptance and loyalty (Bigelow & LaGaipa, 1980). Typically, each individual develops a *repertoire of social relations*, differing in complexity, extent of involvement, and affective character. People do not move through increasingly complex stages of social behavior one by one, discarding the simpler sorts of relations as they mature, but rather, as they mature, adolescents and adults add new dimensions to their repertoire or relations range.

This range, ordered from the most to the least complex, includes the following types of relations: *collaborative interdependent friendships, emotional connections* (brief or extended), *relations based on pragmatic cooperation, relations involving unreciprocated assistance, momentary physical play,* and *simple observation* (Bell, 1981; Rubin, 1980). Observational relations, in which two persons attend only to each others' activities, require the most minimal interaction of all (Bronfenbrenner, 1979). Unfriendly relations such as dislike and rejection are also recognized as occupying a place in the typical relationship repertoire (Bell, 1981; Selman & Selman, 1979).

An individual's social relations are described as problematic when, instead of participating in a wide range of relations, he or she has limited access to sustained successful encounters with peers (Hartup, 1978), has difficulty forming emotional connections or deep friendships (Bell, 1981), or is consistently rejected by others (Strain, 1981). Problematic social relations, especially in the form of limited access to "positive, affectionate, cooperative social contacts with peers," are identified by one authority on the issue as a profound handicap faced by most young people with disabilities (Strain, 1981, p. viii).

Social Relations In School

Anthropologists and sociologists view schooling as a means of *transmitting culture*. In contrast to preliterate societies, in which the family was the major agent of socialization, societies like ours depend on schools to transmit both elements of the "formal" culture (such as history, politics, and literature) and less formal elements such as values and social behavior. In particular, school experiences teach young people *how to behave in nonfamily groups*, and thus prepare them to fit into the *existing* social and cultural system (Henry, 1963; LeCompte, 1978). Therefore, sociocultural theorists argue, schools usually serve a conservative function, reproducing the patterns (e.g., of social stratification or inequality) that exist in the larger society instead of challenging them (Hollingshead, 1949; Landis, 1980; Ogbu, 1974, 1978).

Staff Influences

One way that social patterns are reproduced is through the activities of school staff. Administrative procedures such as *tracking* (counseling students to enroll in a series of honors or remedial classes) serve a gatekeeping function that can be used to sort and stratify students. The effect is to limit social contact between members of different academic tracks and reduce lower-track students' opportunities for upward social mobility (Erickson, 1976; Erickson & Schultz, 1982; Oakes, 1986a, 1986b; Ogbu, 1974; Rosenbaum, 1976). In addition, administrators who equate good classroom management with teacher-dominated lectures and a lack of classroom noise can discourage faculty who want to promote cooperative student interaction through group discussion or joint activities (Benham Tye, 1987).

Teachers, of course, are in a position to influence student behavior and social relations directly (Harrington, 1973; Sieber, 1979). All too often, we communicate our own beliefs and predjudices without an accompanying self-critique. We may not be fully conscious of our influence on student social relations. For example, faculty serving students of different socioeconomic and racial backgrounds have been shown to teach differently, tailoring their discourse styles and discipline techniques to their perceptions of their students' assumed futures: preparing middle-class students for responsibility and lower-class students for submission (Leacock, 1969; Rist, 1970; Wilcox, 1982).

The ways in which we convey our preconceptions to students can be subtle, or they can be quite overt, as in the following instance, recorded in my journal, in which a teacher openly exhibited racial and ethnic predjudices to his pupils:

> I stopped by at the end of 3rd period to ask Mr. Askimos if I could visit his room on the days when I follow Veronica and Noreen as they go to all their classes. He agreed, and then, in the presence of the remedial reading students who were sitting quietly behind us, he said, "I have 35 kids in this class. For most of them, the guidance office was looking for a hole to put them in. I have a few Vietnamese kids who want to learn something, but *otherwise!* Most of 'em have bodies like this one here (I can't believe it but he's pointing to a tall black kid about 3 feet away), and they can't read more than second or third grade level!"

As part of my research, I followed nondisabled students (those who were involved in social relations with the disabled students in my study) as they went to their classes, in order to get an idea of what their days were like. Mr. Askimos was an unusually bitter man who was recognized as such by other teachers and administrators. Unfortunately, three of "my" students (Veronica, Noreen, and Preston) were enrolled in his remedial reading and driver education classes. My data therefore contain dramatic but not necessarily representative examples of the ways in which faculty can negatively influence student relations, such as the following instance:

As we walk to driver education class, which is held in a bungalow on the edge of the school grounds near the neighborhood shops, Noreen (an extremely pretty girl who is a part-time clothing model at a department store) says, "He usually lets us go to the store, but he probably won't since you're here today." As class begins, Mr. Askimos talks about what the students are supposed to be doing (he still has the same things written on the board that he had when I was here last week with Veronica). He says that they may answer questions at the end of the chapter in their driver education textbook, or else read an article in *Scholastic Magazine* on jobs, and if they want to, use it as a preparation for choosing their courses for next year. Mr. Askimos says, "I gave this article to my sixth period remedial reading class (the one Veronica is in). *They can't read well enough to go to English classes, but I was amazed at how well they understood this article, given their temperaments, background, and willingness to go to school!*" None of the students choose to take a *Scholastic*, however.

It's 9:35 A.M. Kids do things at their seats—other homework, reading text-books, talking, eating, complaining about their grades. I go up to Mr. Askimos's desk to get a text and he explains about the blue and yellow books he uses. The yellow book "is used in the bilingual program because it's about third grade reading level instead of eighth. *That's about all most of these kids can handle.*" As I return to my seat, the Asian guy sitting behind me looks at me with raised eyebrows. I wonder if he was listening to what Askimos said and if he is as embarrassed and angry as I am.

A boy from India who speaks English with a strong accent approaches Mr. Askimos to appeal the F he received, saying that he turned in all his work. Askimos says that although he got an A on the test and in class, some assignments are missing. Askimos asks him, "Which period were you in, 'pirst' or first?" This results in loud laughter from the class. Apparently, the kids think that the teacher's imitation of the Indian boy's accent is funny.

One can only speculate about the effects of Mr. Askimos's mockery and low expectations on his students, but the attitudes he modeled obviously made no *positive* contribution to the social climate of a school in which (one hoped) young people of different racial and ethnic backgrounds and varying ability levels were learning to get along with each other.

Form and Function of Student Relations

Observational studies of U.S. and British adolescents offer interesting information about the *forms* of student relations in school. Young people are often observed to enact these relations in groups or *cliques*. Clique members are generally of the same sex, grade, and social class, and hold common values related to appearance and academic or athletic achievement. Depending on the nature of the peer group, however, academic achievement is not always positively correlated with high social status (Hallinan, 1980; Lightfoot, 1983).

Student cliques are also characterized by racial/ethnic polarization. At Explorer, a school whose population encompassed an unusually wide range of racial and ethnic groups, special clubs and informal hangout areas developed along ethnic lines. As noted previously, academic tracking, which often acts to separate racial and ethnic groups into separate academic "streams" within individual schools, can reinforce adolescents' tendency toward homogeneous association (Oakes, 1986a, 1986b; Ogbu, 1974; Schofield, 1982; Shimara, 1983). Teachers' attitudes or example may also reinforce homogenization, as could have happened in Mr. Askimos's case.

Same-sex associations typify cliques in U.S. schools. Because the romantic overtones of boy-girl relations intensify during adolescence, cross-sex friendships become difficult to achieve at this age (Bell, 1981). Instead, girls typically form friendships with other girls in pairs or threesomes, while boys form larger groups. This difference in the size of friendship cliques is explained in terms of the differing "developmental tasks" faced by boys and girls of this age. Girls focus on developing interpersonal skills and relationships, tasks best accomplished in dyadic relations; boys are said to need achievement and independence, best worked through in groups (Douvan & Adelson, 1966; Savin-Williams, 1980).

In secondary school, students sometimes value peer relations more highly than academic learning. One functionalist theory explains this phenomenon by describing the ways in which social relations fill needs unmet in typical U.S. public schools. In such schools, the qualities most rewarded by teachers are punctuality, obedience to authority, perseverance, dependability, the deferral of gratification, tact, and predictability (Bowles & Gintis, 1976; LeCompte, 1978; Sizer, 1984). In large secondary schools, where students are massed and treated as subordinates and routines and rules thoroughly govern activities, positive peer relations are said to offer alternative milieux in which individuality, authority, variety, spontaneity, and other rewards can be obtained (Coleman, 1961; Cusick, 1973; Hallinan, 1980; Henry, 1963; Karweit & Hansell, 1983).

WHAT WE STILL NEED TO KNOW

This overview of background research shows that school integration for young people with severe disabilities is the result of more than 2 decades of effort aimed at reducing the inequality and exclusion experienced by persons stigmatized as disabled. The schools are viewed as an important social setting in which positive intergroup relations, critical to community "absorption," can be promoted. Ethical, legal, and pedagogical arguments support the value of societal participation for all persons with disabilities.

Stigma and negative attitudes can be seen to have obstructed integration efforts. The special education literature emphasizes the need to overcome these obstacles through school-based programs that include attitude-change efforts, peer interaction arrangements, and the use of data-based teaching techniques to instruct disabled students in the social skills they need in integrated environments.

The literature on social relations during adolescence describes this stage as a time when young people first develop the cognitive capacity to base their social relations on moral thought and an idealism that might encourage associations based on more than simple attraction. Typical adolescents are said to develop a range or repertoire of social relations, and lack of access to this full array of relations can lead to problems. Observational studies stress the primacy of peer relations in adolescence, and criteria for peer association that include similarity between individuals and conformity to standards of ethnicity, appearance, athletic skill, or academic achievement. Studies of intergroup contact reveal ways in which administrative policies and classroom practices can affect the development and quality of intergroup peer relations.

Research into social relations between nondisabled and severely disabled adolescents is not yet sufficiently extensive to constitute a body of literature. The studies reviewed in Chapter 2 reveal that most contacts are neutral in nature, and that the structure of the contact situation is also influential. Unfortunately, these research reports contain only brief descriptions of the quality of the social relations observed. A further problem with this literature is that only one study (Voeltz & Brennan, 1983) incorporated the viewpoints of the participants in its assessment of the quality of these social relations.

The purpose of the research on which this book is based, therefore, was to provide a detailed description of the social relations that occur between severely disabled and nondisabled adolescents as a result of integration in high school, with special emphasis on discovering the meanings that participants attribute to these social relations. A second goal was to describe those features of the contact situation (i.e., environmental characteristics, administrative structures, pedagogical practices, and participant characteristics) that affected the development of various types of intergroup social relations. A third goal was to contrast participant understandings and contextual features with the stated and implied goals of the integration program in one high school, in order to improve understanding of current practices and to generate hypotheses for future research.

chapter 5

San Francisco and Its Schools

Social relations in schools are thought to reflect the patterns of the larger society. In transmitting culture, schools tend to duplicate the beliefs, traditions, and social hierarchies of the communities in which they are located. In order to understand the ways in which teachers and students acted at Explorer, then, it helps to know a bit about local demographics, the political history of the San Francisco Unified School District, and the organizational structure of the high school.

THE CITY

San Francisco is a large American city (population approximately 680,000) whose reputation for innovation and social tolerance might lead one to expect that here, if anywhere, people with disabilities would be accepted. As noted in a recent guidebook:

> In San Francisco a long tradition of social diversity has resulted in a widely practiced and genuinely relished tolerance toward—and vast enjoyment in—nearly all the possible permutations of human behavior . . . Though the City's physical space is small, her "social space" is virtually unlimited and constantly expanding. San Franciscans are united only in their cherishing of the exotic, the eccentric, the amusing, and the human. (Delehanty, 1980, p. 6)

Another important characteristic of the City is the mixture of ethnic and cultural groups that coexist within its limited space (the peninsula site occupies only 46 square miles). Gay men and women have a long-established community there; more recently, increasing numbers of persons from Southeast Asia and Latin America have arrived as refugees from political instability and conflict.

The guidebook image of cherished diversity is an attractive one, but not completely accurate. For example, although the City's standard of living is high (the median family income was $20,911 at the time of this study), many poor people live in San Francisco. More than 10% of all families, and almost 14% of the total population, lives in poverty (U.S. Bureau of the Census, 1983; the Census Bureau's 1980 poverty level was $8,414 annual income for a family of four). The "haves" and "have nots" experience the City's social space quite differently, particularly in terms of access to goods, services, power, and prestige.

Indicators of socioeconomic status demonstrate that poverty in San Francisco does not occur equally among racial and ethnic groups. The "have nots" in San Francisco are most likely to be blacks or recently arrived Asian and Hispanic refugees. For example, data in the Youth Needs Assessment recently prepared for the San Francisco Delinquency Prevention Coordination Council gave evidence of black youth's impaired access to livelihood and power: while only 3% of white families lived in poverty in the City, 23% of black families were poor; although black youth made up 21.6% of the youth population, they made up 58% of those who lived in public housing projects (the least desirable housing in the city); black youth between ages 16 and 19 had the highest unemployment rate in the city, a rate twice as high as the city-wide average (Bolton, 1980).

Although the sight of intergroup contact promoted by the City's limited physical space might lead the visitor to believe that diverse groups coexist in peace, San Francisco is actually not much better than other American cities in this respect. The differing needs of the City's population groups put stress on public resources and result in continuing political and social conflict as these groups compete for increasingly scarce resources (FitzGerald, 1986).

SCHOOL POLITICS

The San Francisco Unified School District (SFUSD) is a social-service arena in which *intergroup competition* has been clearly visible. In recent years, demographic changes and cuts in state taxes have shrunk the district's financial base, put stress on school services, and exacerbated competition and conflict among ethnic, racial, and socioeconomic groups.

Following an industrial boom during World War II, San Francisco's population peaked: the 1950 Census reported 775,357 residents in the City. The population declined to 740,316 in 1960 and to 678,794 in 1980 (Bureau of the Census, 1983). School enrollment declined by one-third between 1960 and 1970, as a result of a declining birth rate and rising real estate values that made housing for families with children increasingly expensive within the city limits (Kirp, 1982). State financial aid to the schools, calculated per pupil, dropped concurrently.

During the same decade, racial segregation and inequality in schooling became the focus of political discussion. A 1971 judicial decision ordering desegregation (*Johnson v. San Francisco Unified School District*, 339 F. Supp. 1315, N.D. Cal. 1971), and consequent changes to school district pupil assignment practices (which included extensive busing and redesign of school attendance areas), were intended to create racially and ethnically balanced schools. However, it soon became evident that public policy was being undercut by *informal discrimination*.

During the 1970s, for example, assignment to special education classes in San Francisco schools was shown to be racially disproportionate. Black students, who in the 1976–1977 school year made up 31.1% of the district's enrollment, constituted 53.8% of the enrollment in classes for the educable mentally retarded (EMR) (Levy, 1975; Ogbu, 1982). After apparent racial bias in the assignment of students to EMR classes was successfully challenged in federal court (*Larry P. v. Riles*, 495 F.Supp. 926, N.D. Cal. 1979), the situation improved for EMR students, but the problem of resegregation did not disappear (Kirp, 1982).

Tracking, the practice of dividing students into separate classes on the basis of achievement level, also served to maintain educational inequality (Oakes, 1986a, 1986b). In the words of an SFUSD memorandum, "Black and Hispanic students are disproportionately represented in academic classes, especially advanced placement and honors classes" (1985, January). This was a particular problem in the district's secondary schools, where minority group students were underenrolled in college-prep tracks. In 1985, this problem had become so severe that a district-wide in-service day was organized for the discussion of potential solutions.

In the 1980s, the competition for educational resources was intensified by attempts to provide for the *special needs* of the district's 59,000 students. In 1980, there were some 6,500 school-aged youth in San Francisco who spoke any of 22 different foreign languages, but who required special services because they spoke little or no English (Bolton, 1980; REACH, 1981).

As much as one-third of the school-age population in the City was said to experience some form of learning difficulty, ranging from failure to master a basic skill to severe learning disabilities (Bolton, 1980). In addition, the district was serving approximately 2,000 students with severe disabilities such as hearing, vision, or mobility impairments, mental retardation, or emotional disturbances (Criner, 1981), At the same time, the SFUSD was attempting to provide high-quality academic, business, and technical education to gifted and normally achieving students.

Unfortunately, the effort to serve diverse groups of students was being made in the context of constantly diminishing financial resources. Between 1975 and 1985, the school budget had shrunk so much that teaching staff had to be reduced by 25%. Three factors contributed to the district's long-running financial crisis: the drop in pupil enrollment, poor budget planning, and, especially, the property tax limitation imposed by Proposition 13, a state-wide tax reduction measure (Kirp, 1982).

As resources diminished, competition between interest groups intensified. The ideal of a city that cherished its diverse population groups came into conflict with the reality of scarcity. When one group successfully obtained special services in the City's schools, other groups seemed to lose. For example, the bilingual education budget for 1978–1979 was almost 30% higher than the previous year's budget, even though the total school budget had become smaller (Kirp, 1982).

Within this context, during the 1980–1981 school year, the SFUSD embarked on a program to comply with federal special education legislation by closing segregated special schools and integrating all disabled students into age-appropriate regular schools, one of which was the high school I describe here.

EXPLORER HIGH SCHOOL

Explorer was located south of the downtown business area in a sunny valley. The high school's immediate neighborhood was primarily residential. Low-rise Victorian and Edwardian buildings, divided into large flats, lined the narrow streets. A public housing project with 246 units was nearby. Small businesses catering to neighborhood needs were scattered throughout the area. This factor had influenced the choice of Explorer for the integration program, since easy access to shops and small businesses afforded opportunities for the vocational and community training viewed as essential components of a special education program for students with severe disabilities (Sailor et al., 1986).

The Community

Explorer's neighborhood was not without its disadvantages. It was densely settled, with noisy, ill-kept streets. Almost 16% of its families lived in poverty (compared to 10% city-wide), and 16% received Aid to Families with Dependent Children (Bolton, 1980). It was a high crime area: the San Francisco Police Department's statisticians ranked the area first in reported assaults and family violence and second in reported burglary among the City's nine police districts ("Crime in the Mission," 1985). The neighborhood housed 11.6% of the City's youth population, and, in addition, five large schools (Explorer High School, a public middle school, and three Catholic schools) that brought an estimated 6,000 children and youth into a six-block area every day (Bolton, 1980).

Perhaps as a function of these problems and the other disadvantages discussed above, the neighborhood's population tended to be transient, with a relatively low proportion of home owners to renters (Bureau of the Census, 1983). If they could afford to, families living in the neighborhood would eventually move to more desirable areas of San Francisco, a factor which one of the school's vice-principals identified as contributing to the high transiency rate among Explorer's student population.

Physical Structure

Explorer was a large school, with about 2,100 students and a 110-member professional staff. Established in 1890, it was proudly described as "the first comprehensive high school West of the Rockies" (High School, 1975). The original 19th-century building was replaced in 1928 with an imposing four-story structure built in California Mission style with red-tiled roof and tall bell tower. This structure was renovated to meet earthquake safety standards in 1977, at which time an elevator and ramps were added to make the building wheelchair-accessible.

A large, hand-painted mural (in a style inspired by Mexican political artists) decorated a side wall of the school. It showed black, white, Hispanic, and Asian youth holding olive branches, and seemed to express in iconographic form the high school's commitment to the San Francisco ideal of accommodating and appreciating diversity.

Inside, the building was much less attractive. Students complained about the way the school was maintained, but student carelessness and vandalism seemed to compound the problems inherent in maintaining an old structure of this size. In spite of school rules and periodic cleanup campaigns, the walls were defaced by graffiti, and the floors and stairways were frequently littered with papers, food remnants, and discarded soft-drink cans. According to the school newspaper, a leaking roof, broken, boarded-up windows, and ill-heated and ill-lit classrooms and hallways had gone unrepaired for at least 2 years ("Trip downhill!," 1985). Student bathrooms were very badly maintained, unclean, and too small; their condition had long been the subject of unresolved complaints (Parents Meeting, 1983).

Organizational Structure

Education reform movements had left schools like Explorer essentially untouched—its organizational structure duplicated a pattern that hadn't changed since Henry collected the data for his classic portrait of high school life in the late 1950s (1963). The formal organization was hierarchical; important information travelled vertically, from administrators to department heads, department heads to faculty, and faculty to students. At the top of the pyramid were the principal and three vice-principals. Below them were nine department heads (including the girls' dean and the boys' dean, who headed the counseling department and were responsible for handling discipline problems).

The rest of the professional staff was subdivided into 10 departments by subject matter specialization (creative/practical arts, business, mathematics, science, bilingual, English, social studies, special education, physical education, and counseling). Seven counselors (each with an average case load of 300 students) were responsible for advising students about course enrollment and for monitoring individual student progress toward graduation. One teacher, housed next to the counseling department, maintained student attendance records and administered the Internal Work Experience program (IWE). A nonprofessional staff, including custodians, kitchen workers, and security guards, provided support to the administrators and teachers. The allocation of physical space in the school reflected these subdivisions: classrooms, department offices, and resource rooms were clustered by department around the building.

Departmental divisions, space allocation, and scheduling affected patterns of collegial relations. Teachers formed social cliques, often reflecting subject-matter specializations, that met within the various departmental areas during lunch or preparation periods. The administrators and guidance counselors, who were on duty during 4th period (when the rest of the school ate lunch), formed an informal group that met (and often played bridge) in the staff lunch room during 5th period. The nonprofessional staff groups also had their separate territories and schedules. These cliquing patterns made it difficult for special education teachers to integrate *themselves* in the school's staff, since they belonged to a separate department and sometimes had self-imposed schedules that were different from those of the regular education staff.

Regular education classrooms reflected the school's organizational style and top-down information flow. Typically, the teacher's desk was at the front of the room, with student desks or chairs in rows facing front. Periodic announcements and a "daily bulletin" were broadcast through a loudspeaker on the wall above the teacher's desk, often interrupting class work. Most lessons I observed were conducted as lectures. (The exceptions were English classes.) Usually, students were expected to take their places at the beginning of each class, remain in place until the end of the period, attend to the teacher, and keep discussion with fellow students to a minimum.

Students at Explorer were grouped by grade level (9th–12th grades), and within grades into *remedial, standard,* and *honors tracks* that determined the types of courses in which they were permitted to enroll. Each student's program was organized by a guidance counselor who considered three criteria: whether the program met attendance criteria, whether the courses enabled the student to satisfy graduation requirements, and whether space was available in courses the student wanted. Students had to be enrolled in at least five courses per semester (at least three "requiring home preparation") in order to be included in the daily attendance "head count" on which much of the district's financial aid (and consequently the high school's budget) was based. Typically, a student earned five units for each semester in each class for which he or she earned a grade of D or above. The subject matter distribution of these classes was decided by a formula that allowed counselors some flexibility in designing student programs.

In 1985, in order to graduate, a student had to earn 200 units, of which 110 were required and 90 could be electives (e.g., foreign languages, art, building maintenance, or Internal Work Experience). *Internal Work Experience (IWE) was an elective that had an especially strong impact on the present study because "IWEs" often served as peer tutors in Explorer's special education integration program.*

IWE had originally been set up to provide clerical help for staff while allowing students to earn 5 hours of academic credit for their work as "teacher assistants." During the 1984–1985 school year, approximately 110 students were enrolled in the IWE program, at least 42 of whom were assigned to the three classes for students with severe disabilities. (Figures are approximate because of discrepancies between enrollment statistics and actual student participation.) Other IWEs worked in the attendance office, in the main office, or as assistants to individual teachers in academic subjects.

The school day was divided into seven periods, each 55 minutes long, except for 4th period (lunch), which lasted 40 minutes. Bells rang to indicate the beginning and end of each period, with 5 minutes allowed for students to pass from class to class. School rules prohibited students from being in the halls without a written pass during class time. Other rules prohibited eating, drinking, smoking, or possession of objects such as radios, Walkmen, or skateboards. The school's behavior code detailed in full the kinds of conduct for which students might be expelled or reported to the police. Security guards patrolled the halls, maintaining order and enforcing the rules.

The hierarchical organization, vertical flow of information, subject matter specialization, daily routine, and array of rules designed to maintain the routine were characteristic of conditions found at most large American urban schools (Benham Tye, 1987; Cusick, 1973; Sizer, 1984).

Special Education Programs

Staff and Students Explorer High School had enrolled students with disabilities since 1960. Since 1981, it had offered a continuum of services ranging from less to more restrictive: disabled students might be assigned to a regular class, to resource specialist services (a "pull-out" program), or to a self-contained special day class (SDC). In 1984–1985, the special education department was organized in the same way as Explorer's other eight departments, with a department head who was responsible for conveying directives from the school's administrators to the faculty members. The department was staffed by three resource specialist teachers, four SDC teachers, and seven full-time paraprofessional aides. This staff served approximately 110 students.

Resource specialists provided limited instruction to approximately 75 mildly disabled "Learning Disabilities Group" (LDG) students who spent most of their day in regular classes. One SDC teacher was responsible for seven students with orthopedic problems who, because they were physically but not cognitively impaired, were able to participate in many regular academic and nonacademic classes.

The other three SDC teachers worked with 30 students who were classified by the school district as "severely handicapped," and whose social relations were the subject of my study. These students all experienced moderate, severe, or profound mental retardation, defined by the American Association on Mental Deficiency as "significantly subaverage intellectual functioning existing concurrently with deficits in adaptive behavior, and manifested during the developmental period" (Grossman, 1973, p. 5). "Adaptive behavior" referred to "the effectiveness with which the individual adjusted to the natural and social demands of his environment" (Snell, 1978; p. 4). Twenty-five of these students experienced additional conditions such as sensory or physical impairments, behavior disorders, autism, severe seizures, or Down syndrome.

The 30 severely disabled students were divided into three self-contained classes, each staffed by one teacher and two paraprofessional aides (one full-time, one half-time). Two of these classes (Mrs. Anderson's and Mrs. Wilson's) were composed of students labeled "Trainable Mentally Handicapped" (TMH). This meant that, in addition to deficits in adaptive behavior, they had Stanford-Binet IQ scores between 51 and 36. (The school district discontinued the use of IQ scores during the time of this study.) The third class (Mrs. Miller's) was composed of students labeled "Severely/Profoundly Handicapped" (SPH). In addition to severe deficits in adaptive behavior, these students had IQ scores of 35 or less.

These 30 students with severe disabilities spent at least half of each school day in special classes or vocational training experiences organized by the SDC teachers. Most of Mrs. Anderson's and Mrs. Wilson's students were "mainstreamed" into at least one regular subject (e.g. gym, art, building maintenance), but none of Mrs. Miller's students were. All 30 students, however, had contact with nondisabled peers during free time, lunch, assemblies, school dances, and fairs, as well as during daily peer interaction programs scheduled by the special education teachers. The basic data on these students are presented in Table 5.1.

Curriculum for Severely Disabled Students Contemporary special education practices are shaped by federal and state disability legislation. For example, in addition to being supervised by Explorer's administrators, special education teachers were responsible to district-level special

Table 5.1.   Basic data on students with severe disabilities

Name	Teacher	Age	Label	Other conditions
Dwayne	Anderson	14	TMH	vision impairment
Mimi	"	18	TMH	vision impairment
Jon	"	19	TMH	Down syndrome
Judy	"	20	TMH	none
Ramon	"	17	TMH	Down syndrome
Lin	"	19	TMH	Down syndrome
Hannah	"	20	TMH	Down syndrome
Sally	"	18	TMH	microcephaly
LaDonna	"	15	TMH	speech/language disorder
Phuc Sanh	"	18	TMH	seizure disorder
Juan	Miller	16	SPH	seizure disorder
Lian	"	20	SPH	none
Patrick	"	17	SPH	Down syndrome
Tricia	"	19	SPH	total blindness
Denise	"	18	SPH	paraplegia, seizures
Tiny	"	17	SPH	visual impairment
Fidel	"	20	SPH	deafness, blindness
Xuan	"	18	SPH	behavior disorder
Lucy	"	17	SPH	none
Cathy	Wilson	18	TMH	speech/language disorder
Elayne	"	18	TMH	Down syndrome
Jerome	"	17	TMH	Down syndrome
Renaldo	"	19	TMH	Down syndrome
Maria	"	17	TMH	Down syndrome
Jack	"	15	TMH	Down syndrome
Lawrence	"	15	TMH	hearing impairment
Elisa	"	17	TMH	none
Mai	"	15	TMH	skeletal disorder
Michael	"	19	TMH	autism
Belinda	"	20	TMH	none

Source: Students' individualized education programs (IEPs)
TMH: trainable mentally handicapped
SPH: severely/profoundly handicapped

education supervisors who monitored assessment, assignment, and curriculum procedures designed to bring SFUSD schools into compliance with federal disability law and the California Master Plan for Special Education. The curriculum in the special education classrooms was determined by documents required under PL 94-142 called *individualized education plans*, or IEPs. Federal law required special education teachers to work as a team with parents and specialist staff (e.g., speech therapist, physiotherapist, orientation and mobility therapist, psychologist, social worker) to write an IEP for each student, and to meet at least once a year as a team to evaluate progress toward IEP goals and revise the document.

The IEP was a contract designed to make staff accountable to parents (and the state and federal governments) for student progress. Each IEP was a lengthy document that described in detail a student's classroom performance, motor/perceptual skills, communication skills, behavioral strengths and weaknesses, self-help/independent living skills, health status, response to specific teaching techniques and reinforcers, learning modalities, talents, and interests.

The IEP team was required to agree upon instructional goals and objectives designed to address problems in the previously listed skill areas, describe conditions under which achievement of these goals and objectives could be evaluated, and appoint staff responsible for teaching and evaluating the student program. An individual student might have as many as 15 separate instructional goals written into the IEP, depending on his or her needs.

The curriculum model used in the classrooms for students with severe disabilities emphasized teaching *basic skills* (i.e., mobility, communication) through *functional activities* (i.e., shopping, cooking, traveling) across four *domains* of daily life (domestic, leisure, vocational, and community), in order to prepare the students to live as independently as possible in integrated community settings (cf. Sailor & Guess, 1983; Wilcox & Bellamy, 1982).

Before coming to Explorer, the 30 students in the study sample had little experience of such settings. Because of the assumed severity of their disabilities, they had spent most of their previous school years in development centers for the handicapped (DCHs): segregated settings that offered caretaking and recreation programs to young people ages 5–21 who had been considered "too handicapped" to be served in regular schools. Leisure time, too, had been spent with disabled peers at San Francisco's Recreation Center for the Handicapped. Therefore, when transferred to regular schools, these students lacked the skills needed for interaction in integrated community settings, and so goals and objectives that stressed such skills were written into their IEPs. For high school-aged students, the IEPs emphasized the importance of teaching and learning in naturally occurring settings where age-appropriate materials could be found and functional activities arranged. For example, the students learned to shop, do laundry, clean houses, and do building maintenance in neighborhood stores, homes, and offices, rather than in simulated classroom settings.

As described in Chapter 3, federal legislative guidelines incorporated the least restrictive environment principle (LRE), and therefore stressed the importance of educating disabled children "with children who are not handicapped." IEP goals reflected the LRE principle's "integration imperative" in that they were often *written to require interaction with nondisabled persons.* For example, a student's IEP might contain the following goal: "When given free time with nondisabled peers, Sean will participate for up to 10 minutes in leisure activities without disruption on 85% of the opportunities, four out of five days."

This curricular emphasis on peer interaction was one major way in which the special education curriculum differed from the curriculum for nondisabled students at Explorer. Regular classes emphasized traditional academic subjects, and student social interactions were likely to be forbidden or at least restricted to discussions of subject matter. In contrast, the special education teachers regarded social interaction as an integral part of their curriculum. Nondisabled peers were thought to be able to model social skills more appropriately than adult instructors, and the attention of nondisabled peers was seen as highly motivating to students with severe disabilities. The SDC teachers therefore worked deliberately to involve nondisabled students with their classes.

At the end of the 1982–1983 school year, the REACH project's school involvement and federal funding ended. During 1983–1984, however, the integration program continued with support from SFUSD, and two new classes (Mrs. Miller's and Mrs. Wilson's) were opened for students with severe disabilities. When I began the present study in September 1984, the three teachers were satisfied with the results of their integration efforts, but they welcomed the possibility, promised by my efforts, of learning more about the nondisabled students.

chapter 6

The Students
at Explorer

Once I began to observe the 30 disabled students and started to document their contacts with nondisabled peers, I realized that, in order to understand these "intergroup" social relations, I would have to be able to analyze the school's social system. In other words, in order to say *who* got involved with the disabled teenagers, I would have to know *where* these nondisabled students fit into the formal and informal hierarchies of student status at Explorer. In the school's system, ethnicity, socioeconomic status, and academic standing all seemed to contribute to individual students' "social identities."

ETHNICITY

Descriptions of Explorer High School invariably emphasized the ethnic and racial variety of the student population, and stressed the positive aspects of such diversity. For example, a pamphlet prepared for school visitors stated:

> Today, (Explorer) is a multilingual, multicultural reflection of the community it serves . . . Members of the student body represent geographic areas from around the world. These students provide the school with a cultural diversity that enriches the academic atmosphere and creates an appreciation of ethnic differences. (High School, 1984, p. 2)

The dimensions of the school's attendance area reflected the district's efforts to satisfy state guidelines for ethnic and racial balance, but in spite of these efforts, certain ethnic and racial groups were disproportionately represented at EHS in 1985. Although 17% of the district's students had Spanish surnames, this group made up more than 33% of the high school's population. "Other white" students (so-called because Hispanic students might also be of

Caucasian origin), who comprised 17% of the district's population, were only 5% of the EHS population. In contrast to the student population, the teaching staff was predominantly (66%) white. The school district and high school enrollments are compared in Table 6.1.

Explorer had one of the largest English as a second language (ESL) and bilingual programs in San Francisco. More than 40% of its students were bilingual, and approximately 36% (756 students) were enrolled in limited English programs (LEP) designed to improve their English skills. The languages spoken at Explorer included Cantonese, Spanish, Tagalog, Ilocano, Arabic, Hindi, Samoan, Lao, Cambodian, and Vietnamese.

Social Separation

Ethnicity and race were highly salient population characteristics to both staff and students at Explorer High School. Among the students I interviewed, race and ethnicity were most discussed in relation to patterns of peer association, but individuals were also characterized by ethnic or racial origins or associated physical characteristics. For example, after an incident in which a boy made a pass at me (see p. 9), I was interested in learning if a teenager would have reacted as I had, so I asked two girls (both were members of a black Nasty Girl clique) what they thought. Their first question was about the boy's race:

> After I got up to Mrs. Miller's room, I asked Zita and Latrice what they'd do if someone said something weird to them in the hall. Latrice said, "Who was it— was he black?" I said, "No, kind of light." Zita said, "I'd just talk right back to him."

Individual students reported suffering peer sanctions if they tried to date across ethnic/racial boundaries. The high school's hangout areas also reflected these divisions, with different groups occupying separate territories. Interviews with teachers and school security guards confirmed the social separation of ethnic/racial groups that I had observed.

Expectations

In repeated interviews, teachers and administrators spoke of race and ethnicity as predictive of academic success and behavior. Certain groups could generally be expected to do well in school, while others were more likely to fail. From the staff's perspective, ESL students, especially the foreign-born, enjoyed a positive valuation. As in other schools and other U.S. cities, these young people had a reputation for achieving success in spite of the linguistic and economic barriers they experienced as new immigrants (Lightfoot, 1983). As one Explorer administrator said, "What makes the school are the ESL kids. ESL kids come to class, stay with it, and graduate."

Young people from Asia were considered particularly likely to excel academically. These students had a reputation among their peers for working

Table 6.1. Percentage of enrollment by race/ethnicity, 1985

	Spanish-surnamed	Other white	Black	Chinese	Japanese or Korean	Native American	Filipino	Other nonwhite
San Francisco Unified School District	16.9	16.9	23.3	19.7	2.2	0.6	8.5	11.9
Explorer High School	33.2	5.0	14.0	19.2	0.0	0.6	12.5	15.5

Source: Explorer High School attendance office

hard and obeying rules. As Anita (who was black) said in describing a science class, "You know how the Chinamens usually be sitting and looking at the teacher? Well, this class is so boring, even the CHINAMENS be falling asleep!" Of the 402 students on the EHS honor roll in Spring 1985 (a 3.0 average in academic subjects was required), at least 54% were of Asian origin (High School, 1985; Yearbook Staff, 1985).

Hispanic students as a group were not expected to do as well in school as Asians. One guidance counselor explained that, in his experience, the foreign-born Asian students were slow to mature socially, and so they were able to do better academically. Hispanic students, however, developed social maturity early and therefore would put social priorities ahead of academic achievement. Consequently, their schoolwork would suffer. However, of the 402 students on the Honor Roll, 26% had Spanish surnames—a percentage which roughly equalled the Hispanic proportion of the student population at Explorer (High School, 1985; Yearbook Staff, 1985).

In contrast, black students had the lowest valuation of all ethnic/racial groups at Explorer. They were reputed to lack motivation and cause discipline problems. Although discipline figures broken down by ethnicity were not available specifically for Explorer, in San Francisco schools in general blacks accounted for 63% of the school suspensions and 29.5% of the dropouts (Bolton, 1980). Blacks also had a negative valuation for academic achievement. Of the 402 students on the Explorer honor roll in Spring 1985, no more than 6% were black, although blacks made up 23.3% of the school's population (High School, 1985; Yearbook Staff, 1985).

SOCIOECONOMIC CHARACTERISTICS

In an application for accreditation submitted to the Western Association of Schools and Colleges, Explorer's attendance area was optimistically described as follows:

> The [Explorer High School] service district contains the complete spectrum of socioeconomic descriptions from small packets [sic] of expensive homes occupied by highly paid professionals to old Victorians occupied by skilled and semiskilled workers to housing projects and tenements occupied by the unskilled and poor. (High School, 1982, p. GD 2)

This service district included 37 census tracts, 30 of which were located on the City's southeast side, comprising a roughly triangular area with its apex in the Castro district and its base at San Francisco Bay. Besides this triangle, an eight-block-square area of Chinatown (comprising most of seven census tracts) was also included within the area served by Explorer High.

Since specific socioeconomic indicators were not available for all 2,100 members of the high school's population, I used city and county census data on income and poverty to evaluate the economic status of families within these 37 census tracts, and thereby to make inferences about student poverty (Bureau of the Census, 1983).

Explorer families were poorer than the San Francisco average, as measured by per capita income and percentage of families in poverty (see Table 6.2). Income in 26 of the 37 EHS tracts ranked in the lowest quartile of per capita income in the city, and of the 37 tracts, 14 had more than 20% of families in poverty: double the city-wide rate.

Although it was true that "highly paid professionals" lived within Explorer's service area (particularly in the Castro district a few blocks from the high school), it was my impression that few occupants of the "expensive homes" so proudly touted on the accreditation application had much to do with the high school: the Castro was the City's most successful gay community, and its mostly young, white, male population had few children (FitzGerald, 1986). The students I got to know at Explorer had little contact with gay people, and comments they made revealed feelings of aggression coupled with envy of their perceived economic advantages. For example:

Anita came to my house for lunch and we discussed Melvin—her new love interest. Melvin lives in a halfway house, and when I asked her why, she said, "Well, you know how black people beat up on faggots." I said, "No, I *don't* know!" She said, "Well, they *do*, and Melvin was with a bunch of guys—he said he didn't *do* nothin', he was just watchin' and waitin' to pick up any money that fell out of the faggots' pockets—but he got in trouble for that an' den . . . an' den he had t' go to the halfway house."

Actually, I knew quite well that gay men had been the victims of attacks by groups of black and Hispanic youth that often took place in the immediate vicinity of Explorer. The increasing frequency of these attacks was thought to correlate with the growing fear of AIDS in San Francisco (FitzGerald, 1986).

STAFF-ASCRIBED STUDENT ROLES

Especially when talking with peers, teachers constantly categorize students. It is both a survival tactic and a handicap, this ability to type a kid within 5

Table 6.2. A comparison of economic characteristics

	Per capita income ($)	Percentage of families in poverty
San Francisco	9,265	10.3
Explorer High School service district	7,678	18.4

Source: Bureau of the Census, 1983

seconds of looking at him. Through content analysis of interviews with 25 staff members, I identified more than 100 terms that teachers used to describe students at Explorer. These terms revealed a typology of informal student roles that intersected with ethnic/racial categories, and was structured around the concept of "doing well in school." Student roles and associated expectations for behavior seemed to be assigned primarily on the basis of staff perceptions of who had potential for academic success and the ability to "work up to potential." A description of these roles (in descending order of status) follows.

'Honors Types'

"Honors Types" were characterized by staff as being "sharp" and "academically oriented," and as having good attendance and good behavior. They were most likely to be enrolled in college preparatory programs and honors track classes, and were perceived by teachers as being especially rewarding to work with.

'Newcomers'

Students typed as Newcomers were mostly recent immigrants from Latin America or Asia. They were characterized as "wanting to learn," and were expected to have good attendance and generally good behavior. Although they might engage in intragroup conflict, this generally occurred outside school. Newcomers were expected to have difficulties with English, but to work hard at their studies whether they were academically skilled or not. Because these students were perceived as highly motivated to learn, staff also found them rewarding to teach.

'Bright, But . . . '

Some students were characterized by staff as being "bright" or having "a lot of potential," but also as having undesirable characteristics such as being "a discipline problem," "a cutter," "sarcastic and streetwise," or having "a poor self-image," "a problem home," "a drinking/drug problem," or "priorities other than school." These undesirable characteristics were seen by staff as interfering with such students' ability to "pull themselves up and make the most of their potential." These "Bright, But . . . " students were difficult to have in a classroom, although some teachers enjoyed the challenge they presented.

'Nice, But Not Very Bright'

Students characterized as "Nice, But Not Very Bright" were generally pleasant individuals with good attendance who were "trying hard," but who did not do well academically because they lacked ability. They had "good, quiet behavior," were dependable and "the kind of kid who will show up." Because they were not disruptive in class, they were appreciated by teachers, but they were not as highly valued as the Honors Type.

'The Special Ed. Type'

"Special Ed. Types" were characterized as being less competent than others, and therefore as "needing help." They were considered likely to misbehave or behave in unusual ways in order to get attention. Staff had these expectations of both special education students with mild disabilities who received services in resource room programs (e.g. learning-disabled students), and students with more severe disabilities. Students whom regular education staff found difficult to work with might be characterized as Special Ed. Types, even if they were not so labelled officially.

'Losers'

"Losers" were characterized as "raunchy," or as "troublemakers," and were likely to break school rules, cut school frequently, or be chronically tardy. Most of these students had been involved in infractions of school discipline serious enough to warrant warnings or suspensions, and some were on probation from the juvenile courts. They differed from students in the Bright, But . . . category (who could also be troublemakers) in that they were considered beyond help. One staff member characterized these students as "the kids nobody wants."

The staff-ascribed student role typology is diagrammed in Figure 6.1.

THE 'REGULARS' AND THE 'OTHERS'

My broad, initial, "grand tour" observations (Spradley, 1980) at Explorer helped give me an overview of where students hung out and what they did during the day. Data collected during these observations showed that the 30 severely disabled students in the study population (13 boys and 17 girls), although assigned to self-contained special classes, spent a lot of time in contact with nondisabled students.

Based on later "day in the life" observations during which I followed each of four randomly selected students with severe disabilities for an entire school day, I estimated that these teenagers spent about a *third* of the day in

Students who do well in school	Students who don't do well in school
Honors Types	Bright, But . . .
Newcomers	Losers
	Nice, But Not Very Bright
	The Special Ed. Type

Figure 6.1. Staff-ascribed student role typology.

Table 6.3. Extent of interaction of four randomly selected disabled students with nondisabled peers on a randomly selected school day

Student	Instructor	Proportion of school day spent in interaction
Renaldo	Wilson	35%
Jon	Anderson	34%
Juan	Miller	36%
Maria	Wilson	38%

either proximal, helping, or reciprocal interactions that involved nondisabled peers (Brown et al., 1983; Hamre-Nietupski et al., 1978; Schutz et al., 1984; Stainback & Stainback, 1985). (See Table 6.3.) The amount of time these students spent in contact with nondisabled peers compared favorably with data from a study that investigated daily contact between 104 students with disabilities and their nondisabled peers in a nearby area of the state (Filler, Goetz, & Sailor, 1986). The study of the 104 students found that they spent 27 percent of the average day in interactions involving nondisabled peers.

I identified these "contact situations" as the focus of my study. I categorized the nondisabled students whom I observed in these contact situations into two groups on the basis of the frequency and extent of their contact. I called these groups the *Others* and the *Regulars* (cf. Spradley & Mann, 1975).[1]

The Others were 115 nondisabled students whose interactions with the disabled students were episodic, serendipitous, or involuntary. These students were of both sexes and represented all the ethnic groups present in the high school's population.

Because I had decided to focus on the nature of social relationships among students who were in *regularly repeated voluntary contact*, I didn't collect more detailed data on these casual relations. The frequency with which these casual contacts occurred, however, showed that *the disabled students had more extensive social connections than could be documented given the limitations of my investigation, suggesting an area for future research.*

The Regulars were 32 students (11 boys and 21 girls) who repeatedly and voluntarily interacted with disabled students. The data analysis that I completed at the end of the 1984–1985 school year showed that these *Regulars were involved in 66% of all contact situations observed.* All but two of the Regulars had some connection with the school's Internal Work Experience program (IWE), which supplied teacher assistants to staff members. Twenty-

---

[1] In the terminology of The Seabreeze in Glendale, Arizona, and Matilda's, in Melbourne, Australia—two establishments where I have tended bar (an occupation in which a special education teacher feels right at home)—a "regular" was a customer who repeatedly patronized these hangouts; my use of the term to describe these 32 students reflects that usage and does *not* imply that other students (disabled or not) were in any way "irregular."

five of the Regulars were enrolled in IWE during the time of the present study, and were receiving five elective credits for acting as peer tutors in the special education classrooms. Five additional Regulars were either former IWEs or friends of IWEs.

The Regulars, and their social relations with their disabled fellow students, were the particular focus of the present study.

Racial/Ethnic Characteristics

As previously noted, the high school served students from an unusually wide range of ethnic and racial groups. The students with severe disabilities were similarly diverse, as were the Regulars. However, certain student groups were observed to be disproportionately involved with their disabled fellow students. *In particular, a high number of black students and a disproportionately low number of Chinese and other nonwhite students were so involved.* The high school's enrollment and the racial/ethnic makeup of the sample groups are compared in Table 6.4.

Socioeconomic Characteristics

As stated previously, socioeconomic indicators suggested that Explorer High School students came from families that were, on the average, poorer than others in the city. The same indicators for the census tracts in which severely disabled students lived suggested that the families of these disabled students were similar in socioeconomic status to the Explorer averages for per capita income and percent of families in poverty.

The Regulars, however, came from families that were *much poorer* than the EHS average: 22 of the 30 Regulars for whom socioeconomic indicators were available (data was unavailable for two additional Regulars) lived either in public housing or in census tracts ranked in the *lowest quartile* of per capita income in the city. The mean per capita income in the census tracts from which Explorer drew its students was $7,678, already far below the city's mean per capita income of $9,265; mean per capita income in the census tracts where the 30 Regulars resided for whom data was available was $6,608—only two-thirds of the average income of San Francisco residents. The Regulars also lived in areas of town where high percentages of families in poverty were concentrated. The percentage of families in poverty in these areas averaged *more than twice* the city-wide rate (Bureau of the Census, 1983). Figures for San Francisco, Explorer High School, severely disabled students, and the Regulars are compared in Table 6.5.

Pupil Characteristics: Students with Severe Disabilities

Thirty adolescents with developmental disabilities were assigned to three self-contained special education classes at Explorer because they needed a curricular program that emphasized the acquisition of basic skills (e.g., com-

Table 6.4. Racial/ethnic composition of two groups (students with disabilities and 'Regulars') at Explorer High School (EHS), 1985

	Spanish-surnamed	Other white	Black	Chinese	Native American	Filipino	Other nonwhite
Students with disabilities	23.3	10.0%	23.3%	30.0%	0.0%	6.7%	6.7%
Regulars	25.0%	6.3%	50.0%	3.1%	0.0%	12.5%	3.1%
Overall EHS student population	33.2%	5.0%	14.0%	19.2%	0.6%	12.5%	15.5%

Source: Explorer High School attendance office

Table 6.5. Socioeconomic status of selected groups

	Mean per capita income	Proportion of families in poverty
All San Francisco residents	$9,265	10.3%
Explorer High School area[1]	$7,678	18.4%
The Regulars	$6,608[2]	22.5%
Explorer students with disabilities	$7,768[2]	17.3%

[1]Census tracts from which EHS drew its students
[2]Figure is for census tracts where individuals in the relevant group (for whom data is available) resided.
Source: Bureau of the Census, 1983

munication, mobility, and independent living) rather than academics. The instructional needs of these teenagers varied widely. Some could use complex speech, and some had no systematic communication system at all. Some students could walk and orient themselves independently, both in school and on the streets of the community, whereas others required constant assistance to move from place to place within the school building. The range was equally wide in terms of self-care, vocational, domestic, and social skills. Table 6.6 provides a comparison of these student characteristics.

Pupil Characteristics: The Regulars

As stated earlier, Explorer students compared unfavorably to students at other city high schools on standardized achievement measures. However, approximately 20% of Explorer's students *did* achieve the 3.0 grade point average (GPA) each semester necessary for inclusion on the high school's honor roll during the time of this study (High School, 1985). *None of the Regulars, however, was listed on the honor roll during the 1984–1985 school year.* In fact, an examination of the report cards for those Regulars for whom grades could be obtained showed that most of these students had very poor records. The Regulars' GPAs ranged from 0.23 to 2.58 on a standard 0–4 scale.

In addition to GPA, students at Explorer received a grade for "Citizenship." (actually an evaluation of classroom behavior). This was reported in terms of a 4-point scale in which 4 meant "excellent," 3 meant "satisfactory," 2 constituted a "warning," and 1 was "unsatisfactory." Teacher evaluations showed that many of the Regulars' behavior in their academic classes left something to be desired. Individually averaged citizenship marks for these teenagers ranged from 1.25 to 3.23.

The Regulars' attendance records also were often poor. At the high school, classes met approximately 90 times in each report period. Students whom I interviewed explained that they cut certain classes more than others, depending on the times they were scheduled (first period and the period after lunch were often cut), or their perceptions of the teacher's interest in them.

Table 6.6. Educational characteristics of 30 students with severe disabilities at Explorer High School

Name	Expressive language	Mobility	Independent living skills
Dwayne	simple speech	independent in school	self-care, domestic, social
Mimi	limited speech	independent in school	self-care, domestic
Jon	limited speech and articulation	independent in school and community	self-care, social
Judy	simple speech	independent in school	self-care, vocational
Rodrigo	limited speech and articulation	independent in school	self-care
Lin	limited speech (bilingual)	independent in school	self-care, vocational
Hannah	limited speech and articulation	semi-independent in school	self-care
Sally	simple speech	independent in school	self-care, domestic, social
LaDonna	simple speech	independent in school and community	self-care, domestic, social
Phuc Sanh	bilingual	independent in school and community	self-care, domestic
Juan	10 pictures	semi-independent in school	requires support in all areas
Lian	none	semi-independent in school	requires support in all areas
Patrick	20 signs	limited	semi-independent self-care
Tricia	one-word utterances	limited by vision	semi-independent self-care
Denise	none	limited	requires assistance in all areas

Tiny	none	limited	requires assistance in all areas
Fidel	5 signs	limited by vision	requires assistance in all areas
Xuan	none	limited	requires assistance in all areas
Lucy	5 pictures	limited	requires support in all areas
Cathy	limited speech	independent in school	self-care
Elayne	limited speech and articulation	independent in school	self-care, domestic
Jerome	limited speech and articulation	independent in school and community	self-care, domestic, social
Batisto	limited speech (bilingual)	independent in school and community	self-care, social, vocational
Maria	two-word utterances	semi-independent in school	semi-independent self-care
Jack	limited speech (bilingual)	independent in school	self-care, social
Lawrence	simple speech	independent in school	self-care, vocational
Elisa	bilingual	independent in school and community	self-care, domestic, social, vocational
Mai	bilingual	independent in school and community	self-care, domestic, vocational
Michael	simple speech	independent in school	self-care, domestic
Belinda	simple speech	independent in school and community	self-care, domestic, social, vocational

Source: Student individualized education programs (IEPs)

Some of our Regulars had cut almost every meeting of an individual class in a semester. The highest number of unexcused absences reported for these students ranged from 14 to 85 classes per semester report period. Table 6.7 summarizes these student characteristics.

Informal Student Roles

As described previously, school staff ascribed to students at least six different types of social roles. In addition, the students themselves perceived *further* informal roles. The answer to the research question, "Who were the students involved in integrated social relations?," varied, therefore, depending upon whom I asked: regular staff, special educators, or other students. These three perspectives on the Regulars' social identities are reviewed below.

Regular Education Perspectives Interviews with the Regulars' teachers and guidance counselors showed that the roles ascribed to 30 of these teenagers were *the least desirable in the student typology*. None of the Regulars were Honors Types, and only two belonged to the Newcomer group that "did well" in school. Seven were typed as Bright, But . . . , because they habitually cut class or caused discipline problems. Thirteen Regulars were labelled Nice, But Not Very Bright, because of perceived incompetence in academic or oral skills (or both); these students might also be characterized as "class cutters" or as "having priorities other than school." Three Regulars, considered Special Ed Types, were assigned to the Learning Disabilities Group (LDG) classes. (One of these students was also perceived as Nice, But Not Very Bright, and one was characterized as a Loser.) Seven of the Regulars were typed as Losers because they combined dramatically poor attendance records with repeated infractions of school rules; five of these students had at different times been suspended or expelled from school for fighting or stealing.

Special Education Perspectives In contrast, interviews with teachers and paraprofessionals, who had come to know the Regulars in the context of their relations with the severely disabled students, revealed a different side of these young people. These staff described the Regulars as either peer tutors (students who received credit through the school's Internal Work Experience program for assisting the teachers) or as friends (students whose association with the disabled students was purely social).

Instead of the "doing-well-in-school" yardstick against which regular education staff measured students, the special education staff described the Regulars in terms of *how they interacted with their disabled peers*. I used content analysis techniques on transcripts of my interviews with these teachers to identify three non–mutually exclusive student types that they perceived.

'The Reliable Type' Regulars classified as the "Reliable Type" could be "counted on" or trusted by staff. This quality was determined by two

Table 6.7. Characteristics of 30 nondisabled students at Explorer High School who were considered "Regulars"

Name	Grade	Racial/Ethnic Category	Grade-point ave. (0–4 scale)	"Citizenship" (1–4 scale)	Absences (over 1 report period)
Andi	9 (repeat)	Black	1.48	1.90	80
Andreas	12	Spanish-surname	1.39	2.23	58
Anita	10	Black	2.58	3.08	14
Aretha	12	Black	0.87	1.91	82
Candi	12	Filipina	1.70	2.88	36
Chanel	11 (LDG)	Black	1.92	2.52	80
Doretha	12	Black	1.70	2.90	53
Harold	12	Black	2.27	2.83	15
Hector	12	Spanish-surnamed	1.63	2.96	43
Latrice	9 (LDG)	Black	0.23	1.25	71
Melody	10	Black	0.09	1.47	85
Mendel	9	Filipino	1.27	2.10	75
Monica	12	Other white	2.08	3.23	25
Noreen	10	Other nonwhite	1.14	2.18	40
Preston	9	Black	1.75	1.90	79
Rick	10 (LDG)	Other white	1.50	2.90	32
Rico	12	Filipino	2.19	2.75	60
Sayonara	12	Filipina	1.48	2.78	31
Silvia	12	Black	1.30	2.20	n/a
Tina	9 (repeat)	Black	1.40	2.00	67
Veronica	9	Black	1.90	2.30	46
Virginia	12	Chinese	1.79	2.70	82
Xavier	12	Spanish-surnamed	2.08	3.00	43

LDG = Learning Disabilities Group

Source: Explorer High School counseling office

67

characteristics: class attendance (for IWEs), and the student's demonstrated ability to "take responsibility." Special education staff shared regular education teachers' concern that students "show up," and attendance-monitoring required the special education teachers' continuing vigilance. But special education staff emphasized the importance of the second characteristic in typing individual students. For example, if a "reliable" Regular were accompanying a disabled student while taking attendance slips to the office, or if a disabled and a nondisabled student were engaged in activity and a staff member was not in the immediate area, the teacher could depend on the fact that, in the absence of direct supervision, the Regular would behave responsibly, appropriately, and resourcefully. In this sense, *the special education teachers typed 25 of the 32 Regulars as reliable.*

The 'Type That Takes Initiative' Regulars identified as being able to take initiative were those who initiated intergroup activities without staff prompting. This quality had two salient characteristics: enjoyment and independence. Staff perceived these Regulars to be motivated primarily by enjoyment rather than duty in their relations with the severely disabled students. Although staff members might suggest joint activities (e.g., "Why don't you listen to the radio with Tiny?"), this type of Regular could be depended on to initiate independently other appropriate activities once radio-listening palled. Nondisabled students who "flaked out" or needed constant urging or supervision were criticized by both teachers and aides. Other Regulars were "reliable," but lacked initiative. *The staff typed 23 of the 32 Regulars as the "Type That Takes Initiative."*

The 'Age-Appropriate Type' Staff evaluations of Regulars indicated a constant concern with the quality of student interactions. Regulars who were the "Age-Appropriate Type" were viewed as engaging in positive interactions because they treated severely disabled students "just like anybody else." These intergroup contact situations were characterized by the same physical horseplay and friendly ribbing that occurred between nondisabled friends.

Nondisabled students whose manner was viewed as condescending (such as Rick, who was thought to "use" disabled students in order to compensate for his lack of other friends) were the subject of staff sanctions (see Chapter 7 for further discussion of interactions perceived as problematic). Some of the Regulars who were described as unreliable or lacking in initiative were still appreciated by the special educators for the quality of their interactions. *All but one of the 32 Regulars received positive evaluations for "age-appropriate behavior"* in intergroup contact.

The Student Perspective Interviews with student informants revealed the existence of at least four informal roles into which 29 of the Regulars could be typed: "Popular People," "Nasty Girls and Thugs," "Cholos and Flips," and "New Wavers." Three additional Regulars did not fit these roles. The descriptions of these student roles reflect the fact that my most articulate informants were black girls whose perceptions of other students were colored by their own status as Popular People.

'Popular People' Students typed as Popular People were well-liked by both sexes, well-dressed, and often actively involved in school activities (e.g., cheerleading, sports, drama, or clubs). Nine Regulars fit this category: one Hispanic boy, and seven girls of black or interracial origins who identified themselves as black. The boy was an all-city soccer star who had friendly relations that crossed racial/ethnic boundaries. Preston, a black Regular, characterized him as "raw"—a highly complimentary term. The girls were described as "nice-spoken" (meaning that they could easily "code switch" between Black and standard English) and "nice people." They had light complexions, and "good" (easy to manage) hair that they wore in loose curls. They dressed in fashion magazine-style, earned money in after-school jobs, and had boyfriends and elaborate social lives that were the frequent subject of our conversations.

'Nasty Girls' and 'Thugs' In the double-edged way that such terms were used by students at Explorer, it was not altogether negative to be a "Thug" or "Nasty Girl." For example, Aretha explained that "being bad" was a quality she had cultivated by lifting weights! Negative expectations, however, were frequently associated with this role. Popular People explained that such persons could be expected to start fights, steal, or otherwise get into trouble. Being "bad" or "nasty" had fewer negative implications for boys than for girls. (Three "popular" girls had boyfriends of this type.) However, Nasty Girls were said to "act fast," or get "jealous" and "destroy things you've worked for" because they "can't stand to see anybody else get up."

Eight Regulars fit this category. Two were black boys, six were girls (five black, one—Zita—described herself as "mixed with Mexican, Irish, black, German, and Filipino). The Thugs and Nasty Girls often braided their hair in corn rows, and dressed in an expensive, eclectic style in which leather clothing, designer jeans, or track suits were accessorized with copious and frequently varied jewelry, hats, bags, and sunglasses. Some had jobs outside school; others may have been involved in illegal activities. (One girl was expelled from school for stealing during the time of the study, and the two boys had been on probation for juvenile justice offenses.) *Two of the Popular People said that they had been "totally surprised" to learn that such "thugs" had chosen to become involved with disabled students.*

'Cholos' and 'Flips' "Cholos" (a term used to describe certain students of Mexican or Central American ancestry) and "Flips" (a term applied to certain students of Filipino origin) were characterized by black informants as "square" (serious and boring), submissive to school rules, and exclusively tied to social relations within their own ethnic groups. Such ethnic labels, which were insulting when used by outsiders, were employed by group members jokingly or as signs of in-group status. Seven Regulars fit this category: two girls had been born in the Philippine Islands, one girl and four boys in Central America. Two were members of a school service organization, and others were active in Hispanic or Filipino clubs. These students tended to dress in conservative "preppy" style. The three girls were deeply involved with steady boyfriends, and four of the boys had jobs after school.

'Little Gangs'/'Rappers' Members of so-called Little Gangs, who referred to themselves as "Rappers," could be characterized by their interest in a musical style beginning to become popular in the early 1980s—*rap*, a rhythmic, nonmelodic music whose lyrics are recited to a strong, rapid beat, instead of sung. Three Regulars, who were related by marriage and who came from families of mixed Filipino, white, and black origin, fit this category. They were streetwise boys who survived in school and in the very poor South of Market neighborhood where they lived by involvement in sports-centered activities. They formed what they described as a "Little Gang" that met to play basketball and hang out at a community center that had recreation programs during the day, and at night provided free food and lodging to homeless men. Two of these boys had jobs at the center, and all three were responsible for babysitting younger siblings at home. Rappers typically carried sports equipment and wore mesh-backed hats, inexpensive track suits, and high-topped basketball sneakers tied with elaborately braided, multicolored laces.

'New Wavers' Students known as "New Wavers" adopted a characteristically nonconformist stance reminiscent of the '50s beatnik style they (perhaps unwittingly) emulated. Two Regulars, an Hispanic boy and a Chinese-American girl (both born in the United States) fit this category. Both appeared to enjoy breaking ethnic and sexual stereotypes, and both associated with friends who reinforced these behaviors. Andre, for example, felt himself to be something of an outsider in the school and deliberately didn't hang out with one of the predominantly Hispanic cliques (two of his best friends were a Filipina and a Samoan girl, who were also Regulars). He described himself as being more sensitive than other students, and was looking forward to "getting away" by leaving the school after graduation. Andre often wore imaginative combinations of thrift shop clothes, and frequently changed the color of his hair.

Virginia was described by her counselor as a "real cute girl with a tough personality—nothing fazes her." She did not do well academically, and had attended another school of higher status before transferring to Explorer. She was a good athlete, and hoped to become a policewoman when she graduated. Like Andre, she dressed in New Wave style.

'Best Friends' and 'Molded' Three Regulars didn't fit easily into the above categories. From my perspective, they exemplified the type of young person who wrings the adult heart because of his or her low status in *both* academic *and* peer social systems. Betty and Veronica, the "Best Friends,"

Table 6.8. Perspectives on Regulars' informal roles at Explorer High School

Student	Regular ed. staff	Special ed. staff	Other students
Andi	BB discipline problem	R, TI, AA	Popular Person
Andreas	BB discipline problem	R, TI, AA	New Waver
Anita	BB discipline problem	R, TI, AA	Popular Person
Aretha	Loser	AA	Nasty Girl
Betty	NB cutter	R, TI, AA	Best Friend
Candi	NB not bright	R, AA	Flip
Carmina	NB other priorities	R, TI, AA	Cholo
Chanel	NB Special Ed. Type	R, AA	Popular Person
Denard	Loser	TI, AA	Thug
Doretha	NB cutter	R, AA	Popular Person
Fifi	BB cutter	R, TI, AA	Popular Person
Fino	Newcomer	R, TI, AA	Popular Person
Harold	Loser	R, TI, AA	Thug
Hector	NB not bright	R, TI, AA	Cholo
Latrice	Special Ed. Type, Loser	AA	Nasty Girl
Melody	NB cutter	R, TI, AA	Nasty Girl
Mendel	NB not bright	R, TI, AA	Rapper
Monica	NB not bright	R, TI, AA	Popular Person
Noreen	BB cutter	R, TI, AA	Popular Person
Preston	Loser	R, TI, AA	Rapper
Ramon	Newcomer	R, TI, AA	Cholo
Ray	NB not bright	R, TI, AA	Cholo
Rick	Special Ed. Type	User	Molded
Rico	NB not bright	R, TI, AA	Rapper
Sayonara	NB not bright	R, AA	Flip
Silvia	Loser	AA	Nasty Girl
Susie	Loser	AA	Nasty Girl
Tina	BB discipline problem	R, TI, AA	Popular Person
Veronica	BB discipline problem	R, TI, AA	Best Friend
Virginia	NB not bright	R, TI, AA	New Waver
Xavier	NB other priorities	R, TI, AA	Cholo
Zita	Loser	TI, AA	Nasty Girl

AA = Age-Appropriate
BB = "Bright, but . . . "
NB = "Nice, but . . . "
R   = "Reliable"
TI   = "Takes initiative"

were 9th-grade black girls who formed an inseparable twosome. Although they took great care with dress and grooming, these girls didn't have the appearance, the speech style, or the clothes that seemed to be required for membership in black Popular People cliques. In addition, each had extensive responsibility for younger siblings that took precedence over participation in school social activities or paid work after school.

Even though both girls were perceptive, had inquiring minds, and could be quite articulate once their shyness was overcome, they had fallen through the cracks of the educational system as well. Veronica, for example, who read thick paperbacks for pleasure and who wanted to go to college so that later she could open her own day-care center, was assigned to "dead-end" classes (including Mr. Askimos's remedial reading class!) that would not fulfill university entrance requirements and in which I observed her to be unchallenged, bored, and engaged in endless power contests with her teachers.

Rick, negatively labeled as "Molded" by a male peer, was a white student who was assigned to a resource-room program for students with learning disabilities. He had been an IWE student assistant to one of the special education teachers the previous year, and continued to maintain contact with the staff and students. One special education teacher characterized him as someone who "used" the disabled students to hide the fact that he had no other close friends in school. He was overweight, had a bad complexion, and wore clothes characteristic of many Explorer boys: work pants, t-shirt with a rock band logo, and running shoes.

Rick was also a heart-wringing type, in spite of the behaviors that made staff and peers avoid him. His behavior reminded me of every adolescent attention-getting-device *I* had ever mistakenly employed, and although his posed coolness and condescending treatment of the disabled students made me (and the staff) uncomfortable, at the same time I felt sorry for him because these devices were so ineffectual in gaining him the positive attention he appeared to seek.

Table 6.8 compares informal student roles across the regular education staff, special education staff, and student perspectives presented here.

These data demonstrate that, in spite of their relatively low status in the regular education academic system, many Regulars were positively evaluated by peers, or by the special education staff (or sometimes by both groups).

chapter 7

What Did They Do and Where Did They Go?

During the school year I spent at Explorer, I was present during more than 300 "contact situations" in which interaction occurred between nondisabled teenagers and the 30 students from the targeted special education classes. The interactions I observed varied from brief encounters to long periods of mutual involvement. In order to make sense of the voluminous data describing these interactions, I analyzed the contact situations in terms of the persons present, the activities they engaged in, the duration of their involvement, and the physical settings where the students met.

You have already "met" the young people involved in these integrated social relations—now I ask you to imagine those Popular People, Thugs, and other "Regulars" as they got together with the "Humans Like Us"—their disabled fellow students.

WHAT DID THEY DO TOGETHER?

Over the year, I observed activities involving disabled and nondisabled students which could be classified (according to the stated or implied goal of each individual contact situation) into nine broad types:

1. Leisure
2. Communication
3. Independent living
4. Mobility
5. School meals

6. Classroom chores
7. Special events
8. Vocational training
9. Functional academics

As the following examples show, the interactions that actually occurred within individual activity categories did not necessarily meet the instructional goals identified by teachers writing lesson plans or IEPs. From my perspective, however, the disabled students learned more age-appropriate social behavior from the serendipitous exchanges that occurred when teachers had the pedagogical courage to "let it happen, Cap'n," than had their time with peers been more rigidly controlled. (See Table 7.1.)

Leisure Activities

Leisure activities provided the focus of about 24% of the contact situations I observed. On the average, each activity lasted about 17 minutes. Playing or teaching such games as miniature pool, Battleship, Mastermind, UNO, or Go Fish, looking at magazines together, working on craft projects, and playing sports together were joint activities that were commonly organized by teachers. This activity category also included contacts that occurred between students mainstreamed for physical education classes in exercise, basketball, and weightlifting. More informal leisure activities, such as hanging out between classes or during free time, listening to music, or horsing around, occurred spontaneously.

In the following example, a holiday craft project was combined with a conversation that, besides illustrating the way in which a leisure activity

Table 7.1. What did disabled and nondisabled students at Explorer High School do together?

Activity	N = 311	Percentage of situations*	Mean duration (minutes)
Leisure	76	24	17
Communication (Greetings)	54 (17 of 54)	17 (5)	10 (2½)
Independent living	43	14	19
Mobility	32	10	4
School meals	29	9	8
Special events	22	7	29
Classroom chores	12	4	9
Vocational training	23	7	16
Functional academics	20	6	26

*Rounded to the nearest whole number

could promote informal social contact, gave me new insight into the linguistic skills of a student named Renaldo:

> I come into Mrs. Anderson's room after lunch to find the students cutting pumpkins for Halloween. Renaldo is speaking Tagalog with Candi and Sayonara while showing them pictures of his family that he carries in his wallet. I had only heard him speaking English until now, and even though I don't know what he's saying, I can hear that his speech is fluent and his utterances much longer. Mrs. Wilson comes over to them, saying, "I brought Renaldo's pumpkin down, but you've got to watch him—this knife is dangerous." Renaldo says, "No, no," and jokingly covers his face. He starts to work on his pumpkin with Sayonara while Candi helps Elisa, another disabled student. Renaldo tells Sayonara, "You draw." She tells HIM to draw the face on the pumpkin. Candi says teasingly to Elisa, "Look what you did! Yours is cut ugly, and mine is nice!" Renaldo says something kiddingly in Tagalog as he and Sayonara scoop the seeds out. Tina, another IWE student, has come in, and she asks, "What did he say?" Sayonara interprets, "He says to eat it!" Renaldo says, "Come on, go 'head," as he holds out a spoonful of seeds to Tina. Candi asks, "Did you ever taste that, Renaldo?" Then the girls joke with him, saying, "Who's your girlfriend?" When he points to Elisa, the other girls say "Ooooo—ooooo!" in unison. Later, I get Sayonara aside and ask her how well Renaldo speaks Tagalog. "Not so good," she says, "It's his second language. He speaks Ilocano better." That blew my mind! A guy with Down syndrome who speaks *three* languages!

Communication Activities

Communication activities were the focus of about 17% of the contact situations I observed. Spontaneous greetings, such as saying hello while passing someone in the hall (included in this activity category), were naturally quite brief. Extended communicative interactions, which included conversations, the translation of foreign languages, and communication instruction, lasted an average of about 10 minutes. Students used sign language, picture communication systems, and, of course, speech (English, Tagalog, Lao, or Spanish).

Since six of the disabled students came from non–English-speaking homes, nondisabled teenaged translators were sometimes used in situations that made me feel uncomfortable, as in the following example:

> Mrs. Anderson and Phuc Sanh are sitting in the lunchroom in the area where the Asian kids often sit. She has a note he has handed her, written in Lao. She says that he doesn't look right—his face is swollen—and that maybe his seizure medication has been changed. She is looking for a Lao friend who will translate. Finally she finds a boy, who smilingly translates, poking and touching Phuc Sanh for emphasis. Mrs. A. is asking about medicine and a doctor's appointment. Something makes me real uncomfortable about this interaction—are the other guys at the table laughing at him? It's hard to take proper care of student privacy when you can only find a translator in the lunch room.

Independent-Living Activities

Activities designed to teach skills required for independent living were the focus of about 14% of the contact situations observed. These activities averaged 19 minutes in length. Food preparation and dishwashing, doing laundry, and applying cosmetics were independent living activities organized by teachers, and typically had an instructional focus. One exception was hair-styling or braiding, which nondisabled girls would spontaneously intiate with disabled students. (This was an activity which I also observed nondisabled peers doing among themselves.) For example:

> Veronica, Tricia, and I come back to Mrs. Miller's room after taking the attendance down. Warren, who is finishing a program with Xuan, welcomes us, saying, "You sure do laundry pretty quick." Veronica says, "We didn't DO laundry." He replies, "I know, bone head." "BONE head?," she echoes, as she goes to the cupboard and gets out a comb and cosmetics bag. She tunes in a better station on the radio, turns up the volume, and begins to comb Xuan's hair. After she is satisfied with the hair-style, she starts painting Xuan's nails pale pink. Xuan giggles. Veronica says, "Hold still!—Xuan . . . Xuan . . . look!" Xuan begins acting really silly so Veronica gives up and puts the polish away. Warren sings along with the radio, "Purple rain, hmm, purple rain . . ." Veronica says, "My cousin likes you." He says, "Oh yeah, which one? The one who was here yesterday?" Veronica answers, "Yeah, she told me to tell you."

Mobility

Activities involving movement from place to place made up about 10% of the contact situations I observed. "Passing" independently from class to class or from school to community sites and teaching independent mobility skills were two types of activity included in this category. Contact while passing had a mean duration of about 4 minutes and always occurred outside the special education classrooms. Teachers might promote contact during passing by asking Regulars to assist disabled students in finding their way, or contact might occur spontaneously. Take, for example, an instance in which a student teacher and I were accompanying students to the neighborhood laundromat:

> We exit school and pass "the wall" (a hangout area for kids cutting classes). Juan is ahead of us, carrying a laundry basket. A guy sitting there says, "Sst . . . sst . . . Juan!" Juan laughs and makes a "sst" noise too. We keep walking, and a black guy in a blue track suit calls Juan from behind: "Juan . . . Juan." Juan keeps walking, turns his head and yells, "HEY HEY!" back. I say, "He's working— we're going to do our laundry." The guy says, "He's my buddy! Hey, Juan . . ." He gets up from the wall, catches up to Juan, and puts his arm around his shoulders. They stand at the crossing, waiting for the light to change, and exchange "Sst's" and "Hey heys" (Juan can't speak—he can only makes these sounds and a whistle). They cross to the next corner, the guy's arm still around Juan's shoulders. He turns to me and says, "He goin' over there?" I say yeah. The guy has to hold Juan back until the light changes, and then he walks him over and returns to "the wall," saying " 'Bye, buddy" before he leaves. The owner of the little grocery store next to the laundromat hears us, sticks his head out, whistles, and says, "Hey, Juan!" Feels like everybody knows us!

School Meals

School meals were the focus of about 9% of the contact situations I observed. Meal-associated contacts had a mean duration of about 8 minutes. Waiting in line outside the cafeteria, purchasing food, and eating breakfast or lunch in the school cafeteria were activities that often resulted in contact between severely disabled students and others.

The special education teachers or their aides always supervised school meals, and I often saw them deliberately separating their students in line and distributing them around the cafeteria. Students separated in this way were harder to supervise, but the special education teachers believed that in order to maximize opportunities for contact with nondisabled peers, they should prevent their students from forming "retard tables"—groups composed only of teenagers with disabilities. Since some of the moderately retarded "TMH" kids were quite good friends—they had gone to school together all their lives—the integration ideal sometimes struck Mrs. Wilson and Mrs. Anderson as conflicting with the students' association patterns. They often discussed this concern, and reached a compromise by encouraging small groups of disabled students to share tables with cliques of nondisabled teenagers. The following notes, which illustrate my interest in these issues, was taken from my "day in the life" observation of Maria's contacts:

> **11:26** Going down to lunch. Maria gets in the long line on the right side of the hall. Kids in line are a normal distance in front of and behind Maria—there's about a foot of space between students. Mrs. Miller, Tricia, and Tiny line up behind Jack (another disabled student) on the opposite side of the hall, next to three cute Chinese girls. Tricia touches Jack's hair, but he doesn't object. After Mrs. Miller's group, there are three nondisabled kids, then Jerome, Ramon, and Elisa, then two more nondisabled kids, then three disabled kids. This strikes me as a good dispersal pattern with good interpersonal distances—not like some other times I've observed.
>
> **11:33** Maria shows her ID card to the security guard who is acting as a line checker, selects cutlery, and moves through the cafeteria line as fast as everybody else. She chooses a seat at a table where a teacher aide has grouped eight members of the orthopedically handicapped class. Maria sits alone at a far end of "their" table. Mrs. Wilson makes Maria move, telling me, "She was isolating herself." Maria comes over to Mrs. Wilson's table, which includes both disabled and nondisabled kids. She finishes lunch. Mrs. Wilson makes her say where she's going—"out"—then she joins the other kids on the basketball court in back of the school.
>
> **11:50 to 12:00** There are about 25 regular ed. kids on the court, some sitting on the benches, some playing basketball. Lin, Michael (off on a bench by himself), Lawrence, LaDonna, Belinda, Elayne, and Maria sit on a bench together, and then begin playfully taunting and chasing each other. For example, I record this dialogue:
>
> **Jack:** You stink!
> **Lawrence:** Stinky Cooster!

Jack: Come 'n get me . . .

Their play is conducted in proximity to nondisabled students, but only disabled students are more directly involved.

12:00 The bell rings, signaling the end of lunch hour, and all the kids begin to leave the basketball court.

Maria: C'mon, Lawrence!

Lawrence: (to me) Maria is MY GIRL—write that down (as we're coming in the door).

Special Events

Special events were the focus of about 7% of the contact situations observed. Contacts in this category, which occurred during assemblies, sports events, food fairs, and concerts, lasted the longest of all the activities I observed, with a mean duration of about 29 minutes. As during school meals, teachers would try to improve their students' opportunities for intergroup contact by positioning students (e.g., scattering small groups in different areas of the auditorium) and by inviting Regulars to accompany disabled peers. This proximal contact was not always easy, as my experience with Xuan shows:

We go to an assembly to see the school's dance group perform. I am with Xuan, who is acting up—maybe she's testing me because she doesn't know me well? In the hall on the way to the auditorium, she strikes the arm of an Asian girl who is just passing by. The girl just turns and looks at us (this counts as a negative interaction when I later analyze my data). Meanwhile, Preston goes into the auditorium with his arm around Patrick's shoulders, taking him to sit in the front row. Veronica had walked in with our kids, but then went to sit with her girlfriend Betty.

I follow Xuan, who goes by herself upstairs and sits in an empty aisle seat next to a tall Asian boy. I ask him to move over one so I can sit next to her. I sit between her and these other kids (preventing contact, ironically), but I'm worried about what she might do, and want her on the aisle side in case a quick exit becomes necessary.

Before the music starts, Xuan is grabbing me and crying. Then she reaches back and puts her hand on the knee of an Asian girl behind her—the girl speaks quietly to her. She grabs the girl's books—the girl pulls hard to free the books while speaking nervously in Chinese to some friends next to her. I don't blame her! I'm nervous too, wondering what I'll do if Xuan gets too disruptive and I have to wrestle her out of there, down the aisle in front of everybody, disrupting the assembly.

Mrs. Wilson's class comes in as a group and sits four rows in front of us. I know it's supposed to be better to distribute the kids around, but I sure wish that *I* had some company at this moment!

The assembly is VERY difficult for me, but this is what anyone might go through sitting with Xuan. The potential for embarrassment is the worst thing about situations like this. Maybe this is why teachers who have worked in special schools have such a hard time adjusting to integration! I spend my lunch hour luxuriously alone, recovering from the assembly and rewriting these notes.

Classroom Chores

Routine chores, such as taking attendance slips to the office, helping to make teaching materials, or preparing notes to be taken home made up about 4% of the contact situations observed. These activities had a mean duration of about 9 minutes.

I'm in Mrs. Miller's class, where we are writing notes to tell the parents about tomorrow's bowling trip. Lucy comes over and hits Monica's arm. Monica turns around and cries out, "LUCE!," but at the same time she's smiling. She goes back to writing, then Lucy hits her again. Monica says, "I'm 'na put Juan on you!" She looks at my note and says, "I don't know why—all ADULTS have better handwriting than kids."

Mrs. Miller says, "Lian, I have some notes to go home—will you come help me? Ramon, will you work with Lian? I'll tell you what I want . . . (She explains how Lian should put one notice about the Special Olympics bowling tournament in each bag). That's right Lian. Come help me please." Then to all of us she says, "What I'd like you to do tomorrow is help the students make the balls hit the pins, 'cause those bowling balls are hard to lift."

We begin to fold and staple the notes. Mrs. Miller explains to Ramon, "She needs to staple one on here, fold it in half, and then put it together. It's a lot of work so I'm gonna steal Tricia away from you. (Tricia has been next to him, trying to get his attention.)

Mrs. Miller says, to Tricia, "Kinda like Ramon, huh?" Mrs. M. takes Tracy away and Ramon and Lian start stapling and folding. Actually Ramon folds and sets the notes up, and Lian is supposed to hit the stapler.

2:17   Ramon is trying to work and Juan is teasing (poking) him.

2:20   Lian leaves the table; Ramon is finishing the job himself.

2:24   Ramon says, "Where'd Juan go?"

Mrs. Miller replies, "Oh, he just went to the restroom."

Ramon says, "Does he DO that? By himself?" He and Lian come over to the table to get a letter. He says, "Come on, come on Li."

Mrs. Miller says to Ramon, "Juan likes you a lot! It's really hard for him because he really likes to wrestle."

Vocational Training

Vocational training, involving instruction in clerical, janitorial, or restaurant skills, was the focus of about 7% of the contact situations I observed, and had a mean duration of about 16 minutes. These activities were organized by teachers, commonly had an instructional focus, and involved IWE students. Spontaneous contacts with nondisabled "others" could and did occur, however, when vocational training took place in common school areas or in the community.

Renaldo has a job in the cafeteria, busing the tables. He's working the cleanup job, drinking a soda as he stacks trays. Hector, a Hispanic boy who is carrying a portable tape player, comes up to Renaldo and puts one of his earphones to Renaldo's ear. Renaldo listens and laughs. Hector and his friends also laugh and then go on to the front of the cafeteria to get in line. A few minutes later, as

Renaldo clears a table, he gestures to Hector, asking him to throw one of the oranges lying there, left over from somebody's lunch. He does, Renaldo catches it, juggles the orange in the air, then throws it to another guy who catches it and then throws it to hit Hector on the back. Renaldo leaves their table, clears some more trays, juggles another orange he has found, and then overhand, pitches it hard across the room so that it splats on the wall by the teacher's lounge!

Functional Academics

Simple academic skills, such as recognizing numerals, telling time, reading basic vocabulary, writing personal data (name, address, telephone number), or calculating quantities of money, were involved in about 6% of the contact situations observed. These activities were the focus of long-lasting interactions whose mean duration was about 26 minutes. These contact situations were organized by teachers who often asked IWEs to help disabled students practice skills that the teachers had previously taught; nondisabled students might also be asked to "take data" on student achievement and to administer reinforcers in such instructional situations. The following sequence was taken from the "day in the life" observation I made with Jon:

Mrs. Anderson tells Doretha how to help the students practice telling time, using little toy clock faces. She says, "You can set these to any time you want— just make it 45 minutes after the hour. Try to set the hands so they look like the hands on a real clock. Mrs. Anderson demonstrates, showing a clock to Ramon and asking him, "What time is it?" Ramon doesn't answer correctly, and Mrs. Anderson says to Doretha, "This is real hard for 'em—when it's just before the hour—so he gets a minus. He has to say it RIGHT on the spot! Right away!"

8:45 Jon works on writing his name and address on a dittoed work sheet. Mrs. Anderson asks Doretha to work with Jon and Helen on reading "survival words" (common signs and labels).

8:59 Jon and Hannah sit with Doretha, taking turns reading word cards, and being marked with plusses or minuses on their individual data sheets. Meanwhile, another group of three students is working on numeral-quantity association at a far table, matching quantities of pennies to the numbers on playing cards.

9:05 Jon gets bored. Pointing to his head, he makes a circle with his finger, as if to say to Doretha, "You're crazy."

Doretha:	I'm not lookin' at you (Jon hides his completed ditto sheet).
Jon:	Go down there (they are both teasing each other).
Doretha:	We're fin' t'do s'more words.
Jon:	Don' look at my paper.
Doretha:	There's nothin' on your paper I wanna see excep' your BEAUTI-FUL handwriting.
Doretha:	You don't have to sit nex' to me. Dwayne's MY frien.' He stays across the street from me. (Jon hides his paper from her, anyway. Dwayne comes and whispers in Jon's ear.)
Doretha:	What'd you say 'bout me?
Jon:	He says you havin' a baby.
Doretha:	SHUT your mouth!

They go on like this until the bell rings to signal the end of the period. I wait until after class, and then ask Doretha more about the students' contacts outside of school.

Carola: Who does Dwayne hang out with at home?
Doretha: Oh, everybody, he's in and out of everybody's houses, because we all live on a street that ends (a dead-end street) and we're all out there all the time. He has three brothers. They real cute—they have girlfriends and everything. He has a younger sister in eighth grade.
Carola: Where does he get his way of talking?
Doretha: I guess from his mother. He gets all that "I love you Jesus" talk from church. His mother takes him to a Holiness church all the time.

WHERE DID THEY GO?

Intergroup contact was observed to take place in three kinds of areas in and around the high school: special education classrooms, common areas of the school, and community areas. With a few exceptions, all categories of activity could be observed to occur in any of these three areas. (See Table 7.2.)

Special Education Classrooms

The students with severe disabilities were assigned to three self-contained classrooms for their daily programs. Mrs. Anderson's (a former home economics room) was equipped with full kitchen and laundry facilities, and the teachers had improvised simple food preparation areas in the other two classrooms. A computer, used to run numeral recognition and alphabet memory software, and materials used in the simulation of clerical tasks, were installed in Ms. Wilson's classroom. Grooming supplies (e.g., cosmetics) and leisure supplies (e.g., board games and magazines) were available in all three special education classrooms. The teachers shared the facilities and often scheduled peer tutoring sessions in one of the three special education classrooms. *Fifty-one percent of the contact situations observed took place in one of the three special education classrooms.*

Table 7.2. Where did disabled and nondisabled students at Explorer High School associate?

Location	Percentage of situations
Special education classrooms	51
Common areas within the school	38
Community	11

Common Areas of the School

In order to promote intergroup contact, special education teachers tried to make sure their students ate lunch and took breaks between classes when and where the regular students did. Sixteen of the more independent students with severe disabilities were mainstreamed into nonacademic regular classes such as physical education, art, and typing. Disabled students also attended school assemblies, food fairs, concerts and, in some cases, lunchtime club meetings. *Thirty-eight percent of the contact situations observed took place in regular school settings such as halls, the cafeteria, and gymnasiums.*

The Community

Because the curriculum model used in the special education classes emphasized teaching with functional materials in integrated community settings, the teachers also scheduled instruction for their students in local churches, stores, and the neighborhood laundromat. Therefore, even the most severely disabled of the special education students spent some instructional time outside their special classrooms and thereby had opportunities to interact spontaneously with nondisabled people in the community. During school hours, however, few students were (or should have been) in the community. *Eleven percent of the contact situations observed took place in community settings, mostly as a result of IWE students accompanying students with severe disabilities.*

As these observations illustrate, disabled and nondisabled students engaged in activities that varied widely according to their stated and unstated goals.

STUDENT PERSPECTIVES ON INTEGRATION

I repeatedly interviewed the Regulars about their involvement with disabled fellow students, both casually and formally, over the course of the school year. Their responses to my questions demonstrated that *the Regulars understood most of these activities to be designed to help students with disabilities to fit into integrated environments; they also indicated that the Regulars perceived these joint activities to be of benefit to themselves and to other nondisabled students at Explorer.*

Benefits to Students with Disabilities

The Regulars understood specific intergroup activities as being beneficial to their disabled schoolmates. For example, communication activities such as learning to express feelings or make requests, learning to shake hands, or give other appropriate greetings such as the "high five"; independent living activities such as learning to wash and fold clothes, learning to purchase and prepare food, learning to apply make-up and nail polish, learning to do domestic chores; leisure activities such as playing sports, playing board games, and generally being around or hanging out with nondisabled students were all viewed as appropriate and educational.

The Regulars understood these activities to be beneficial for four reasons. First, they helped prepare disabled students to "have a better future" by helping them "fit in," to "have games that they would know how to play so they won't be alone." Second, these activities helped to make the students more self-sufficient and less dependent on their parents, which was viewed as important because "sometimes your parents—even though they want to help you, sometimes they don't have time—they can't take care of you *every* day." Third, these intergroup activities helped the students learn how to "act right" by giving them a chance to see "if they can make it with 2,000 other kids" so they would later be able to "get out in the streets around more normal people" than they could if they spent all their time with other disabled people. Fourth, the Regulars recognized that, "These people are not good in some points and we just try to help them get better." They felt good when they could help disabled students acquire practical skills.

Benefits to Nondisabled Students

Regulars described three kinds of benefits they and others experienced through their contact with severely disabled students. First, as Rico said, "You can learn off them, they can learn off you." Regulars emphasized the ways in which they had learned to be patient or had learned more about their own strengths, and had been surprised by the unexpected skills they had seen severely disabled students display. Second, Regulars repeatedly said that they had felt good because of being able to help someone else or because of successfully meeting a challenge. Third, several Regulars mentioned future benefits to themselves or others. For example, Aretha said, "If I had a handicapped child I would know how to treat it." She added that it was good for others to learn how to get along with disabled people now because they would "have to grow up and learn about getting along with other people and stuff."

Learning Opportunities

Regulars generally emphasized opportunities for learning when asked to explain why they thought disabled students were attending the high school. For example, in formal interviews, I asked them to imagine a hypothetical situation in which a new freshman who had never had any contact with disabled people came to Explorer and met the Regular walking down the hall with a disabled student. The Regulars were asked to imagine how they would answer if the freshman asked them why the disabled student was going to this high school.

Some students replied quite vehemently. Mendel thought that he wouldn't know what to say, so he'd probably just beat the freshman up! Anita replied:

I would say, "That's a STUPID question—shit! What do you THINK they're doin' here? The same thing that YOU'RE doin' here! You know, they came to LEARN stuff!"

In their answers the Regulars emphasized the similarities between disabled and nondisabled teenagers. For example, Fifi (a Regular who had been an IWE the year before) said:

"They GO here!" That's the first thing I'd say. "They're not different from us except they minds, you know." I'm sure that person would know but they'd say, "This is a public school, right? Why don't they go to a handicap school?" I'd say, "They don't cheat, they're no different from us you know, except that they need more help!"

Other students emphasized equality of opportunity when they responded to this question. For example, Monica said:

Well, I would tell them, "To learn, just like WE are!" I mean, they're people too, and they need to learn just as well as we learn. . . . It's not FAIR if, you know, people who don't have emotional or physical handicaps are going out there and doing things—I mean, the handicapped person can do good just like WE can!

Veronica responded similarly:

I'd just say, "They're here for an education like you are, 'cause it's not like they're not supposed to be in the school! The school's open to ANYONE. So they come here to get an education like anyone else." They COULD go to a school for all handicapped kids but, you know, Tricia and them, I think they can improve the way they ACT here.

Value of the Integration Program

When I asked Veronica whether she thought the integration program was good or bad for Explorer High School, she emphasized the benefits to other nondisabled students in her answer:

It's not bad (for the regular students), it's good, because, see, they should learn about how Tricia will react to other people and things like that. Because Tricia and them have to grow up and pretty soon life's gonna be getting hard, so you have to learn about sharing—you know, not being selfish—and the regular students can learn from what she does.

Candi, a Regular in Ms. Wilson's class, explained that she thought the program at Explorer was good for some disabled students but that the school was perhaps too tough for others. She was a slightly built, shy girl who had immigrated from the Philippines 5 years before, and based on her own negative experiences in the school (her locker had been robbed and she had been hassled by more aggressive students), she said, "Some people, if they know you're kind of, you know, they're gonna mess you up. They're gonna go 'Oh, she's like that . . . he's like that . . . he's easy to beat up,' you know."

Regulars repeatedly emphasized the importance of treating disabled students just like nondisabled people their age. Take, for example, this discussion that occurred when I asked twin sisters for their views on the program:

Tina:	I think ALL of them (the schools) should have it! I mean because WHY are you going to send them to a school, you know, where they feel like, you know, it make them feel like they're *handicapped* . . . ?
Andi:	They're not any different from *us*!
Tina:	. . . Like they're *incompetent* or something!
Andi:	*Yeah*! Jut put 'em in a public school, you know, where they be around other normal kids, you know . . .
Tina:	Well, they're normal too!
Andi:	Of course, they're *humans like us*, you know.
Carola:	Uh-huh?
Tina:	It isn't like they can't understand what you're saying!
Andi:	That's why you shouldn't put them *inside*!
Tina:	Or put 'em *down*!
Andi:	They got a right to be here just like anybody else! And like I said, they smarter than *half* the people they got here anyway!
Carola:	(laughs)
Andi:	I'm *serious*!
Tina:	And see, the people at (Explorer), they don't even think of them like that, you know. Everybody speaks—you know some may not *work* with the kids, but they know who they *are*, you know. It's not like they go around harassing them or teasing them or anything . . .
Andi:	No, it's not like *that*!
Carola:	They seem to get along pretty well.
Tina & Andi:	(simultaneously): Yeah!
Andi:	Yeah, with everybody. From the *Thugs* to everybody!

As Candi had pointed out, Explorer could be an intimidating place. But as the twins had accurately observed (and as is confirmed by data reported in the next chapter), the student community's responses to its severely disabled members demonstrated the *goodness* that even a troubled school could achieve.

Schools teach moral lessons in addition to the Three R's (Benninga, 1988; Bronfenbrenner, 1970, 1979, 1986; Lightfoot, 1983; Sizer, 1984). As the author of a recent review of the "moral education" literature has said, "The role of the school is not simply to make children smart, but to make them smart *and* good" (Ryan, 1986, p. 233). *Good* schools do this in two ways: by modeling moral values (through equitable treatment of staff and students, for example) and by providing young people with opportunities to practice the "fairness, generosity and tolerance" that are central to the American value system (Sizer, 1984, p. 121).

Although (as I document in Chapter 11) Explorer could have improved on the values it modeled, the school's acceptance of the special education integration program gave students lessons in moral education that experts say are rarely available in contemporary schools (Bronfenbrenner, 1979; Ryan, 1986). For example, as in the discussions reported in this chapter and in Chapters 3 and 4, Regulars reported that through their contact with disabled fellow students they learned important lessons in how to get along with others. As Harold, Doretha, and Monica said, they also learned patience and developed a new tolerance for individual differences which would come in handy when, as Veronica said, "life got hard." Through the challenges they met as peer-tutors, the Regulars built self-esteem, found unexpected strengths in themselves as they overcame the fear of disabilities "that might rub off," and learned to feel good, "knowing that you're helping someone."

This growing strength of character served the Regulars well when situations arose—because of Lucy's hugs or Tricia's shoe-flinging, for example—in which they had to choose between sticking up for their disabled schoolmates or slinking away in embarrassment. Although one sometimes needed patience to keep from "going off on" (getting angry at) nondisabled students in such situations, the empathy that the Regulars developed enabled them to act diplomatically, as Monica had, on such occasions.

The twins' dialogue, raising as it did the issues of separate schooling and equal rights for people with disabilities, seemed to encompass many of the ethical, legal, and pedagogical questions adult advocates continue to debate. When Tina and Andi recognized the implications of the phrase, "normal kids"—rejecting it in favor of "humans like us"—their discussion exemplified the 'smartness and goodness' that every school should aim to instill in its students.

chapter 8

Was It Only
'Helping the
Handicapped'?

W hen I talk about my work to people who have never had a chance to see an *effective* integration program, their questions reawaken me to the assumptions that inexperienced persons typically make about the quality of contact that can occur between disabled and nondisabled people. Because individuals with disabilities are typically assumed to be incompetent across the board, "helping the handicapped" is seen as the only way nondisabled persons can interact with them. This assumption is inaccurate because it fails to take into account the diverse personalities and communication styles displayed even by those individuals with the most severe intellectual impairments. The data summarized here document a richly varied range of student interactions that should surprise those with no experience of integration.

TYPES OF INTERACTION

As has been shown in previous chapters, contact between disabled and nondisabled teenagers occurred in the context of nine different kinds of activity, located in school and community settings. All but one of these 311 "contact situations" that I observed (a meeting of the school's Filippino Club that involved multilingual, simultaneous interactions) could be further categorized in terms of one of five mutually exclusive types of interaction: *proximal, helping, reciprocal, mediated*, and *negative*. The first three categories had already been described in the special education literature as being of potential benefit to students with severe disabilities (Brown et al., 1983; Hamre-Nietupski et al., 1978; Schutz et al., 1984; Stainback & Stainback, 1985). The last two categories emerged from my data.

Because the sampling strategy I used led me to seek out interactions involving students identified as Regulars, and because the majority of Regulars were enrolled in the school's IWE program, and were ascribed the role of teacher assistant or peer tutor by staff, this strategy *could* have led to the observation of a predominant number of interactions involving instruction or the provision of assistance. Also, given the severity of the impairments experienced by the disabled students, one might have predicted that "helping" would characterize most contact situations. Actually, *less than half* of the total contact situations I observed were characterized by this sort of interaction (see Table 8.1.). To gain a more accurate picture of student relations, it is useful to compare the proportionate incidence of these varied interaction types, as follows:

Proximal Interactions

When some form of sensory contact was made between a severely disabled student and a nondisabled peer, this was defined as a *proximal interaction* (Hamre-Nietupski et al., 1978). Of the 311 contact situations in which severely disabled and nondisabled students were observed, *63 situations (20.5%) involved proximal interaction*. Most often, students identified as "others" were observed in these situations. The activities in which most proximal contact occurred were participation in special events, hall passing, and school meals. In the following example, Juan and Michael initiated proximal interactions (they were in visual contact) with other boys, and a group of Asian girls initiated proximal contact with Fidel, Xuan, and Lian.

> I'm sitting with Fidel (who is deaf and blind) at an empty table in the cafeteria. Xuan and Lian (two other students from Mrs. Miller's SPH class) come to sit with us. I'm worried that Fidel will grab at the girls' lunches or else start smearing his food on the table in that gross way that I saw in October, so I give him a quarter of his tuna sandwich at a time to make it last longer (and to give him less to play with), and all is okay.
>
> Meanwhile, I watch Juan (another of Mrs. Miller's students) go and find a group of boys to sit with. I see Michael (who has autism) go and sit by some Asian boys—they ignore him but they don't move away. A group of Asian girls sits at the table next to us (I'm somewhat surprised, given what I've seen of Fidel's eating techniques); they remain there for the next 10 minutes.

Helping Interactions

When one student voluntarily provided direct assistance or instruction to another, this was defined as a *helping interaction* (Hamre-Nietupski et al., 1978). *Of the 311 situations observed, 115 (36.9%) involved helping contact.* Most often, Regulars who were also IWEs were observed to help disabled students. I also witnessed a few reverse situations—for example, when a

Table 8.1. Kinds of interactions between disabled and nondisabled students

Type	n	Proportion of contact situations
Proximal	63	20.5%
Helping	115	36.9%
Reciprocal	83	26.4%
Mediated	30	9.6%
Negative	20	6.4%

student with severe disabilities would open a door for an "Other," or when a disabled student would show a Regular how to run a computer program. Helping situations occurred most often during instructional periods. For example, in the following excerpt from my notes, Preston (one of the Rappers) is helping Tiny use simple sign language:

> Preston is playing the radio with Tiny while Sylvia (the speech therapist) works on picture discrimination with Ling. Preston says, "Show me whatcha *want*." He guides Tiny's hands into the sign for "music" and then turns on the radio. They listen for a bit and then Preston turns down the volume. "Whatcha want, Tin'— ya want some hometown down home ra ra ra?" Tiny laughs, but doesn't sign. Preston turns up the volume anyway, saying, "Y'like that music, don't you? Y'like that *music*." He prompts Tiny to make the sign again. She rocks in her chair. He says, "Try'na dance?" He changes the station. "Tiny—wanta hear The Beat?" He turns the sound up anyway, even though she hasn't signed as she should have. He tells me later that The Beat and Run-DMC are his favorites.

Reciprocal Interactions

When the contact situation resulted in mutual though not necessarily similar benefits, and the nondisabled student was not primarily assisting or instructing the severely disabled student, this was defined as a *reciprocal interaction* (Hamre-Nietupski et al., 1978). *Eighty-two situations (26.4%) involved reciprocal contact.* Both Regulars and Others were observed in this type of situation. Reciprocal contact occurred most often during communication, hall-passing, or leisure activities. In the following incident, Mrs. Wilson and I accompanied three of her students to a wrestling match held after school in the gym. In this example, Jerome (a student with Down syndrome) initiates a reciprocal interaction with one of the contestants:

> **5:10 p.m.** The match is over and Mrs. Wilson, Belinda, Jerome, and I walk out together. In the main hall, Mrs. W. gestures to get my attention and points to a wrestler who sits, still in his brown and gold uniform, head hanging, hands between knees—the picture of dejection—on the steps leading to the outside doors. We make sympathetic faces at each other, but we've just seen this guy in a tremendous display of anger and bad sportsmanship—first restrained by teammates as he tried to turn the wrestling match into a fistfight, and then refus-

ing the ritual handshake with the opponent who beat him, so we hesitate to approach him. Mrs. Wilson and I stand, pretending not to notice him, chatting about my Christmas trip while we wait for Renaldo. Jerome interrupts us, saying, "Talk to him," and starts walking towards the wrestler. Mrs. W. tries to stop him, saying, "Jer . . . ," but it's too late. Jerome's already there. He speaks to the guy, and the guy nods his head. We can only catch the words "You try . . . you try . . . ." When we're outside the building, I ask Mrs. W. what she thought was happening, and she says that Jerome was telling the wrestler that he had *tried*, and that that was good.

Mediated Interactions

When a "helper" without disabilities was present and promoted positive proximal or reciprocal contact between another nondisabled student and a severely disabled student, I defined this as a *mediated interaction*. *Thirty situations (9.6%) were characterized by mediated contact.* These situations could occur within any type of activity, and often involved friends whom the Regulars introduced to disabled students, as in this example in which Anita, a vivacious member of a Popular People clique, brought her Thug boyfriend into the class where she was assigned for IWE credit:

> Sixth period. Anita asks Mrs. Anderson if Denard (who has dropped out of school) can visit the class. Mrs. A. suggests that they play a game of UNO with Dwayne, Phuc Sanh, Mimi, and me. The kids are messing around as usual. Dwayne calls Anita "Buffalo Butt" and she replies with "Nigger." (Both are black.) When the game is over, Denard wants to try out the computer. Anita says, "Phuc Sanh knows how to do it," and so the two boys go to work. Phuc Sanh uses single word utterances to help Denard: "Load . . . run . . . 5." Anita comes to sit with them. Dwayne comes over to watch and puts his hand on Anita's shoulder. Denard says, "Hey! Don't you touch my *woman!*" Dwayne removes his hand. Denard says, "I was just kiddin'."

Negative Interactions

When the contact situation resulted in injury, when feelings of strong dislike, fear, or anger were expressed, or when the goal of one individual was to tease hurtfully or condescend to another, I defined this as a *negative situation*. *Twenty situations involved negative contact (6.4%)*. Of these, six were the result of aggressive contact initiated by severely disabled students (e.g., grabbing food, throwing objects, or hitting a passer-by, as in the example given on p. 78). In six additional situations, also initiated by disabled students, nondisabled students jumped back or otherwise appeared fearful of students who came near them or touched them unexpectedly. In eight situations, nondisabled students teased or condescended to the severely disabled students. One Regular (Rick) was involved in two of the teasing/condescending situations; otherwise, negative situations involved nondisabled students labeled as Others. These situations occurred most frequently during hall passing, school meals, or during special events.

On one occasion, members of the school's Chinese Club were preparing chow mein to sell at a lunchtime food fair while Mrs. Miller, Preston, and Lucy (a Chinese girl who was severely mentally retarded) were cooking nearby.

Mrs. Miller's Independent Living Club is going to sell nachos. We're in the former home economics room, sharing the stoves with the Chinese Club. Lucy (who loves to eat) keeps trying to get into their food. By mistake, Mrs. M. drops a plastic bag into a garbage can full of ice and canned sodas. As she takes it out, she says, "Oops! I put garbage in the wrong can." One of the Chinese kids tells her, "Take it out!" Preston says to him, "Hey, Blood, you don' talk to a teacher that way!" As we're leaving, Lucy finally succeeds in putting her hands into a portion of chow mein. The kids go, "Oooo, uck, it's *that* one! Gross!" One says to Mrs. M., in a hostile tone, "Were you going to buy one? Here it is." Preston sees me writing this and says, "Will I get in trouble for saying 'Blood'?" I say, "I was interested in how those kids talked to Mrs. M. and how you stuck up for her."

These results were more varied than would have been predicted from my sampling strategy and the disabled student population. Although the largest proportion of the contact situations observed involved helping interactions, these were *less than half* of the total situations observed. More than one-fourth of the contact situations observed were reciprocal, dominated by the type of interaction believed to be at once the most valuable and the most difficult for special educators to promote. Although mediated situations were relatively rare, they exemplified the ways that peer relations (described by students as one of five types of influence on the initiation of intergroup contact—see Chapter 10) worked to include disabled students in existing student cliques. Finally, it was interesting to note that negative contact was the type least frequently observed, and was initiated by nondisabled students in only eight (2.5%) of the 311 situations observed between October 1984 and June 1985.

All in all, these data demonstrate that interactions between disabled and nondisabled persons are more interesting and complex than the "positive/negative/neutral" range or "acceptance/nonacceptance" commonly reported in the disability research literature.

TYPES OF SOCIAL RELATIONS

Wouldn't you hate it if people were always helping you? Wouldn't it be awful if everybody pretended to accept everything you did, even when you were boring or obnoxious, just because you were "special"? How would you like it if other people always initiated and terminated the interactions that involved you? Worst of all, how would it feel to experience that omnipresent strained politeness, lingering like a damp fog that obscured your individuality from every new person you met?

It seems to me that the normalization principle, when applied to the analysis of intergroup social relations, offers a standard against which we can measure the outcomes of our integration efforts. Normalization refers not only to each individual's need for a normal daily rhythmn and normal life-cycle changes, but also to the fact that each individual needs access to the normal array of relations with other people (Nirje, 1969, 1988). As summarized in the literature reviewed in Chapter 2, this range of relations goes far beyond polite tolerance, and includes experience with strong feelings of both positive and negative types, balanced by a healthy measure of middle-ground acceptance and acquaintance.

What kinds of social relations did the students experience at Explorer? Besides the characteristics related to activity, interaction, and setting that I have already described, an important ecological theory of human development (Bronfenbrenner, 1979) identifies four additional elements that can be used to analyze social relations between pairs of people: *participant roles, mutual balance of power, reciprocity* or *mutual adaptation*, and *quality of affect*.[1] When I compared these elements across the transcripts of student interviews, staff interviews, and my own observations, I was able to identify five contrasting types of dyadic social relations involving disabled and nondisabled teenagers: *observational, negative*, two types of *working* relations, and *friendship* relations.

Most of the Regulars engaged in various types of relations with their disabled fellow students, depending on *who* was involved. Three Regulars, whose relations were observed to be limited to a single type (Latrice, Candi, and Rick), exemplify problems that can occur in intergroup social relations. Characteristics that differentiate the five types of social relations I observed in the present study are summarized in Table 8.2 and described in the pages that follow.

Type I: 'I Like to Watch 'Em!'

Participants in these observational relations shared a common formal role, that of high school student. However, expectations associated with the student roles varied, depending on if the student was disabled or not. Balance of power was unmarked but *potentially* equal, in that either student could have controlled the relation through initiation, maintenance, or termination of contact. Reciprocity, or mutual adaptation and feedback, was unlikely to occur given the distance inherent in Type I relations. Affect expressed by nondisabled students ranged from tentative/cautious to curious/interested.

Anita participated in working and friendship relations (Types III and IV) with some of Mrs. Anderson's students. She had Type I relations, however, with some students from Mrs. Miller's class. She was particularly interested

---

[1]See endnote, p. 103.

Table 8.2. Types of relations between disabled and nondisabled students

Types of social relations	Occurrence of play	Role of nondisabled student	Balance of power	Mutual adaptation (reciprocity)	Quality of nondisabled student's affect
I (observational)	None	Student	Not noted	None	Tentative
II (negative)	Rare	Tutor	Fixed	Problematic	Dislike
III (working/businesslike)	Occasional	Tutor	Fixed	Problematic	Bored/cool
IV (working/sociable)	Occasional	Tutor	Fixed	Frequent	Engaged/warm
V (friendship)	Frequent	Friend	Flexible	Frequent	Friendly

in Tricia and Fidel because, she said, "I like to watch 'em. I'd like to see what they do next!"

Anita expressed her desire to get involved with these students throughout the school year. For example, the following conversation occurred when, sitting in the park across from the high school, Anita and I saw Fidel crossing the street with a nondisabled student:

Anita:	See, now, if I was workin' with Mrs. Miller's class—see what they get to do—come outside 'n help the BLIND! That's what I wanted t' do!
Carola:	You're interested in that, huh?
Anita:	Ye-ah!
Carola:	What, like . . . ?
Anita:	See, I LIKE Hannah 'n them—they're, they're okay, but they don't really need that much HELP, like they (Mrs. Miller's class) do. So I wanted, to, you know, to work with THEM where they needed a little more HELP!
Carola:	Uh-huh?
Anita:	I—'cuz I think it'd be HARDER 'n everything working with them.
Carola:	It'd be harder, but I think you like to DO things that are a little bit hard.
Anita:	Yeah! 'Cuz, you know, I be lookin' FORWARD, like, 'Hey, I wanta help HIM,' you know.
Carola:	That's INTERESTING! How come—how come you'd like it better to work with somebody that's harder t' work with?
Anita:	'Cuz they need more HELP than Hannah 'n them.

As in Anita's case, *Type I relations tended to remain static until subjected to some additional influence that acted as a catalyst for closer contact.* As an English student had written after Mrs. Miller lectured to his class (see Chapter 9), differences paired with disability made him unsure about how he should approach special education students. Anita herself waited to initiate closer involvement with Fidel and Tricia until the end of the school year, when I invited Anita to go to a Special Olympics bowling tournament with Mrs. Miller's class.

Other Type I relations evolved more quickly into other types of contact—often facilitated by mediated interactions involving the Regulars. For example, Veronica's best friend Betty, an IWE in Mrs. Miller's class, began casually visiting the class in November. At first, she just hung around the classroom door with Veronica during the 5-minute break between class periods, but toward the end of November she began to come into the classroom during her free period, watch what was going on, and make occasional comments such as "He CAN do it! He CAN do it," or "She's combing her hair! She can turn on the radio!," when she was surprised at the students' activities. Veronica was observed to promote closer contact between Betty and Tricia in the following way:

Veronica is getting a hug from Tricia. She brings her over to where Betty and I are sitting and says, "Say 'Hi' to Betty . . . Say 'Hi.' " Tricia says, 'Hi,' but Betty doesn't say anything. Veronica shows Betty how to put out her hand and let Tricia touch her fingers. Veronica then says, "Let's get your stick," and then, "Give Betty a hug." Tricia puts her arms around Betty's neck and kisses her cheek.

Betty continued her association with Mrs. Miller's students the rest of the year, regularly joining in leisure activities such as games, picnics, and excursions.

Type II: 'Sometimes They Just Get on My Nerves!'

Participants in Type II relations held disparate roles characterized by different role expectations. The nondisabled party (always an IWE) held the role of peer tutor, the disabled party the role of learner. The tutor was expected to assist or instruct and the student was expected to cooperate and learn. Balance of power was fixed and unequal, with the nondisabled party controlling the contact. Reciprocity was problematic; given role expectations that required a high degree of mutual feedback and successful adaptation (especially by the learner), the absence of easy and frequent reciprocity was perhaps the major source of irritation in Type II relations. Affect expressed in these relations ranged from exasperated to critical, and play rarely occurred.

Preston, a 9th grader, was a Regular and an IWE in Mrs. Miller's class. He was involved in a continuum of relations with severely disabled students, ranging from an affectionate, protective relationship with Patrick (a student in Mrs. Miller's class) to casual "buddy" associations with Jon and Renaldo (students from Mrs. Anderson's and Mrs. Wilson's classes). Preston's Type II relations with Juan represented the negative end of the continuum. Juan was very sociable, but he expressed himself through loud vocalizing, frequent whistling, and occasional pinching, spitting, and poking. In an interview at the end of the year, Preston described his relations with Juan:

> **Preston:** Yeah, but sometimes they just get on my nerves! You know, I just want to say 'SHUT UP!' Make me feel like punching them right in the mouth!
>
> **Carola:** Well, to tell you the truth, they get on my nerves sometimes too! What do you do when you feel like that?
>
> **Preston:** I just don't trip, I just look away. Juan be yellin' in the hallway and I keep on tellin' him t' be quiet and he thinks it's FUNNY! Keep on laughin', I swear! I just feel like just backhanding him!

Not all nondisabled students dealt with Type II relations as Preston did. For example, Latrice, Zita, and Susie were Nasty Girls who enrolled as IWEs in Mrs. Miller's class for one semester. While they attended IWE sessions fairly regularly, they typically maintained distant relations with her students, physically separating themselves, engaging in separate activities, and ignoring staff efforts to engage them with the disabled students. Their relations were observed as follows:

> Tricia and Tiny are sitting at the table, eating oatmeal that Eliza (Mrs. Miller's aide) has made. Tiny has oatmeal on her face. Latrice and Susie stand over by the counter, eat candy they have brought with them, and talk. Latrice looks at Tiny and says, "She's the WORST." Susie says, "I like the way she laughs!" Latrice answers, "You LIKE her? I can't stand it when she has oatmeal on her nose and her face!" Eliza talks to Tricia and Tiny, getting them to wash and put away the dishes they have used and clean their faces. She tells Latrice and Susie to help them put the chairs away and then asks them to start making some program cards for Mrs. M. Zita has now arrived. Susie takes out her portable tape player and starts listening to it. Zita is wearing some glittery adhesive stars on her cheek. She takes some out of her purse and gives them to the other two to put on. Meanwhile they stand by the counter and draw lines on the program cards.

Latrice was one of the Regulars, but she also exemplified the type of person most likely to be threatened by close association with severely disabled teenagers. She was a 9th grader who *herself* was assigned to a special education "resource room" for students with learning disabilities, and had frequently been involved in physical fights with her peers. Her relations with severely disabled students were limited to Type II, and were characterized by a mixture of disgust, fear (remarks like "she look mean" were common), and self-consciousness if other nondisabled students (especially boys) were present.

The special education teachers were naturally troubled to observe Type II relations such as Preston's and Latrice's. They attempted to modify such relations by making the joint activities more attractive (e.g., Latrice was asked to help Tricia and Tiny apply nail polish or make-up instead of with food preparation), or by trying not to pair students who didn't get along well together (e.g., Preston would be given a choice of students with whom to do errands). They also tried, with varying degrees of success, to involve the nondisabled students in discussions of the problems they were having with the disabled students.

In Preston's case, because he developed a range of relations with disabled fellow students, these efforts were successful. With Latrice, they were not. She gradually stopped attending IWE, received a grade of "D" from Mrs. Miller, and later in the year, if she met disabled students in passing, would act as if she just didn't see them.

Type III: 'I Start to Get Bored'

I observed two types of task-centered working relations at Explorer, the first (Type III) characterized by businesslike, bored affect, the other (Type IV) by warm, engaged affect. In both kinds of working relations, the participants held the roles of peer tutor and learner. The balance of power was fixed and unequal, with the nondisabled party in the controlling position. Mutual adaptation or reciprocity, which facilitated the exchange of information and assistance that was implied by role expectations, could be problematic in Type III relations. Although some playful reciprocal interactions occurred, the focus of activity was task completion, as the following example shows.

Candi, a 12th grader from the Philippines, was an IWE in Mrs. Wilson's class. Although she was a friendly, affectionate person in other situations I observed, she maintained distant, businesslike relations with the disabled students, keeping control of interactions and resisting being drawn into personal contact. Mai, a disabled student who had recently moved to the United States from Southeast Asia, was mainstreamed into an ESL (English as a second language) class. In response to an assignment made by the ESL teacher, Mai had dictated sentences describing her former life to Mrs. Wilson, who had then assigned Candi to help Mai copy the sentences, using cursive (script) writing.

Candi: Do your homework! How can you write like that? God, not like that, like this . . . (shows her). Like THIS . . . Make it big! . . . That's small . . . that's small. Make it BIG! Like THAT! "My father died . . . " Write that! (Mai copies) . . . "in" . . . write "Cambodia"—C . . . a . . . write that! Start number 2. Put the period after you write that, always write that. "My mother . . . my mother . . . "

Mai: D . . . i . . . e . . . d.

Candi: Right! "In Cambodia" . . . Cam . . . bo . . . (Mai writes). Okay, number 3. "My sister . . . "

Mai: S . . . i . . . s . . . t . . . s . . . t . . . no, no, no . . .

Candi: Straight! Straight! " . . . has four children."

Mai: (echoes as she writes) Has four children.

Candi: (dictates) "My two big brothers died in Cambodia."

Mai: B . . . r . . . o . . . t . . . h . . . e . . . r . . . s—b–brothers.

Candi: Write "brothers died." Copy that.

Mai: D . . . i . . . e . . . d . . . (A bell rings, ending the period.)

Candi: Look! "In Cambodia!" Bye! (She leaves)

The content of the "handwriting lesson" makes this example unusually dramatic, but the balance of power and affect were typical of Candi's interactions with disabled students. In an interview, when I asked her if she was having any problems in her relations with Mrs. Wilson's class, she mentioned two potential reasons for her Type III relations:

Candi: . . . With them, sometimes you're gonna say something, and like they don't hear you or if they say something I have trouble to understand it . . .

Carola: Uh-huh.

Candi:	. . . and sometimes if you're teaching them you're gonna say it 100 times and they still don't know!
Carola:	Like what would you be teaching them?
Candi:	You know, like math or English, you know.
Carola:	Uh-huh.
Candi:	And like I'm trying my best to explain it to them REALLY, really good and they still don't GET it, you know . . . I don't get mad, but at least, you know, I start to get BORED!

While almost all the Regulars who were IWEs were observed from time to time to be engaged in businesslike Type III relations, Candi's relations appeared to be limited to Type III only. Candi's remarks suggested that *mutual communication problems (she herself spoke English imperfectly) and frustration with tasks she was assigned contributed to the negative affect she expressed.*

Although I saw Candi's relations as problematic, Mrs. Wilson did not. Perhaps our opposing views originated in different interpretations of the integration program's goals. Mrs. Wilson believed that it was better for IWE students to feel like teacher assistants than like buddies, and evaluated their relations with her students accordingly. I, on the other hand, felt that warmer, less businesslike relations were desirable, and would have liked to have seen Candi involved in a wider range of relation types.

Type IV: 'They Teach You as Well as You Teach Them'

Monica was an IWE in Mrs. Miller's class. Her relations with the disabled students were characterized by fixed balance of power, frequent and easy mutual adaptation, occasional playfulness, and warm, engaged affect. One day at the end of the year she brought Kim, her "godsister," to visit the class and in a tape-recorded conversation explained her relationship with Fidel to her godsister and me:

Carola:	. . . Say Kim said to you, "Well Monica, why do you go to the laundromat with those people? What are you achieving by that?" What would you say?
Monica:	Well, I'd say . . . sometimes what I'd achieve by going there—sometimes they help YOU learn something instead of them—instead of YOU helping THEM learn something.
Carola:	Uh-huh?
Monica:	They teach YOU just as well as you teach them. And that's what I like . . .
Carola:	Huh!
Monica:	. . . You know, you just know something new with them every day with them.
Carola:	What do you mean, Monica? That's neat!
Monica:	Oh, well, let's see, like um, just like sometimes you—like Fidel—(to Kim) Fidel is blind—he'll have, like I'll show him to put one hand on one part of the clothes and then the other, and he'll do it just right

> then and it's so NEAT and everything. It's like "Huh! That's REAL good!"

Carola: Uh-huh.

Monica: And just like, when they smile—Fidel sometimes just doesn't laugh or smile—and he'll surprise you with a smile and a HUG!

(This theme continued for six turns until a new question was asked.)

Carola: . . . If you were gonna talk about your relationship with, say, Fidel or Tricia, to someone else, how would you . . . what kind of relationship would it be? Would you say, "Well, I'm her teacher, or I'm her friend," or . . . ?

Monica: I'd say, "My friend."

Carola: Friend is the better word?

Monica: Yeah, um-hm. 'Cuz I'm not a teacher, I'm just a student myself, so . . .

Carola: Uh-huh?

Monica: . . . So I would consider the students in here FRIENDS. Or I'd say—if somebody asked me, you know—"The kids that I work with."

Monica's comments indicated that she recognized the conflicting expectations associated with her role in Mrs. Miller's room. She viewed herself as a fellow student, a friend, or a "worker," depending on which of the disabled students she was with. Monica interpreted behaviors that would ordinarily be viewed negatively (such as Juan's poking or Lucy's habit of strongly grasping passers-by) as being these students' ways of expressing happiness or affection, and so was able to maintain Type IV relations with even the more "difficult" members of Mrs. Miller's class. In addition, she had an affectionate, closer relationship with Tricia, another of Mrs. Miller's students.

Type V: 'I Respect Her for What She Is and for What She's Doing'

Participants in Type V relations held either tutor/learner roles or mutual student roles. Both IWEs and non-IWEs were involved. The balance of power was flexible, which afforded the disabled party frequent opportunities to control interactions. Feedback occurred easily and mutual adaptations were frequently perceived. The affect expressed was warm, ranging from friendly to protective. Spontaneous, playful behavior commonly occurred, even during tasks or instructional activities.

Veronica was a black 9th grader and an IWE in Mrs. Miller's class. She participated in a range of relations with disabled students that spanned all the types described here, but had developed a particularly close relationship with Tricia, a student with visual impairments who was well-liked by nondisabled students in spite of characteristics that might be assumed to interfere with the development of peer relations. Besides having limited expressive language and being incompletely toilet trained, Tricia habitually expressed negative feelings by throwing heavy objects with painful effect at people nearby. In an interview, Veronica described their relationship:

> **Carola:** Soooo . . . like, how do you, uh, see Tricia—say, in comparison to somebody like Betty who's your real good friend?
>
> **Veronica:** Well, Tricia, she's very intelligent—she's a bright person even though sometimes she gets upset. But in other words, as I grow and as she grows I would still respect her for what she is and for what she's doing by being the person she is.
>
> **Carola:** So you kind of feel she's . . .
>
> **Veronica:** She's just like Betty. She can't see, but Tricia, she KNOWS things and she'll catch on to it quick.
>
> **Carola:** Mm-hm . . . . Like, would you consider Tricia a FRIEND? Or would she be something else to you?
>
> **Veronica:** Well, if she was with me, you know, living with me in my own apartment, I'd consider her as a close—a very close friend . . .

Some Type V relations, like Veronica and Tricia's, developed out of Type III contact. Others developed more spontaneously. For example, Salvador was an Hispanic student who had moved to the United States a few years before the time of the study. He was a 12th grader and an outstanding athlete, with city-wide awards for his soccer skills. He had never been an IWE, but had gotten to know certain severely disabled students through casual contact. In particular, Mrs. Miller had observed him interacting regularly with Juan. In a brief conversation with the investigator, Salvador described their relationship this way:

> **Carola:** So, um, how did you get to know Juan?
>
> **Sal:** I don't know, I just see him around sometimes, he say "Hey." I found out he comes from Nicaragua, so I speak Spanish with him.
>
> **Carola:** Does he like it when you speak Spanish?
>
> **Sal:** Yeah . . . I think he understands me pretty well.
>
> **Carola:** What kind of things do you guys do together?
>
> **Sal:** Sometimes we play a little football, hang around, I don't know. I see him in the park, or when we're in the hall he'll come up, say hello. You know Hector? The guy with me in 105?
>
> **Carola:** I don't know . . . Oh! You mean when you came in with the award? Was he wearing a net on his hair?
>
> **Sal:** Yeah! He knows him (Juan) too!

Type V relations were particularly likely to involve either horsing around (nonverbal physical play) or playful verbal interactions. For example, Dwayne, a student with impaired vision, and Anita, one of the Popular People who was an IWE in Mrs. Anderson's class, had a running joke in which the two students (both were black) would use exaggerated "Southern" accents and vocabulary while working on tasks the teacher set up. In this instance,

Anita was to "take data" (i.e., evaluate Dwayne's achievement on each step of an instructional program) while Dwayne made scrambled eggs:

Anita:	(mock-seriously) Now YOU know what you got t'do . . .
Dwayne:	(shakes his finger at her) Now jus' a minute!
Anita:	Don' you "Jus' a minute" me! You know what you got t'do, nigger! (She drops her voice dramatically on "nigger.")
Dwayne:	All right, all right . . . (He begins to assemble utensils and ingredients, bringing them to the table where she sits.)
Anita:	(to Carola and Dwayne) The BELLS are ringin.'
Carola:	What?
Anita:	(pointing to Dwayne's unfashionable bell-bottomed pants) The bells are RINGING!
Dwayne:	(Ignores implied criticism)
Anita:	Honey, you need a bowl.
Dwayne:	Honey, I KNOW that, sugar pie. (He mixes milk and egg in a bowl.)
Anita:	Here, take this and take this . . . (He should return dirtied utensils to sink at this stage of the task analysis.)
Dwayne:	I'm not nobody's maid around here . . . 'cept myself. (He takes the things to the sink and then goes to the stove.)
Anita:	Scoot over some, baby, so I c'n see what you're doin.' (He lights the fire.) Tha's cool. (He pours eggs into the pan with her help.) Oh Dwayne, you got a giant-size eggshell in there . . . 'd you get it out? (He finishes cooking and sits down with her to eat the eggs.)
Dwayne:	(He points to Anita's data sheet as he clears his throat theatrically) A-he-he-hem!
Anita:	I MARKED your sheet! I gotta wait until you done eatin' t' mark some more.
Dwayne:	Now I'm finished—now are you happy?
Anita:	You know I LOVE you, Dwayne.

IWEs in Type V relations sometimes spoke as though they perceived a conflict between the duties expected of them as teacher assistants and the activities they preferred to engage in with Type V friends. For example, in a conversation with Andi and Tina, sisters who were also IWEs in Mrs. Wilson's class, Anita said that when she was supposed to take data on Dwayne or Hannah, she would "just make plusses on the sheet and then say, 'go on, Hannah, tell Susan (Mrs. Anderson's aide) we're done and then we can do somethin' else.' " Tina said that sometimes, when she and Dwayne were supposed to clean tables in the cafeteria, she would say, "C'mon, don' do those tables! I'll just mark your sheet all plusses and we can go hang out— don't tell Susan!"

Exceptions

Not all relations fit these five categories perfectly. Rick's relations, for example, were particularly hard to categorize. He was a 10th grader classified, like Latrice, as "learning disabled." He, too, appeared to have problematic relations with nondisabled peers at Explorer. He had been an IWE in Mrs. Anderson's class during the 1983–1984 school year, and had regularly eaten lunch with Mrs. Miller's students during that year. Although he had tried to re-enroll as an IWE with Mrs. Miller in 1984–1985, she had resisted his attempts to join her class. For one thing, she didn't like the feeling that he was "using her and her students because he didn't have any other peer relations." However, he maintained contact with several of the disabled students.

Rick's relations with the disabled students made me uncomfortable also. Although they were similar to Type III relations in role, reciprocity, and balance of power, the feelings he expressed were similar to the negative affect displayed in Type II relations. Although Rick was observed to initiate play with disabled students, his playful interactions had a teasing, condescending tone that made me, and others, uneasy. His relations with disabled students had the same peculiar character, regardless of whom he chose to interact with. For example, Rick was enrolled in a building maintenance class in which Lin, a severely disabled boy, was also enrolled. The students in building maintenance received elective credits for sweeping the halls and picking up trash after lunch. Tina, one of Mrs. Anderson's IWEs, had a Type IV relationship with Lin, and was accompanying him when the following interaction occurred:

Lin is sweeping the hall while Tina picks up the big pieces of trash. Lin makes a gesture at Tina that means, "Go ahead" . . .

Tina:	He makes sure I pick up every little scrap—won't let me leave NOTHIN'!
	(Rick comes along with a broom and sees them.)
Rick:	Lin! You are so STUPID!
Tina:	WHO you callin' stupid? (Two hall guards come up, hear the exchange, and come to Tina's support.)
Guard:	Rick, don't call anybody stupid. You aren't so smart yourself!
Lin:	(to Rick) Shut up, boy! (He performs a Michael Jackson-style spin. Another kid sees us and speaks to Tina.)
Kid:	Michael Jackson ain't supposed to sweep, he's supposed to make money. Don't you push Michael Jackson into anything!

The studies of social interactions between disabled and nondisabled adolescents that I reviewed in Chapter 2 reported three types of social relations differentiated by affect: *negative, positive,* and *neutral* (e.g., Breen et al., 1985; Brinker, 1985). The data presented here, however, show that we can expect more from integration. Students at Explorer had access to at least *five* types of relations, differentiated by participant roles, balance of power, mutual adaptation, occurrence of reciprocal play, and kind of affect expressed.

ENDNOTE

In Bronfenbrenner's analysis of social relations and their contribution to individual development (1979), the following concepts are defined: "Participant role" refers to an individual's position in a social system and the expected activities and relations associated with that position. Some examples he cites are the varying expectations associated with the roles of Mother, Baby, Teacher, or Friend (p. 84). Roles in Explorer's system could be either formal or informal, and varied depending on the perspective from which an individual was described. The formal roles of "high school student" and "special education student," and the informal roles of "peer tutor" and "friend" were influential elements in the student relations typology.

"Balance of power" refers to control of joint activities. The balance may be fixed, in which one individual consistently controls the dyadic interactions, or flexible, in which the developing (less powerful) individual experiences increasing opportunities to exercise control. Bronfenbrenner views situations characterized by *flexible* balance of power as optimal for learning (p. 58). At Explorer, flexible contact situations were those in which I observed the disabled participant to initiate, redirect, or terminate joint activities.

"Degree of reciprocity" refers to mutual coordination of activity. In situations characterized by a high degree of reciprocity, "What A does influences what B does and vice versa. As a result, one member has to coordinate his activities with another" (p. 57). Reciprocity between disabled and nondisabled high school students took both verbal and nonverbal forms of feedback and mutual adaptation.

"Affective relation" refers to the participants' mutual feelings about each other. Bronfenbrenner hypothesizes that, "As participants engage in dyadic relations, they are likely to develop more pronounced feelings toward one another. These may be mutually positive, negative, ambivalent, or asymmetrical" (p. 58). Feelings voiced by students or inferred in my notes included more than 30 descriptors that I collapsed into five general affect labels associated with the relations at Explorer: *tentative/curious, dislike, engaged/interested, businesslike,* and *affectionate.*

chapter 9

Obvious
Influences

By Christmas, I could see that my earlier doubts about REACH's choice of Explorer as an integration site had been unfounded. I hadn't gotten mugged and the special education classes had come a long way from the bad old days when Mr. Tetrowski's students sat watching *Sesame Street* while the teenagers who volunteered to help them were taunted in the halls. Now, instead of being isolated and babied, disabled young people were active participants in a variety of social relations that paralleled those that typical adolescents might be expected to experience. Student interactions weren't always ideal, but the daily rough-and-tumble I witnessed had a natural, *teenaged* quality that seemed more realistic (and therefore more valuable in the long run) than any "special" treatment could be.

The months I had spent earning the Regulars' trust had paid off, too, in the candor with which they answered my questions. Even remarks like "sometimes they get on my nerves" or "sometimes I get bored" showed that the Regulars were relating to their disabled fellow students as fallible, multidimensional "humans like us" rather than as idealized, infantilized Poster Children.

What had happened here? Federal legislation had led to Explorer's desegregation, but integration—in the sense of positive intergroup relations—can't be legislated. What had influenced the development of the relaxed and normal social relations between disabled and nondisabled students? As a teacher-cum-researcher trying to analyze this change, I naturally expected that my research would identify ways in which teachers and administrators had affected the situation—professional problem-solving seemed to be the most obvious source of influence.[1] In fact, several of the school's administrators (the principal, three assistant principals, and the dean of boys) were

[1]See endnote, pp. 115–116.

quite vocal in their support for the presence of the students with severe disabilities at Explorer. A lower-level administrator—the teacher who served as head of the school's special education department—was, however, not so supportive.

ADMINISTRATORS' INFLUENCE

'They Have to Learn to Live with Others'

The school's principal and three assistant principals made contact possible between disabled and nondisabled students in at least three ways. First, they publicized their support for the integration program in documents expressing school policy, such as the school's accreditation application, the information bulletin given to visitors, and in the orientation materials prepared for all new students. Second, they established safety procedures that made it possible for the special classes to be housed in the school, such as emergency building evacuation procedures or directives to be followed in case a severely disabled student had a medical emergency. Third, they authorized the special education teachers' efforts to involve nondisabled students in their classrooms, and they observed and evaluated these programs when they included the special education teachers in their teacher supervision rounds.

I appreciated the ways in which regular-education administrators expressed their understanding of the integration program's goals. As the dean of boys said, when I asked him what he thought of the program, "I see them as part of the school—not as handicapped—just as students. Years ago, handicapped students would have been ridiculed, but here, the students are more accepting of a range of abilities. For example, nobody makes a big deal over the little blind girl, they just move out of her way."

I told Dean Roberts that I had thought it was great, when one of Mrs. Anderson's disabled students got in a fight, that he had suspended him just as he would have suspended a nondisabled student—this equal treatment was REAL acceptance, in my mind. When I asked the dean about what benefits and drawbacks he saw to integration, he said, "I think the program is good for the students. Unless they're going to live separately all their lives, they have to learn to interact with others. This way each one learns to understand each other. If you stay around the same kind of people as you are, you emulate those people. This way the handicapped kids see how to act. People shouldn't treat 'em like dogs—they want to be loved and cared about like anybody else."

'I'll Watch Them, but I Won't Touch Them'

Mrs. Anderson, Mrs. Wilson, and Mrs. Miller perceived the regular education administrators positively, but unfortunately had little daily contact with them. Their department head could have provided them with more direct, concrete support; however, she was a member of the special education "old guard" who believed that children with severe disabilities had been served better in separate, special schools, and expressed her belief by treating these teachers as though their efforts were unimportant or useless. The following instance is from Mrs. Miller's third period class:

> Veronica sits next to Diane. Tricia is seated on the opposite side of the table. Tricia throws off her shoes, and then starts to strip off her clothes. Mrs. Miller intervenes, repeatedly giving Tricia chances to put her shoes back on.
>
> Fidel (a deaf and blind student) is in a bad mood today. Veronica is acting calm and trying to go on with Battleship while Mrs. Miller holds down various pieces of furniture as Fidel tries to flip them over. I'm trying to ignore these behaviors too, but I just go leaping out of my seat, feeling that Mrs. M. needs help when he lifts a table with a record player and radio on it—he's so strong! Fidel is really tantrumming now—stomping his feet and wailing. He tries to pick up and throw an area rug. Mrs. M. tries to hold his hands still. Jesus! Tricia, meanwhile, is throwing her shoes.
>
> Incredibly, Mrs. Ringwald, the head of the special education department, has interrupted *three* times during this period, looking for a list of parent names for IEP notices she wants to send out. First, she sent her teacher aide down, then she telephoned our room, and then came down in person! While all of the above is going on, she is standing there trying to get Mrs. Miller to say that she'll turn in the names Monday—which Mrs. M has already promised!

The teachers resented Mrs. Ringwald's habit of interrupting them during their classes without any regard for what might be going on, but they were most upset about the attitudes of the extra staff she had chosen. For example, a teacher had been hired to substitute and, when necessary, cover single classes on a daily, rotating basis while each special education teacher had a "preparation period." This teacher said that he would not come into physical contact with severely disabled students, his exact words being, "I'll watch them, but I won't *touch* them." Mrs. Ringwald refused to replace him, and this made the teachers very unhappy.

REGULAR EDUCATION CLASSES AND CLUBS

The research literature on attitudes toward disability tells us that many people *still* believe (as I suppose the substitute teacher did) that disabled people are sick, or that their disabilities are contagious. Therefore, educators are advised to correct this (and other) misinformation if they want to promote better acceptance of such individuals. For that reason, regular education classes and clubs were targeted for informational presentations by the REACH project during the early days of Explorer's integration efforts, and in 1984, regular education teachers continued to promote intergroup contact in at least three ways.

First, at least 16 of the students from Mrs. Anderson's and Mrs. Wilson's classes were accepted by regular education teachers for mainstreaming in physical education, art, reading laboratory, typing, and English as a second language classes. Unfortunately, because no extra teacher aides were available to accompany them to their mainstream classes, only the most independent disabled students could participate. Second, the teachers who served as advisors to the student ethnic clubs (e.g., the Black Student Union, Chinese Club, and Filipino Club) accepted disabled students' memberships, and the advisor of the Bears Society (a school service club) prompted the Bears to sponsor a Christmas party and a series of lunchtime visits designed to acquaint club members with members of the classes for students with severe disabilities. Third, two teachers in the English department incorporated units on disability into their lesson plans, and invited the special education teachers to speak to their classes.

'. . . To Rid Some of the Ignorance of Most of Us'

The visits sponsored by the service club appeared to have been much appreciated, both by the special education teachers *and* the students, who welcomed the chance to talk with nondisabled teenagers at length. For example, in one visit I observed, a class for honors students was working on a unit in which they were to write about "parts of the high school we are not often exposed to." They heard a series of lectures by various building staff, including Mrs. Miller, who, as described in Chapter 3 (pp. 19–20) explained her program as she showed slides of students using age-appropriate materials and working at community job-training sites.

Mrs. Miller's lecture stressed two themes: the importance of learning *functional* skills in school, and the reasons for using appropriate community settings in which to learn these skills. In dealing with these two themes, she stressed the similarities between disabled and nondisabled students (e.g., both types need to be independent from parents and want to have a job and friends). She emphasized that the students were integrated at Explorer so that they could "see what normal life was like, to learn normal behavior, and also to get regular friends."

The students' reactions revealed that they had all seen the disabled students around school, that they had long been curious about them, and that they welcomed the chance to ask questions. As one boy commented, "I am presently able to view the students in a new light. Maybe you should give more lectures on your students to rid some of the ignorance of most of us." Students asked repeatedly about the severely disabled students' ability and motivation to communicate. For example, one girl asked, "Can Juan talk?," and, "When you say he can't talk, does that mean he doesn't want to talk?"

Students also asked how they should act toward people with disabilities. For example, one boy wrote a note saying: "I have often seen a certain student in a wheelchair going up and down the halls with a little difficulty but I have always refrained from helping for fear of making him upset in some way. Do you think my fear is unfounded?"

Comments revealed that the honors class had learned important new information about the disabled students' activities and abilities. For example, one student wrote, "I was surprised to find out that the students of Special Ed. didn't learn or aren't taught the kinds of things regular students learn at school. And some of them work at a time when we regular students are trapped in class. How lucky they are . . . and intelligent also." And another commented, "I always wondered what these students did when they weren't in school. I also didn't know that they clean other people's homes and they are much older than they look. They are also much more intelligent than I thought."

Mrs. Miller was especially pleased to find that the presentation had also served to help her involve more nondisabled volunteers with her students. As one girl wrote:

> I'm really looking forward to meeting Juan, Ling, Lucy, Tricia, Tiny, and the rest of the gang and perhaps becoming their friend, that is if they accept me. If you ever need a volunteer to ride the MUNI (streetcar) in the morning with one or more of your students I'd be willing to do so. I'm so happy to see that finally there are some changes being made in the society in favor of the handicapped. All I can say is that it's about time. After seeing a presentation like that I am proud to go to Explorer High again knowing that there are people like you and your helpers. I'd be delighted to be of any help to you.

'We ALL Got a Handicap'

In a second set of "attitude change" presentations (which included the dialogue reproduced on p. 31), three English classes worked on a unit about disability in which they saw films, spoke to the mother of a disabled child (the sister-in-law of the teacher), participated in disability simulation activities, and were visited by Mrs. Miller and some IWEs assigned to her class. During these visits, the special education teacher encouraged these peer tutors to talk about their experiences with their disabled fellow students, and then answer questions.

Again, Mrs. Miller and her copanelists stressed the reasons for the differences between special and regular education curriculum, and again, similarities between disabled and nondisabled students were stressed. As one student said, "They just got a little handicap, that's all. We ALL got a handicap. They try over and over and so they get the hang of it, and then we learn something too."

The students speculated about how they would feel if they had a retarded brother or sister. For example, Preston said, "If I had a brother like that I wouldn't let anybody make fun of him . . . If anybody did, I'd STICK 'em" (stab him).

Lectures, panel presentations, and other contact with regular education classes was an effective and rewarding means (the special education teachers especially enjoyed it) of promoting better understanding of people with disabilities at the high school.

'SEVERELY HANDICAPPED' TEACHERS

The three "SH teachers" (as teachers of severely disabled students were casually termed) exerted the most obvious and ongoing influence on student social relations. In contrast to Mr. Tetrowski, all three *chose* to teach students with more severe handicaps, and all three had recently been enrolled in courses taught by San Francisco State University faculty (two as master's students and one in an in-service program) that stressed methods of teaching in integrated community environments. All three were good teachers who were highly rated by the high school's administrators.

As I've already documented, Mrs. Anderson, Mrs. Miller, and Mrs. Wilson promoted integration in many ways. First, they organized age-appropriate activities that involved both disabled and nondisabled students. Second, they modeled humane and dignified ways of relating to people with disabilities. Third, they worked to disseminate accurate information about their students' abilities *and* limitations in a positive but casual manner.

The teachers most frequently used informal means of transmitting information about their students. Although all of them had, at different times, tried to set up more formal meetings at lunch or after school in order to answer questions, discuss problems, and train students to act as peer tutors, Explorer teenagers just wouldn't show up! In the end, the teachers found themselves quickly teaching the basics whenever a moment presented itself. Mrs. Miller was particularly good at packing important information into a few words.

For example, when Betty stopped by to see Veronica, who, as an IWE in Mrs. Miller's class was helping Lucy to use a picture communication system, the teacher said to the visitor, "Betty, this is Lucy. She's learning to make her own lunch. Because most of the students can't talk, they have to use pictures. She's hearing what the picture means so she can turn around later and use it to get what she wants." In this way, Mrs. Miller got across the idea that Lucy was expected to be able to learn, and that she could communicate in a systematic way.

On another occasion, Mrs. Miller told Preston how to play Battleship (an electronic board game) with one of her students, and at the same time conveyed the basic social goal of her peer tutoring program. She did this by saying, "One of the things that's important is that you are a TEAM. You're kind of in the role of a teacher as well as a friend. You want to teach her what to do as well as enjoy her company."

Another time, Mrs. Miller re-emphasized a social goal and an important special education concept when she explained how Veronica should play Mastermind with Tricia (Mastermind is a board game that requires one opponent to guess the design another has made in a peg board). Mrs. Miller said, "What we usually do is, when the students are playing we show them where the pieces belong, and then *they* place them . . . Basically, the students are *partially* participating. It isn't as important that they know the game as that they are playing it with everybody else."

Teachers and students rarely discussed the specific disabilities experienced by the disabled students. It seemed impolite to talk about the students' problems in front of them, and besides, the teachers felt uncomfortable with diagnostic labels, as Mrs. Miller explained one day.

In this instance, Mrs. Miller had asked each IWE student to write a letter to a hypothetical friend describing one of the severely disabled teenagers. This assignment provoked an unusual discussion among the teacher, Preston, Noreen, and me. When asked about one student's disability, I responded with a medical/scientific definition of Down Syndrome. Mrs. Miller overheard and gave an alternative definition, and then explained her reasons for avoiding such labels when giving information about her students:

Noreen: What does Ling have?

Mrs. M: Ling is labeled as developmentally disabled. It's a catch-all term. Her major disability is that she's mentally retarded—that means that she learns slower or at a different rate than other people. The trouble with categories is that labels make you think that that's all there *is* to a person—that you can fit them into a little box!

Preston: Run that back again?

Noreen: (to Mrs. M.) He talks so ugly!

Mrs. M: It's hard to categorize someone with a label like 'Down Syndrome' because the label makes you think they have all the same characteristics. It's the same as saying that someone's black. Maybe they all have something in common—they all have black skin—but maybe there are different shades. It's a stereotype.

The letters these teenagers composed—in spite of their problems with written English—eloquently expressed the understanding, accuracy, and empathy with which these peer tutors evaluated the most severely handicapped members of the high school's population:

April 29, 1985

This particular student that I'm gowing to be telling my friend about is Xuan. She is a very small girl from Japan with long Black hair which sometime she'll where it in a braid or other styles.

I really don't know what her disability is. I know that she can not talk she always just like mumbles, but she does not get the hole word out. She walks just fine. Sometime she will drag her feet and I hate when people drag their feet. I notices that sometime she will just come right out and push you for no reasion. She can see and hear just fine, and she does a good job with her close from what I have seen. I thank that she has a mintral disability.

Her parents dress her nice sometime but sometime they just put enny kind of cloes on her like a big sweater that does not match her top or her pants. Will I thank Xuan realy likes me and sometime when where walking down the hall she likes to hold my hand or just put her head on me and walk, and she does not like for a nother student to come and stand by me, she will try to push them a way and then she gets made at me and does not what me to touch her. But she gets over it soon. And a lot of times she will try to test you.

She does not realy tell you when she has to go to the bathroom most of the time you would just have to send her, and she'll go. Sometime she will just go and open up thee door and try to leave.

She trys to comb her hair sometime but she realy can't get into it as good as if someone did it for her. She eat very well on her own. And she can dress her self. I don't see her wash dishes to often as Tricia. she realy does not need help with enny thing to me she is dowing just fine.

She likes me to comb her hair but she does not like enny one to put hair spray on her hair. She also likes to do the cup thing with me. I like to do everything with her. She is a very fun *person*.

Will she is not always in her best mood but every one has their up and downs. And you would love to work with her too.

Noreen

I'm gonna tell you about Tricia. First I'll tell you how she looks like. She's short brown hair. Her disability is that she's blind and doesn't walk too good, I think because one of her legs is shorter than the other. Her other disability is that she can't speak.

Tricia dresses O.K. She dresses like if she was 15 or 14 and I couldn't believe that she was 20 when Mrs. Miller told me.

Tricia likes to sing this song I don't know I was surprise when I heard her singing, she also likes to play pool and get attention. Sometimes it's a problem because she gets mad when she thinks she is not getting attention and she hits her self and throws her cane and takes off her shoes.

With her is not a problem knowing what she wants because she makes sings with her hands that I understand and sometimes makes some sound.

She can feed her self, but she needs someone to help her walk. I think she likes when I ask her to sing with me and I like it too because it's got a good rythm. I can tell when she's happy when she claps her hands.

Andreas

Dear Darryl,

How you been I been fine. I'm just out here in frisco going to school and waiting to graduate out of High School.

I go to my first period to sixth and I'm out at 2:00 pm. But in my third period class I have a Special Ed class. It's students with a disability. Like one student Juan he's a student that's a little slow in the mind and can't all the way speak yet. He's about 59 inches and black hair he's Spanish and he dress average. Sometimes he likes to play games or go out side for a walk, but sometimes he just likes to Kick back. When he wants something he yells and gives you sign language. He can go to the restroom by his self he know his way around the school and sometimes he goes to lunch with a peer tutor or to the wash house or to the store. He's kind of slow learning but he catches on sooner or later. He needs a little help with yelling out loud or whistling, and he needs help with his way of approaching people. Sometimes I will go to the church and he likes to come along with me. He likes too go just about everywhere with any of the peer tutors. I like to take him places with me because even though he's disabled we still are good friends and I wouldn't mind taking him anywhere with me. I like to play games and baseball or running after each other. I can tell he's happy because everyday he comes in smiling about anything. And he always wants to go somewhere with me or play a game of battleship with me.

P.S. Write back soon. Sincerely yours, Preston

One of the many things that touched Mrs. Miller and me about these letters was the way in which negative behaviors that once had been cited by professionals as evidence that Tricia and Xuan were "not ready" for inclusion in integrated schooling (incomplete toilet training and aggression, for example) were accepted so matter-of-factly. At the same time, "dressing okay" was revealed to be at least as important a part of mainstreaming to these teenagers as the social skills adults had established as priorities.

SECURITY GUARDS

Surprisingly, the school staff (besides the special education teachers) who did the most to promote integration were the 11 members of the school's security staff! Because the guards patrolled the school during all times that students were free to associate (e.g., during passing periods, at lunch, and before and after school), and because it was in fact their job to monitor student social relations, *they spent more time in informal contact with students than any other staff in the school.* The senior security guard, Mr. Prince, and at least two others took a personal and particular interest in the school's disabled students, modeled positive behavior toward them, tried to get other teenagers involved with them, and intervened in problematic or negative situations.

Mr. Prince was a long-time observer of Explorer's young people, playing a fatherly role when needed, for example, by giving out his telephone number and saying, "Call me *any* time you need help." In the spring, I asked him for his views of the integration program, and about one of the disabled students—a young man from Laos who had been suspended from school for fighting with a nondisabled friend. Mr. Prince's answer illustrated his concern and understanding:

Carola:	I know that you know the kids pretty well—like I remember you were talking to Phuc Sanh about calling people names the other day.
Mr. Prince:	His friends are into karate-type fighting, kicking and punching.

	Phuc Sanh has gotten into a negative stage now, just defiance, kicking, and running away.
Carola:	(I ask to clarify what he means about stages.)
Mr. Prince:	Well, I see five stages involved in getting into a new school: 1) set-up, 2) getting acquainted, 3) learning the rules of how to act, 4) getting to know/meeting more people, 5) feeling secure, so feeling defiant. Phuc Sanh has gotten to the fifth stage now. In the case of the fight where he got his head cut, both boys were suspended.
Carola:	This was a pioneering program here at Explorer, that's why I'm interested in how it's going.
Mr. Prince:	Oh yeah, wasn't Jerry (a student who had been in Mr. Tetrowski's class) the first person with Down syndrome to graduate from high school in San Francisco? He really changed a lot. At first has was really manipulative—saying stuff like, "Oh, buy me this because I'm handicapped," but he improved.
Carola:	(I ask if he has any advice for other schools' security staffs.)
Mr. Prince:	It's important to build their self-esteem. If they try to cop out, like Jerry used to do, get on their behinds!

I felt that Explorer was terribly lucky to have someone like Mr. Prince working to help its students, and rebuked myself for waiting until the year was almost over to interview him.

PEER TUTORING

Peer tutoring, an activity much analyzed in the special education literature, was the final obvious source of influence on student social relations. At Explorer, the special education teachers drew volunteers from the school's Internal Work Experience (IWE) program, which provided a formal structure through which special education teachers could organize and monitor daily contact between disabled and nondisabled students. Each IWE student spent one period (55 minutes) daily with the disabled students. During this time the teachers would organize the joint activities described earlier. During the year I spent at Explorer, Mrs. Miller, Mrs. Anderson, and Mrs. Wilson recruited more than 40 IWE students, sometimes using more than one per class period; in fall 1984, Mrs. Anderson enrolled IWEs during five class periods, Mrs. Miller during six periods, and Mrs. Wilson during three periods.

IWE/peer tutoring proved to be an important variable influencing the development of social relations between disabled and nondisabled students. Of the 32 students identified as regulars, 25 were enrolled in the program during the 1984–1985 school year, two others were friends of IWEs, and two were former IWEs.

Peer tutoring did not always lead to the development of intergroup social relations. At least 10 of the 42 students assigned to these special education classes dropped the class after a few weeks, or remained enrolled but just didn't attend. However, Internal Work Experience interacted with the demands of the school economy to provide a powerful influence for the development of Regular relations: 30 of the 32 Regulars observed in this study had some connection with the IWE program, either as former or current members, or as friends of IWEs.

Although my past experience in the REACH project had led me to view peer tutoring as an obvious source of influence, *the motivations and influences that led IWEs to prefer to assist disabled students over helping in the principal's office or in computer class were less obvious, as the next chapter shows.*

ENDNOTE: PROFESSIONAL PROBLEM-SOLVING

In trying to make sense of the ways in which teachers, administrators and other staff influenced integration at Explorer, I hypothesized that the professionals' problem-solving response to the social situation experienced by students with severe disabilities was composed of four elements. The first element was *recognition* of the mismatch between integration goals and reality. As established in the Project REACH memorandum quoted in Chapter 1 (pp. 5–6), a much hoped-for goal of the integration program was the development of positive intergroup social relations. Staff believed that by encouraging "positive accepting attitudes towards disabled students" and by increasing "interactions between nonhandicapped and severely disabled students in school and in the community," such relations would develop.

However, the language of the memorandum revealed a subtext to these goal statements. Staff recognized that, given the reality of the disabled students' limitations coupled with the stigmatizing effect of disability on interpersonal relations, this goal would not be achieved without special efforts on the students' behalf. Positive attitudes needed "encouragement" and interactions needed to be "increased."

The second element was therefore *the organization of special efforts*. The teachers were encouraged, by the REACH project staff, the special education professors from San Francisco State who placed student-teachers in their classes, and by the authors of popular textbooks (such as Sailor & Guess, 1983, and Wilcox & Bellamy, 1982) to define these "special efforts" quite broadly. In order to promote long-range community integration, teachers were advised to see themselves not only as instructors, but as managers, responsible for working with community agencies and local businesspersons to arrange a smooth transition from high school to adult life for their students.

The special education teachers at Explorer worked in a variety of ways to encourage contact between disabled and nondisabled students. For example, they wrote individualized education plans (IEPs) that documented social relations as a legitimate educational focus. They scheduled instruction so that it took place in common areas of the school rather than in their separate, self-contained classrooms. They gave lectures and slide shows, and organized panel discussions on disability. They recruited nondisabled peer tutors or buddies through the high school's IWE program. They placed disabled students in mainstream nonacademic classes. They tried to make sure that the special education students would attend assemblies, carnivals, food fairs, wrestling matches, and other special events.

The third element in professional problem-solving was *administration of the contact situation*. As I have documented, these special efforts resulted in contact situations, which could involve proximal, helping, or reciprocal interaction between students. By monitoring the nature of these joint activities and by informal transmission of information, the special education teachers worked to make the quality of student interaction in the contact situations compatible with their views of the integration program's goals.

The fourth element was the *evaluation of social outcomes*. Over the year, the teachers and I talked constantly about daily goings-on in the school. Both special and regular education staff seemed to be fairly satisfied with the social outcomes of the integration program, saying that student attitudes and interactions were about as good as they could make them, given existing school structures and student characteristics. My analysis of student interviews seemed to substantiate the staff's perceptions: most teenagers I talked with believed strongly in the benefits of school integration for both nondisabled and disabled students, and many seemed to value their increased opportunities to know "different kinds of people." Judging from these responses, the mismatch between integration goals and reality had apparently been recognized and resolved with some success through the neat four-part process I tentatively identified at Explorer.

What is wrong with this picture? Close examination would show that it's more tidy than accurate! When I write about education, the tendency to superimpose logical order on the messy reality of daily life in school is almost irresistible. While it is true that staff recognized the existence of potential problems, organized special efforts, kept an eye on the contact situations, and speculated about the results of their efforts, this analysis depends on a mechanistic model of classroom interaction (teacher-input, social-outcome) that lacks "ecological validity," an important concept used in evaluating the quality of research which means, in everyday English, that "things don't work that way in the real world."

As the next chapter shows, cultural beliefs, federal laws, family experiences, and the immediate example of peers were factors that, *in addition to professional influences*, contributed to the situations I observed at Explorer.

chapter 10

Less Obvious
Influences

As a special education professional, I must have
heard it 10,000 times: "Oh, you must have such patience! I could never do
your job!" In 9,999 of these situations, that question has been followed with,
"What ever made you get into helping the handicapped?" I've given many
different answers to these questions, but until fairly recently, I used to respond to the implicit flattery by supplying the sorts of (semi-)saintly answers
my interrogators seemed to expect. The kids at Explorer were less likely to
give those sorts of answers when I tried to find out how they had gotten
involved with Mrs. Miller's, Mrs. Anderson's and Mrs. Wilson's students.
When I analyzed their interviews, and the interviews I had taped with administrators, teachers, guidance counselors, and security guards, I found that
students and staff described five types of influences on intergroup social
relations—less obvious explanations than I had expected.

THE SCHOOL ECONOMY: 'I DIDN'T LIKE CERAMICS'

Both school staff and the Regulars who were IWEs often mentioned the
school's credits, grades, and graduation requirements (elements of the
"school economy") as factors influencing the initiation and development of
intergroup contact. For example, concern with obtaining "economic rewards" led students to enroll in the IWE program, and then, in some cases,
to become involved as teacher assistants in the special education classes. Of
the 32 Regulars, 25 were enrolled as IWEs during the time of this study.

Credits

Students at Explorer were required to earn 50 units of credit each year to
pass from grade to grade, and had to earn at least 200 credits to graduate.

Students who failed classes, however, would often come up short as they approached graduation time. In these cases, a student's counselor might advise him or her to enroll in more than the usual load of five classes per semester. Electives, such as fine arts, building maintenance, or IWE were especially good for an "overload" because, as one guidance counselor said, they were "not too solid," that is, they didn't require homework or exams.

Because the special education classes could absorb almost unlimited numbers of volunteers, they had permanent openings for all the IWEs they could get (at least 42 out of a total enrollment of 110 IWEs were assigned to the three SH classes during 1984–1985). When other classes were full, the counselors would suggest that students try "helping the handicapped." As Andre, a Regular in Mrs. Miller's class, said, "My counselor told me I needed the hours and the only thing open was this." Eight of the Regulars were seniors who enrolled in IWE for this reason. One senior (Harold) was enrolled as a special education IWE for two periods each day!

Electives

Each student at Explorer was supposed to be enrolled in at least five courses each semester. This was not only so that they would complete their graduation requirements in 4 years. State funds were allocated to the city school district on a per-capita basis and a student had to be taking at least five courses in order to be included in this "head count."

The guidance counselors were therefore obliged to enroll students in classes whether they wanted them (e.g., to satisfy graduation requirements) or not. In these cases, students were given a choice of electives. If the student was dissatisfied with one elective, he or she could go to the counselor and ask for a change.

Carmine, a freshman of Central American origin whom the special education staff valued for being responsible, taking initiative, and acting age-appropriately, described this process when she spoke to an English class about her experiences with the disabled students:

> **Teacher:** How'd you get started doing this?
> **Carmine:** I didn't like ceramics. The guidance counselor said, "I don't have no more classes for you to take." I'd see the students around the hall. I'd see Juan, he'd laugh, I'd laugh. Other kids might say, "Carmine, why you talkin' to them?" Mr. Wang said, "Why don't you work for Mrs. Miller?" I don't know, I really like them. I just have a feeling.

Grades

Students enrolled in IWE were graded and received credits just as in any other class. The special education teachers graded primarily on the basis of attendance and behavior. This meant that students who had poor academic skills could earn A's for their work as teacher assistants if they attended regularly and behaved appropriately.

Mr. Wang, a teacher of Chinese origin who was in charge of the IWE program, believed that grades constituted the most important motivation behind IWE enrollment. I showed him a list of the students who had been assigned to the special education classes and asked him what *he* thought might have influenced them to choose involvement with disabled students instead of one of the other positions available through IWE (e.g., working in Mr. Wang's office, the principal's office, in phys. ed., or in one of the school laboratories):

Mr. Wang:	They just take this because it's an easy grade! (He drops his tone dramatically.) These are not the very best kids! (He picks up a red pen and starts to mark my list of names.) Show me that list—I'll show you the losers. THIS one I WARNED her about! (He checks off 18 of my 42 names.) Loser . . . loser . . . Next year, to be a student teacher assistant you must have a C average or be a junior.
Carola:	What about the other teachers—what about you? Won't you lose yours?
Mr. Wang:	Oh, no! MINE are top notch! I have 11 working for me and only two didn't make the honor roll. But THESE (my list) are the kids nobody wants, so I say to the teachers: "You have a chance to interview them—good luck!"
A Secretary:	(Working next to Mr. Wang) Come on! I've seen some of them with the kids and they do a GOOD job!
Mr. Wang:	Oh yeah, they're not all losers, only 70%!

In fact, *for 11 of the 42 IWEs assigned to the special education classes that I studied, their grades for IWE were the highest they had ever received in their entire high school careers* (High School, 1985).

PROXIMITY: 'I JUST USED TO SEE THEM IN THE HALLS'

Several young people reported that, after seeing the students with disabilities in school, they were sometimes motivated to initiate further contact. *The fact that severely disabled students were not isolated in their self-contained classrooms, but were present in so many school and community areas, had a positive influence on their access to intergroup relations.* The special education teachers promoted proximity by scheduling as much instruction as possible outside the special education classrooms, by using common facilities at the same times as regular students, and by making sure that their students participated in special school events. As reported in Chapter 4, 62% of the intergroup contacts observed took place outside special education areas.

Noreen's comments provided an example of the way proximity combined with other influences. Noreen was a 10th grader of mixed black and

Pacific Island origins who was an IWE in Mrs. Miller's class. She reported that she had first gotten to know some students with severe disabilities when she was a 9th grader:

> I asked Noreen how she got started coming to this class. She said that last year she just used to see Mrs. Miller and her kids in the halls, and one day she went up to Mrs. Miller and asked if she wanted any help. When Mrs. Miller said yes, Noreen arranged it with her counselor. I said, "Why Mrs. Miller?" Noreen said, "Well, I'd seen her the most and she seemed to need the help, and the other kids [I assume Mrs. Anderson's and Mrs. Wilson's classes] seemed much more competent! Besides, my mother used to run a board-and-care home for old people so I'd had some experience—I mean, they were disabled, too!"

Including Noreen, 11 of the Regulars reported that they had been influenced in part by proximity. These data confirmed for Explorer's disabled students the hypothetical benefits of proximal interactions discussed in the special education literature (Hamre-Nietupski et al., 1978; Schutz et al., 1984). As in the case of Noreen, who reported her experience in her mother's "board-and-care" home, proximity was usually combined with other influences.

**HOME INFLUENCE: 'DIG DEEP AND YOU WILL
FIND THAT THAT ATTITUDE OF CARING COMES
FROM THEIR FAMILIES AND THE CHURCH THEY GO TO'**

Both students and staff members referred to home influences when explaining the initiation and development of intergroup contact. For example, students commonly spoke about the direct influence of family members. Besides Noreen, five other Regulars mentioned that members of their families worked with disabled persons in some way. Three additional Regulars had siblings or cousins who were themselves disabled. *In total, 28% of the Regulars reported this type of influence.*

School staff, in contrast, were likely to speak in a more abstract way about home-taught *values*. As one of the school's vice-principals, an Hispanic woman, said, "I just have the feeling that these students come from homes where moral values are strongly taught." (Some research actually indicates that Hispanic homes *may* be more successful than others at teaching accepting attitudes toward human differences [Cowardin, 1986].) Not only professional staff held this viewpoint. For example, Bob Goodfellow was a young black security guard who was often observed to interact with the disabled students. I asked Bob what kind of kids he saw getting involved with the disabled students. He said, "I think they are those who need to love or care for someone!" I told Bob that a large proportion of the kids I observed to be involved were black, and asked him why he thought that was. He said, "Dig deep and you will find that in the majority of kids, some member of the family goes to church. That well-rooted attitude of caring comes from their families and from the church they go to."

However, I could not pursue Goodfellow's idea further because I was constrained from questioning students about "their parents' . . . family life, morality, (or) religion" by the terms of my agreement with the school district (SFUSD, 1984). Casual remarks the Regulars made, however (talking about the Bible or their participation in a church choir), and behaviors they were observed to engage in (e.g., blessing themselves before eating) suggested that at least nine of the Regulars came from families where Judeo-Christian religious practices were commonly observed.

Other staff members spoke about influential home *experiences* when explaining the initiation and development of intergroup contact. Many staff members (e.g., six of the seven guidance counselors) theorized that because Explorer's students "had it hard," they were more accepting of others with problems. Mr. Prince, the senior security guard, articulated this viewpoint most clearly. "Mr. P" had been extensively involved with the disabled students since the integration program began 3 years before. When asked for his views on student relations, he said:

> "Explorer is a good place for that (integration)—EVERYBODY has problems! They're 98% minority and most are under some kind of duress. They know what it's like to have troubles, and so they're more accepting." I ask him why more blacks are involved than any other group. He answers, "These kids come from the Fillmore, Potrero Hill, or over by 3rd Street. They've had some hard knocks themselves."

The data on race/class stratification and socioeconomic status presented in Chapter 3 seemed to support Mr. Prince's contention, in that *the Regulars, of all the students at Explorer, were especially likely to live in neighborhoods where family poverty and "hard knocks" were common.* A study of socioeconomic differences in student acceptance of peers with mild retardation provides further support for this argument.

PEER INFLUENCE: "WE USED TO COME UP HERE TO BE WITH RICO AND 'THE HANDICAPS' "

Students often reported the influence of peer relations on the initiation and development of intergroup contact. For example, Regulars who were members of peer cliques might speak with their nondisabled friends about their relations with disabled students, and later bring their "buddies" into contact with the disabled students. In some cases, these buddies themselves might also become Regulars, further linking peer group and special education settings. Rico, Preston, and Mendel provided a good example of this phenomenon. Rico was a 12th grader of mixed Filipino, black, and Caucasian origins. Two of his siblings had disabilities. He had been an IWE in Mrs. Anderson's and Mrs. Wilson's classes for 2 years before the present study, and had maintained friendly casual relations with some of their students. Preston and Mendel, both 9th graders, were Rico's cousins. In an interview, Preston reported that he had actually gotten to know some of the severely disabled students when he was in the 8th grade at a neighboring middle school:

Carola: Who's your best friend around here?
Preston: Well I don't got just ONE best friend. I got some buddies. I always be with my cousins—Rico 'n them, Mendel. . . .
Carola: Oh, Rico! Rico with the long straight hair? He's your cousin? . . . I'd be interested in getting to interview him, actually, 'cause he had a lot to do with the handicapped classes last year and the year before. Did he ever tell you about that?
Preston: Yeah, that's how I got into it.
Carola: Oh really? Tell me about it!
Preston: Well, last year I used to come here after school, 'cuz we used to get out before him 'cuz he had a 7th period class, and we used to come up here to be with him and "the handicaps" . . . the ones that they be walkin' around and nothing's really wrong with them . . . Jon, Batisto, 'n them.

The special education teachers sometimes worried that nondisabled peers would compete with the disabled students for the Regulars' attention. They wondered aloud whether they should agree when the Regulars asked to include their friends or boyfriends in activities with the severely disabled students.

In one case (that of Latrice, Zita, and Susie, Nasty Girls who were IWEs in Mrs. Miller's class), the clique structure *did* appear to detract from and compete with the goals of the integration program. Otherwise, my observations suggested that the advantages of accommodating existing student association patterns outweighed the disadvantages. *The inclusion of student clique members, boyfriends, and others had the effect of both widening the severely disabled students' circle of acquaintances, and of providing positive experiences to members of the nondisabled student population who in some cases became more deeply involved with their disabled schoolmates.*

At least six separate pre-existing friendship cliques were observed among the Regulars. Each clique was made up of same-sex friends who also shared common ethnic origins. Girls' cliques had two to three members, but boys' cliques were larger, with four members or more. These patterns reproduced the "rules" governing adolescent peer relations reported in other studies discussed in Chapter 1 (Hallinan, 1980; Savin-Williams, 1980; Shimara, 1983). In four cases, the cliques developed close relations with specific disabled students, appearing to "absorb" disabled peers into clique activities. In all four cases, the disabled peer was the same sex as the clique members; there was ethnic similarity in two of the four cases. *These data suggest that at least the "rules" governing cross-sex contact be considered by staff who wish to promote intergroup social relations involving students with disabilities,* just as they would be considered in efforts involving nondisabled students.

THE INFLUENCE OF UNIVERSAL HUMAN NEEDS

Both students and staff referred to universal human needs when they tried to explain the initiation and development of intergroup relations. Mrs. Wilson, who taught one of the two classes for "trainable" mentally handicapped students at Explorer, had gotten to know many nondisabled students through her work in the integration program. She told me that she had observed that three kinds of students got involved with her class: 1) those who were motivated by the challenge of teaching, 2) those who had fun with the students and were motivated by interpersonal contact, and 3) those who were the "caring type" and were motivated by a desire to help someone else.

'It's the Challenge'

Statements by the Regulars supported Mrs. Wilson's observations. For example, Andi and Tina were twin sisters, leaders of a Popular People clique, who were IWEs shared by Mrs. Wilson's and Mrs. Anderson's classes. They were described by their regular teachers as "bright, but attendance problems . . . appear hard as nails." When asked what they liked about their relations with the disabled students, they said:

Andi:	Well, it's a CHALLENGE!
Tina:	It's a challenge!
Carola:	It's the challenge?
Andi:	That's true.
Tina:	It's a challenge, you know. 'Cause if you LIKE it, then it wouldn't really be hard . . .
Andi:	And it's hard if you THINK it is, otherwise it wouldn't really matter.
Tina:	Like, "Oh my goodness, he's having a tantrum, what'll I do?" Just have patience enough to hang with 'em and help 'em overcome it . . .
Andi:	And not, when it get BAD, to just say, "I can't TAKE it no more," and LEAVE! You can't do THAT!
Tina:	It doesn't work that way!

Although Andi and Tina found the sense of meeting a challenge motivating, observations showed that they also enjoyed interpersonal contact and the sense of responsibility that developed as a result of their association with disabled students.

'I Like Working with People'

Anita, a black 10th grader and one of the Popular People described by her teachers as "bright, but a discipline problem," was also motivated by personal contact. She had originally been assigned to act as an IWE in the school's computer lab, but had disliked the experience and had transferred to Mrs. Anderson's class. She explained the feelings that had influenced her:

> I like working with people, that's why I like this class. 'Cause before I was working with computers, but that was SOOOO boring. You do the same thing every day, helping them do the SAME thing (she adopts a teacher's tone): "Sit down RIGHT there—there's a COMPUTER, and to ERASE, press this button . . ." Now that was DEAD! So then Mrs. Hammond (her counselor) said, "Do you want to work with the retarded kids?" And I said "Sure, I'd LOVE to work with them."

Anita's style of "working" was characterized by frequent verbal play. She reported that the relationships she had developed with two of the disabled students (Dwayne and Hannah) had evolved over the year from being working relationships to being "very close."

'Knowing That YOU'RE Helping Someone!'

Monica was a 12th grader, assigned as an IWE to Mrs. Miller's class. She was one of the Popular People, a sociable girl who was active in school clubs, and who was described by her counselor as "a nice girl but not very bright." In an interview, I asked her how she felt about the disabled students she knew:

Carola: So did you notice any changes in your feelings, like from when you first started until now?

Monica: No, I just—at first—you know, at FIRST when I just got into the class, it was like, you know, it looks kind of TOUGH, you know, the way how they ACT and . . .

Carola: Yeah.

Monica: You know, when they get into their bad moods. But as I WORKED with them and you know, HELPED them, I understood . . . It's, you know, it's fun. Just, you know, just to be out there knowing that YOU'RE helping someone. It makes me feel good.

Carola: I know, when I think of it, if somebody asked ME why did I go into special ed., I probably would say the same things . . .

Monica: I think it's fun, though! I mean, you don't stay in the classroom, and—you know how it is . . .

Carola: Is that something that people like about the class? That you get to move around?

Monica: Yeah, you get to move around and HELP, you know, while you're moving around, you're still HELPING?

Comments made during the interviews suggested that during "the rest of school," opportunities to satisfy these human needs were rare. My own observation of some of the Regulars' other classes supported their observations and paralleled the results of Cusick's analysis of high school culture (1973). At Explorer, *students like the Regulars* lacked opportunities for personal involvement with staff or for meaningful activity in general. As in Cusick's study, students sought alternative means of obtaining those rewards that they did not get in the "rest of school."

At Explorer, involvement with the special education classes seemed to provide an officially sanctioned means of obtaining social rewards that satisfied universal human needs. In this context, students who were viewed negatively by their regular class teachers were able to display abilities and sensitivities that had gone unrecognized in other school situations.

The data discussed in this chapter showed that, in addition to the obvious influence of special education staff, several unexpected influences affected the initiation and development of intergroup contact. While the expected sources of influence (proximity and the school economy) had been addressed by staff working to promote the integration program, other, unexpected (and evidently positive) influences had not been addressed.

Participant responses that explained relations between disabled and nondisabled students, and the influences that shaped them, were less obvious than conventional teacher-centered explanations. However, none of the students' responses were greatly puzzling or surprising. In fact, once I thought over these responses, my findings made sense, because they paralleled the influences I had felt and the range of social relations I had experienced with persons who had disabilities.

chapter 11

Puzzles,
Contradictions,
and Speculation

PUZZLING RESULTS

Three questions came to puzzle me during the course of my study: Why were *disproportionately high numbers of black students* involved as Regulars? Why were *disproportionately low numbers of Asian students* so involved? Why were so many young people, otherwise considered problem students by regular education staff, observed to display such positive qualities in their interactions with disabled peers?

Disproportionate Involvement of Black Students

Although only 14% of Explorer's students were black, 50% of the Regulars were black. All but two of the Regulars were or had been involved in some way with an Internal Work Experience (IWE) peer tutoring program. Repeated contact through IWE was shown to have had a strong influence on the development of intergroup relations. Therefore, I hypothesized that some informal selection process involving the IWE program was channeling certain kinds of kids into involvement with the severely disabled students.

Interviews with the guidance counselors, a vice-principal, and the teacher in charge of IWE revealed the existence of a two-step selection process: 1) sorting out potential IWE students from those who need more academic subjects, and 2) deciding which IWEs should receive particular jobs. Counselors, in advising students about their programs, were active at the first step. Counselors (and students) perceived classes as either "solid" or "easy." Solid classes were more difficult and time-consuming because they required academic effort, but they were necessary for satisfaction of college entrance requirements. Easy classes were both less demanding and less likely to be useful to a student who hoped to attend college, but they filled the "head count" requirements and provided a source of easy A's that would help students graudate. *IWE was not considered a solid class.*

Counselors became instrumental in the first stage of the selection process, when they advised "honors types" and others whom they perceived to be university-bound to take college prep classes rather than IWE. Therefore, relatively few honors types were enrolled in IWE. These findings paralleled the results of Ogbu's (1974) investigation of school failure in a smaller California city, in which he observed similarly reasoned selection procedures used by guidance counselors.

Those Honors Types who *did* enroll in IWE were naturally in demand as teacher assistants. This supply and demand problem led to the second stage of the selection process. Mr. Wang, the teacher in charge of approving assignments in the IWE program, explained to me in an interview his part in this second stage:

Mr. Wang:	If I get a real sharp kid—I can usually pick 'em, I was only wrong once this year—and I know they'll show up, then I send 'em to the front office. Or I interview 'em, screen 'em—I keep them here!
Carola:	If they don't go to the front office or stay with you, why would they join the special education classes?
Mr. Wang:	(laughing) They get 5 units!
A Secretary:	(sitting next to Mr. Wang) Yes, but some of them really LIKE it.
Mr. Wang:	We have some real RAUNCHY kids who are good in there. In their other classes, their teachers go (he covers his face with his hands in mock fear), "Oh, no! PLEASE don't come in here!" But in special ed., they can control someone; they feel important.

Mr. Wang's "raunchy kids" were, as he dramatically pointed out, the students whom teachers found most difficult to work with. These were the Losers in the hierarchy of student roles described earlier, members of the school's "underclass." From the teachers' perspective, such students were expected to be truant or frequently tardy, to argue, fight, or otherwise cause discipline problems, and were unlikely to have good academic skills.

Why *would* a teacher want such a person to act as his or her assistant? It made sense that Mr. Wang didn't keep "raunchy kids" in his attendance office or assign them to the principal's "front office," where they might misbehave and thereby damage his relations with his superiors. It made sense that he deliberately selected the "sharp" kids for positions that directly affected him (as he was previously quoted as saying of the 11 IWEs assigned to his office, nine were on the honor roll).

The special education teachers were not so choosy. Because of IEPs and curricula stressing the value of peer interactions, the special education teachers *needed* large numbers of nondisabled student volunteers. In order to recruit and reward volunteers who would interact with their students on a regular basis, the teachers turned to the IWE program. Because they needed large numbers of students, and because they would give almost any willing student a chance, the special education teachers ended up being assigned students whom Mr. Wang regarded as "losers . . . the kids nobody wants."

Many members of the school's underclass were black. As reported in Chapter 6, black students were less likely than members of other ethnic groups to achieve academic success at Explorer. Although 14% of the school's population was black, only 6% of the students listed on the school's honor roll (students with a B average or better) were black.

Although specific figures for Explorer were not available, black students may also have been more likely than others to incur serious disciplinary sanctions. In trends reported for the school district as a whole, black youth accounted for 23.3% of the district's student population, but 63% of the school suspensions (Bolton, 1980). Remarks by staff members also seemed to suggest that ethnicity was perceived to be a factor in student status. For example, during a previously described interview when Mr. Wang marked all the "losers" on the interviewer's list of IWEs, all but one of the students so identified were black.

In the competition for teacher approval and academic status at Explorer, students perceived to be Losers were most likely to be black. As Losers, they did not need "solid" classes to prepare them for future university enrollment, and were therefore more likely to be selected by counselors for enrollment in "easy" classes like IWE. Once they were in IWE, the second level of the informal selection process worked to *pair students with the lowest-status teacher-ascribed role in the student hierarchy with another low-status group: the students with severe disabilities.*

Underinvolvement of Students of Asian Descent

Observations showed that although 19.2% of Explorer's students were of Chinese descent, only 3.1% of the Regulars were of Chinese origin. Although approximately 15% of the high school's students were of Southeast Asian origin, none of the Regulars came from Southeast Asia (SFUSD Attendance Office, 1985). IWE involvement, apparently a strong influence on the development of social relations, only brought one Asian student into contact with the disabled students. Data from two other integrated high schools in San Francisco also showed that students of Asian origin were underrepresented in comparable programs. At one of the schools, although approximately 48.5% of the students were of Chinese or Southeast Asian origins, only 18% of the nondisabled volunteers were. At the other school, approximately 52.6% of the students were Asian, but only 30% of the volunteers were (G. Evans & A. Vitali, personal communication, May 1985).

Interview data also pointed to a problem with students of Asian origin. When a security guard and a regular (Noreen) were asked in separate interviews if they had experienced any problems involving the disabled students, both said that the only problem they had observed was that certain Asian students appeared to be afraid of the students with disabilities. As the security guard (who was responsible for keeping order in the cafeteria at lunchtime) said, "Little Chinese girls fall back in line—even if they have a number, they stand back there," thereby keeping a distance between themselves and students with severe disabilities.

Participants offered a number of explanations for this phenomenon. The security guard said that she had heard that "something in their culture makes them afraid, maybe it's a bad omen for the family." Noreen thought that faculty communication might explain it, because "they may have a language problem." Two vice-principals guessed in separate interviews that, because so many Chinese students were enrolled in honors courses and college prep programs, they were too busy with academic work to do anything else. The single Chinese Regular seemed to feel that all these explanations had validity. She said, "It's hard for some kids. Maybe they're busy, or they feel afraid."

The cultural explanation receives some support in the anthropological literature, and from anecdotal reports. Traditional societies' responses to disability range from veneration to euthanasia (Dybwad, 1968). Brief references in a few ethnographic studies suggest that responses in traditional Asian societies could be negative, given that disabled individuals (particularly those perceived to be mentally retarded) might threaten the marriage prospects of their family members (Edgerton, 1968). Furthermore, the chairman of the Cross-Cultural Committee of The Association for Persons With Severe Handicaps (TASH), who is himself of Chinese descent, reports that, during an in-service special education course he was teaching in Taiwan, some teachers told him that they were even afraid to let people know that they *worked* with retarded children (J. Lian, personal communication, September 1986). It was not within the scope of my investigation, however, to ascertain how responses developed in traditional societies might apply to Asian families living in San Francisco.

The explanations involving language problems and competing academic demands also could be supported in part. As reported in Chapter 6, about a third of the school's students came from non-English speaking homes. Such students had to work doubly hard in school in order to perfect their English while at the same time completing graduation and college entrance requirements. Of all the ESL students, Asians were the most successful academically at Explorer. This kind of achievement *did* take time, and may have left these students less time for socializing with other students (including fellow students with severe disabilities). Also, according to the TASH expert, "Chinese students tend to be told and expected to do a good job in academic work rather than to 'fool around' in nonacademic activities. They may be told that a student's job is to 'study the book' and make good grades (J. Lian, personal communication, September 1986). Lian's opinion is compatible with the results of a Northwestern University study (Asian Americans lead, 1986).

I developed a further explanation, based on my observation of the informal selection process operating within the IWE program. As stated earlier, relatively few Honors Types were enrolled in IWE. Given the choice between it and other electives, these students were likely to enroll in courses that would strengthen their college applications (e.g., foreign languages). Interviews with Mr. Wang and one of the vice-principals showed that the honor roll students who *did* enroll were likely either to be assigned to the administrators' "front office" or to Mr. Wang's office.

A majority of the Honors Types at Explorer were of Asian descent. Although approximately 34% of the school's population was of Chinese and Southeast Asian origins, such students accounted for at least 54% of the names listed on Explorer's honor roll (High School, 1985; Yearbook Staff, 1985). All but a few of the eleven "sharp" students assigned as IWEs to Mr. Wang's office had Asian surnames. Therefore, although there *were* Asian students with time to spare for IWE, these students were being selected to assist in areas other than Special Education.

Therefore, a combination of factors, including culture, responses to the school economy, and informal staff procedures combined to prevent Asian "straight-A type" students from developing peer relations with severely disabled students.

Why Did So Many 'Bad' Kids Do Well?

Contradictory images typified the Regulars. At least 21 of the 32 Regulars were viewed as problem students by regular education staff, and were typed in undesirable roles such as "Bright, But . . . ," "Nice, But . . . ," and "Loser." Five of these Regulars (Veronica, Denard, Melody, Silvia, and Preston) had been suspended or expelled from Explorer or from previously attended schools for such serious infractions as fighting and stealing. Not surprisingly, students who cut school, failed their other classes, or otherwise got into trouble sometimes posed management problems for the special education teachers.

But in 17 of these 21 cases, observations by the special education teachers and myself contradicted these negative valuations. In their interactions with disabled students, the majority of these problem students were revealed to have skills and personal qualities that had been overlooked in the regular education hierarchy, based as it was on grade point averages and "citizenship" marks.

What was it in this context that allowed "bad kids" to reveal another side of themselves? Participants stressed the differences between "the rest of school" and time spent with disabled students. For example, Mr. Roberts, (who as dean of boys interacted with some of the most troubled students at Explorer) explained it this way:

> In my opinion, choosing what you want to do is important. In the rest of school, kids don't have a choice. It's 'You GOTTA be in here or else!' For a lot of kids, school is too confining. Kids say, 'Gimme a chance, gimme a choice.' Also, they may see the rewards of helping. You know they NEED you. With this kind of work, you get immediate gratification. You're not waiting for a grade, you see progress right away.

The Regulars' responses presented in Chapters 4, 7, 8, and 10, besides confirming Mr. Roberts' insights, provided other clues about the rewards the Regulars perceived to exist in their contacts with disabled fellow students. In contrast to the "rest of school," Regulars valued the *physical freedom* they were given in the contact situations. Also, apparently in contrast to their other school experiences, Regulars stressed the positive value of *meeting real challenges* and overcoming them successfully, both by conquering initial feelings of fear and by teaching someone else to do things that were both difficult to learn and of practical value.

Finally, Regulars were motivated by *interpersonal contact* with the disabled students, with other Regulars, and with the special education teachers. In the "rest of school," interpersonal contact was generally subordinate to academic activities. Peer interaction was seen to conflict with academic goals except in controlled discussions or occasional group projects. It was difficult to develop a personal relationship with adults in the school during class time, when one had to compete with 30 other students for a teacher's attention. Peer relations generally had to be conducted on the sly or during noninstructional time. But the special education teachers, unlike regular education teachers, considered interpersonal interaction a central element in their curriculum, and therefore actively encouraged it. In their smaller classes, too, there were more opportunities for students and staff to interact, and the Regulars' responses testified to the value they placed on these more cooperative relations.

Mr. Prince, the head security guard described earlier, explained the issue of contradictory images best. When asked if he thought there were benefits to the regular kids from the intergroup contact he had observed, he said, "People need to be needed—you can't always be yelled at and put down. When somebody says, 'C'mon here and let's do this together,' then even the BAD kids respond."

QUALITY, DIVERSITY, AND INEQUALITY

Generally the nationwide debate over the quality of high school education has focused on the academic rather than the social goals of schooling. But a few persuasive critical voices have raised the issue of *the kind of human being* that United States schools produce. Theodore Sizer, the chairman of a national study of secondary education and author of a book-length report on the dilemma of American high schools, has been particularly vocal in this respect. He identified "decency" as a central value in American cultural traditions that advocate "a fair shake for all" (1984, p. 120). He argued that a secondary school should be judged not only by the efficacy with which it cultivates students' intellects, but by the efforts it expends to nurture students' character and decency.

Unfortunately, it is "difficult to find many schools today that both formally articulate decency as an aim and precisely outline how the students can achieve it" (Sizer, 1984, p. 20). Instead, too many high schools pay lip service to social values such as "ethical conduct" and "good citizenship" while engaging in daily practices that fail to embody these values.

Sizer's argument recalls an earlier criticism of U.S. schools that originated in Bronfenbrenner's cross-cultural research on child development and schooling (e.g., Avgar, Bronfenbrenner, & Henderson, 1977; Bronfenbrenner, 1970). Bronfenbrenner noted that, although U.S. schools carried primary responsibility for preparing young people for adult life, they neglected to give young people practice in two critical areas: meaningful work and social responsibility. Bronfenbrenner said:

> It is now possible in the United States for a person eighteen years of age to graduate from high school without ever having had to do a piece of work on which somebody else truly depended . . . without ever having cared for, or even held, a baby; without ever having looked after someone who was old, ill, or lonely; or without ever having comforted or assisted another human being who really needed help . . . No society can long sustain itself unless its members have learned the sensitivities, motivations, and skills involved in assisting and caring for other human beings. (1979, p. 53)

If one accepts Sizer's and Bronfenbrenner's arguments, and if the participants in the present study were telling the truth about their experiences, then Explorer High School offered SOME of its nondisabled students an unusual opportunity to cultivate character and decency while doing meaningful work and practicing valued social skills. At the same time, school structures helped students with severe disabilities gain access to a broad range of relations with nondisabled peers, relations hypothesized to have a positive effect on the disabled students' learning opportunities and social integration.

The high school's support for the integration program was congruent with the institutional ideal of cultural diversity articulated in the school's publications and expressed in iconographic form on the school's mural-decorated wall.

In spite of a limited budget, too many responsibilities, and all the problems inherent in running a large urban school serving low-income students from diverse cultural and linguistic groups, many of Explorer's staff worked to support a program designed to promote the assimilation of one more minority group into U.S. society. In spite of all the problems inherent in *being* a student in such a school, many of Explorer's young people found the time and courage to bridge the gap between themselves and their severely disabled schoolmates.

The only flaw in this happy vision of diverse groups finding harmony was the existence of informal practices that offered various student groups different degrees of access to some of the school's programs. If, for example, interaction with disabled students provided a chance to fill the needs identified by Sizer and Bronfenbrenner, then informal selection strategies that failed to make these benefits available to Honors Types as well as to Losers were inequitable.

Explorer High School had, in the integration program, a unique means of promoting social equality for persons with disabilities, giving nondisabled students an opportunity to practice valuable social skills, and demonstrating congruence between daily school practices and social values. It appeared, however, to have failed to make the fullest use of these means.

SPECULATION: THE SOCIAL GHETTO

The term *ghetto* refers to a neighborhood in which minority individuals, who otherwise have little in common, are forced together because they share one or more characteristics deemed undesirable by the majority. In much of Europe until the end of the first half of the 20th century, for example, people of different linguistic, cultural, and social class origins were forced to live in ghettos because of their shared Jewish heritage. Ghettoization was rationalized as functioning to benefit both outsiders and inhabitants by protecting them from each other.

At Explorer High School, informal staff practices grouped students who were dissimilar in socioeconomic status, ethnicity, and intellect: the Losers and the students with severe disabilities. What was their common characteristic? I speculate that it was *shared deviant identity* and associated low status in the staff-determined system of social stratification. The integration program was thereby seen to function as a *social ghetto* for undesirables within the high school population.

Deviant Social Identity

Deviant social identity and stigma have often been ascribed to individuals who fall to meet or abide by societal norms (Goffman, 1963). Multiple norms provide the bases for the assignment of deviant identity in modern society. Among these norms are several that are clearly related to the population of the present study: norms related to appearance, social behavior, and interpersonal relationships. For example, individuals with disabilities are among those most commonly labeled as deviant. Individuals who form relationships with stigmatized individuals or who otherwise fail to conform to expected behavior acquire deviant social identity as well (Berreman, 1981; Goffman, 1963).

The "hidden curriculum" of U.S. schools (Jackson, 1968) establishes further norms and bases for deviance relevant to the present study population. These norms are said to extend the conventions of the work place to the classroom, rewarding student traits in school that will later be conducive to proper performance on the job (Oakes, 1986a, 1986b). School norms emphasize punctuality, obedience to authority, perseverance, dependability, the deferral of gratification, tact, and predictability (Bowles & Gintis, 1976; Cusick, 1973; LeCompte, 1978).

Even if only some of these norms regulated the social system at Explorer (which I believe was the case), then it was clear that the students with disabilities *and* the majority of the Regulars violated these norms in many ways. Therefore deviant identity was ascribed to them by persons in power, and therefore they belonged together. *In this sense, the integration program functioned like a ghetto within the high school.* Although there were no physical barriers between the ghetto dwellers and other students, staff beliefs and practices acted to keep the "deviants" together.

The Functions of the Ghetto

To me, it seemed that Explorer's ghetto functioned to "benefit" denizens and others as Europe's Jewish ghettos had once been said to "protect" both residents and outsiders (residents were said to be protected from outsiders' hostility, outsiders from disease or racial contamination). From the administration's point of view, relations with disabled students benefited nondisabled students by keeping them busy, out of trouble, and enrolled in enough classes to keep the attendance head count high. Unexpectedly, these relations proved to be rewarding from the students' perspective too, by making the students more content with their time in school.

Disabled students benefited from their access to frequent contacts with nondisabled peers, and from the range of social relations that thereby developed. From the administrative perspective, these relations satisfied the federal and state special education regulations regarding LRE (education in the least restrictive environment).

Ghettoization benefited the school's elite by removing Losers and disabled students from competition for scarce educational resources (e.g. access to teacher attention, places in college prep classes). This, in turn, helped maintain the most successful students' disproportionate access to the best the school had to offer. Furthermore, disabled students and Losers helped maintain the school's economic base by keeping the head count high, thus allowing the school to provide academic and college prep classes to those categories of students who *did* conform to the school's behavioral and academic norms.

At the same time, because the system encouraged disabled students to form relations with the lowest-status nondisabled students while discouraging relations with elite students (who, because of their skill at using education to gain upward status mobility were more likely than any other members of the student population to have future access to real societal power), ghetto-ization served the function of preserving the societal status quo as well.

In spite of the negative picture that has emerged here, the staff at Explorer were *not* ill-intentioned people. From their perspective, their beliefs and practices made sense, given the daily realities of their situation. Some staff members acted as they did because they were attuned to the needs of the school's elite students. Other staff members, including those whom I perceived as truly liking disabled students and "bad kids," acted as they did because they perceived benefits to students who otherwise had more than their share of hard knocks. Sadly, efforts to *integrate* one devalued student group (efforts involving wide-ranging efforts by competent teachers and committed administrators) had the unexpected result of contributing to the *segregation* of another devalued group.

It was ironic that the significant benefits actually provided by the integration program, especially those related to the character and decency issues raised by Urie Bronfenbrenner (1979) and Theodore Sizer (1984), among others, were offered to the least powerful, lowest-status members of the Explorer student body. Had the school's "gatekeepers" *really* recognized the existence of such benefits, Losers would have been systematically *excluded from* rather than *included in* the group known as "Regulars."

FURTHER SPECULATION

The present investigation involved extensive negotiations with classroom teachers, district administrators, and university-level special educators, during which I developed my research questions. Repeatedly, these professionals stressed their interest in knowing more about the "who, how, and why" of student social relations.

During the course of this study, I often wondered what my answers would have been, had someone asked the same questions about *me* and my involvement with disabled persons. When the Regulars described their feelings about disabled students and explained what had influenced them to initiate and develop these unconventional social relations, I compared their explanations to the relations and influences I could remember having experienced.

In general, I felt that my responses would have been much the same as the Regulars': I had participated in Type I through Type V relations with different severely disabled persons, and my motivations for involvement had included proximity, expediency, familial influence, peer relations, and human needs.

In fact, as I reviewed the bases for stigmatization described by Berreman (1981) and Goffman (1963), I could recognize myself and, indeed, my profession! I speculated that the societal forces and personal needs I had documented at Explorer might be part of a larger pattern that could be applied to adult professionals as well as adolescent students.

Could it be that people who had *themselves* experienced deviant status in some form, who, as Mr. Prince had said, "knew what it was like to have troubles," were more likely to choose the job of "handicapped teacher" (as special educators are sometimes informally called) in an already low-status occupation? At the same time, did cultural-ecological influences operate through "gatekeepers" in school districts or universities, encouraging persons who were in some way unconventional or deviant to choose, in Berreman's terms, a "stigmatized occupation"?

If the arguments developed here were correct, then additional questions arose about *all* persons who developed social relations with severely disabled individuals, and about the kinds of barriers advocates need to surmount in their efforts to promote integration.

chapter 12

Where Do We
Go from Here?

This chapter provides a summary of the study's results and explains their implications for special education research and for sociocultural studies of schooling.

I had two immediate goals when I began my study at Explorer: 1) to provide a detailed description of the social relationships that were the outcome of an integration program in a U.S. high school, and 2) to identify those features of the cultural-ecological context that influenced the development and quality of these social relations. Because mine was an exploratory investigation, conducted on a small scale in a single school, my findings do not yield general rules for teaching or general laws about schooling (tasks achieved with questionable efficacy even by larger-scale investigations). However, my data do allow me to draw conclusions about the situation I observed which, when related to current educational theory, suggest hypotheses for future investigation.

BASIC FINDINGS

Students Involved in Intergroup Social Relations

I observed 30 students with severe disabilities at Explorer High School in San Francisco during the 1984–1985 school year. Using "day in the life" observations of four randomly selected disabled students as my basis, I estimated that the students spent about a third of each school day in contact with nondisabled peers, and I identified these "contact situations" as the focus of my study. One-third of the contact situations involved approximately 115 nondisabled students whose interactions with the disabled students were episodic, serendipitous, or involuntary. These students were of both sexes and represented all the ethnic groups present in the high school's population.

Because I had decided to focus on the nature of social relationships among students who were in *regularly repeated voluntary contact,* I did not collect detailed data on the students involved in these more casual relations. However, the frequency with which these casual contacts occurred showed that *the disabled students had more extensive social connections than could be documented given the limitations of the present investigation, and thereby suggested an area of investigation for future research.*

Two-thirds of the contact situations involved 32 nondisabled students (11 boys and 21 girls) whom I called "the Regulars" because I regularly observed them interacting with their disabled peers. Socioeconomic indicators showed that these students came from families that were likely to be poorer than the family of the average Explorer student. They were an ethnically mixed group, including numbers of Hispanic, Other White, and Filipino students proportionate to the size of these ethnic groups in the school's population. A disproportionately high number of black students (14% of Explorer students were black compared to 50% of the Regulars), and a disproportionately low number of Chinese and Other Non-White students were so involved. A total of 19.20% of Explorer students were Chinese, compared to 3.12% of the Regulars, and 15.50% were other Non-White, compared to 3.12% of the Regulars.

The 30 disabled students classified by the district's pupil assignment services as severely handicapped had needs that required them to spend at least 50% of each school day in self-contained special education classes. Twenty of these students, those assigned to Mrs. Anderson's and Ms. Wilson's classes, had moderate mental retardation (Stanford-Binet IQs between 36 and 51), limited speech, and problems getting around in unfamiliar settings. They also needed instruction in various skills required for independent living. These 20 students seemed quite capable in comparison to the students assigned to Mrs. Miller's class. These 10 students had severe-to-profound mental retardation (IQs below 36) and severely limited communication skills, and required assistance or supervision in almost every area of daily life.

Although disability researchers had often assumed a correlation between degree of mental retardation and participation in social relations (Arkell, 1979), *the more severely impaired students in this study were observed to be included in the same wide range of social relations as the students with more moderate impairments.* These observations were confirmed in interviews with the Regulars and the special education teachers. Additionally, at least three Regulars who were IWEs *preferred* to be involved with Mrs. Miller's students because they perceived them to "need more help."

Socioeconomic indicators showed that the disabled students came from families similar to that of the average Explorer student in per capita income; they, too, were likely to be of higher socioeconomic status than the Regulars.

In terms of grades, "citizenship" (classroom behavior), and attendance, the 32 Regulars as a group did not do well. Academically, a majority of the Regulars had grade point averages lower than "C" (below 2.0). Only three for whom such records were available had a "citizenship" rating of satisfactory or better. At least 16 Regulars had extremely poor attendance records, having cut more than half the meetings of a single class in one semester. In terms of informal roles or social types described by school staff, none of the Regulars fit the desirable category of "Honors Type." Instead, they were likely to be typed as "Bright, But . . . ," "Nice, But . . . ," or "Losers."

The special education teachers tended to view the Regulars differently. While conventional teacher wisdom might have suggested that students like these would cause nothing but trouble to the special education staff and would model inappropriate social behavior for the disabled students, in general the contrary was true.

Although Regulars who were having problems in "the rest of school" sometimes brought these difficulties with them into the contact situations, the special education staff generally evaluated their interactions with the disabled students quite favorably; attendance problems, tardiness, and transiency, however, were the characteristics of IWE Regulars that caused the staff the most trouble.

Fellow students saw yet *another* side of the Regulars. Twenty-three of these students belonged to high-status cliques in the student social hierarchy in which looking good, dressing fashionably, or playing sports well contributed to popularity.

Regarding social expectations, *staff and students at different times expressed pleased surprise at the positive nature of student interactions and behavior displayed by individuals otherwise typed quite negatively.* These observations were corroborated by school security guards who had more frequent and extended opportunities to observe student social interactions than any other school staff.

The Nature of Intergroup Activities
Activities, Durations, and Settings Analysis of more than 300 contact situations revealed that disabled and nondisabled students engaged in a wide range of activities together. Contact was observed to occur all over the school building and in the surrounding community. Approximately 51% of these contacts occurred in special education classrooms, 38% occurred in common areas of the school, and 11% in neighborhood shops and on the streets. Social contact occurred most commonly when leisure, communication, and independent living skills were being used.

Intergroup activities could be also be typed according to the quality of interaction they involved (cf. Brown et al., 1983). I observed *five types* of contact situations, which I categorized on the basis of the interactions observed and the interaction goals expressed or implied. *Helping interactions* were the most prevalent, typifying 36.9% of the contact situations. These occurred when one student provided direct assistance or instruction to another during, for example, an IWE peer tutoring activity. *Proximal interactions* (20.5%), *reciprocal interactions* (26.4%), and *mediated interactions* (9.6%) were additional types of positive interactions I witnessed.

Only 6.4% (n = 20) of the contact situations I observed involved *negative interactions*. These incidents occurred most frequently during hall passing, school meals (especially while students were waiting in line to enter the cafeteria), and during special events, and were initiated by nondisabled students in only eight of the 20 instances.

Participant Understandings

Peer Perspectives   Analysis of data I obtained through formal and informal interviews conducted with Regulars throughout the school year revealed that these individuals perceived the disabled students' presence in the school and their joint interactions from both humanitarian and pragmatic perspectives. This positive evaluation was particularly significant in terms of establishing the "social validity" of the integration program's goals, procedures, and effects at this high school (Wolf, 1978).

The Regulars repeatedly stated that *it was more fair and more effective for disabled students to attend school in the company of nondisabled people rather than to attend "all handicapped" schools.* Only one Regular voiced the opinion that some (more severely disabled) students might be better off in a protected setting than in a school like Explorer, which, because of her own experiences there, she considered a dangerous place.

The Regulars saw that severely disabled students had needs similar to their own (e.g., to learn, to be independent from parents), and often stated the view that people with disabilities deserved the same chances available to anyone else. The Regulars understood the integration program as having been designed to help disabled students satisfy their needs more readily than those needs would be satisfied in segregated schools; even their occasional criticisms of special education practices demonstrated the ways in which *the Regulars had internalized the idea that persons with severe disabilities, such as the students at Explorer, were destined for independent living in community settings rather than for life in institutions.*

Interestingly, many of the Regulars clearly perceived the effects of the integration program not only in terms of benefits to the disabled students, but also in terms of benefits to themselves and other nondisabled students. They emphasized mutual learning, preparation for the future in which they might have employment or social contact with other disabled persons, and the benefits of feeling good because of helping someone else and coping successfully with a challenging situation.

Since the Regulars were, in general, strikingly unsuccessful at finding opportunities for mutual learning, positive preparation for the future, or feeling good about themselves in conventional classroom situations, the fact that they reported gaining these benefits through their contacts with disabled students made their evaluation of the integration program all the more meaningful.

Kinds of Relations   My observations at Explorer High School showed that students with severe disabilities had access to a range of social relations that paralleled the adolescent repertoire described in Chapter 1 (Bell, 1981; Rubin, 1980; Selman & Selman, 1979). Analysis of observations and interviews with the Regulars revealed that they engaged in at least five distinct types of relations with disabled fellow students: *friendships*, two kinds of *working relations*, and *negative* and *observational relations*.

As described by the Regulars, friendship relations were based on emotional connections. The two types of working relations the Regulars engaged in had a common element of pragmatic cooperation, but in addition, one type was distinguished by a positive affective component and the occurrence of mutual playful behavior. The other, more businesslike type of working relations did not include positive affect and play and frequently took the form of unreciprocated assistance. When negative relations occurred, they took on a tone of dislike or rejection. Observational relations described by Regulars were tentative and based on curiosity. They sometimes led to the development of more elaborate contact between disabled and nondisabled students.

Given the prevailing reports of negative attitudes held by nondisabled persons toward individuals with disabilities, one might have expected these negative relations to have been initiated solely by nondisabled students. At least three of the Regulars, however, reported feeling that specific disabled students initially disliked *them*, but that over time, they were able to overcome these feelings and build positive emotional connections that they described as friendship relations with these same disabled students.

My analysis of contact situations involving disabled students and "Others" suggested that variety and a range of affect also characterized these relations. Pragmatic cooperation, unreciprocated assistance, momentary play, negative interactions, and observational relations were the types of relations that appeared to characterize these more casual, serendipitous contacts. As in situations involving Regulars, even students with very severe disabilities were capable of playing an equal part in establishing the character of the relation.

The Cultural-Ecological Context

Ecological theory emphasizes the *reciprocal* relationship between context and human behavior. While we act to change our social or physical context (as the teachers at Explorer High did when they brought students with disabilities into common school areas), the way we act is simultaneously affected by characteristics of the context. This ecological system includes elements that interact with interpersonal behavior both directly and from a distance.

Figure 12.1, which is adapted from a schematic John Ogbu designed (1982) to explain Bronfenbrenner's ecological model of child development (1979), illustrates the relationship between participants in the Explorer integration program (symbolized by the central human dyad) and their cultural-ecological context. Bronfenbrenner describes this context in terms of macro-, exo-, meso-, and microsystem elements which he envisions as "a set of nested structures, each inside the next, like a set of Russian dolls" (1979, p. 3). In Figure 12.1, macrosystem elements appear in the outermost ring, exosystem elements are in the next concentric ring, and the mesosystem and microsystem elements encircle the central dyad. (For a more detailed

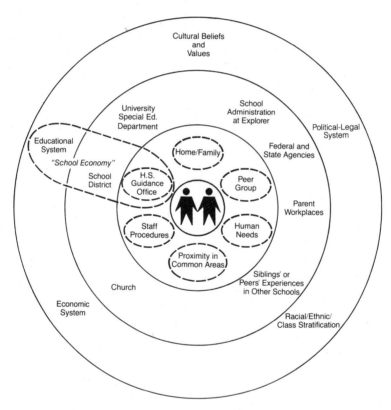

Figure 12.1. Influences on social relations, a social/ecological model. (Adapted from Bronfenbrenner, U. [1979]. The ecology of human development: Experiments by nature and design. Cambridge, MA: Harvard University Press; and from Ogbu, J. (1982, April). [An ecological model of child development]. Unpublished lecture notes, University of California, Berkeley.)

discussion of Bronfenbrenner and Ogbu's theoretical models, see the appendix, "Research Methods and Design," following Chapter 13.)

Cultural beliefs and values (especially our response to deviance or disability), our democratic political-legal system (with its emphasis on equality and civil rights), patterns of societal stratification by race, ethnicity and class, and the structure of the United States economic system (including student perceptions of the behaviors it rewards) were four of the macrosystem (more distant) elements in Explorer's social ecology.

Federal and state education agencies whose policies led to the desegregation of San Francisco schools (with the result that disabled students were placed in physical proximity to nondisabled peers) constituted exosystem (more directly influential) elements. The exosystem also included SFSU's department of special education (through teacher training and research projects), high school and district administrative offices, and the influences of parental, workplace, church, and sibling experiences that Explorer participants identified during interviews. The *school economy* (a combination of American cultural norms and the educational system's structure that functioned to shape both school district policies and guidance office practices at the high school) interacted with student behavior at the three levels of the ecosystem.

Of all the systems elements I identified, the mesosystem, which surrounds the human pair in Figure 12.1, had the most direct effect on the development of social relations between disabled and nondisabled students in the high school. My data showed that the following mesosystem elements were critical to Explorer's cultural-ecological system: staff procedures (including guidance counseling, regular education classes, and actions by individual staff), home and family experiences, peer group activities, and individual human needs.

Administrative Structures Practices at the school-district level promoted integration in that district administrators, guided by a liberal interpretation of federal special education regulations, closed the district's segregated special education sites. District administrators further supported integration by conveying expressions of board-level support to site-level administrators, assigning severely disabled students to chronological-age–appropriate schools, encouraging university involvement in the workings of the integration program, and permitting extensive research efforts (including the present investigation) to occur in district schools.

Administrators at the high school promoted integration by providing information about the program in school-site publicity, establishing basic procedures designed to ensure the safety of disabled students, and by incorporating the special education teachers into the administrators' regular teacher-evaluation responsibilities.

The existence of a separate special education department at the school site, and differences in responsibilities assigned to special and regular education teachers (e.g., lunch supervision) were structural characteristics that appeared to *deter* integration in that they served to segregate special education faculty and thereby discourage the informal collegial contacts with regular education staff necessary to support efforts designed to promote the development of intergroup student social relations.

Staff Procedures Participation in the school's Internal Work Experience (IWE) program was an important influence on peer relations. IWE involved a series of interdependent actions by guidence counselors and the IWE coordinator that strongly influenced the selection of nondisabled students who became involved in extended intergroup contacts at the high school.

Regular education teachers promoted integration by "mainstreaming" disabled students into their classes, teaching regular education curricula dealing with disabilities, incorporating disabled members in school clubs, and involving disabled students in club projects. Explorer's security guards were particularly visible among the staff, in that they took personal interest in promoting positive intergroup contacts.

Special education staff employed teaching procedures that led to physical proximity and extended interactions between disabled and nondisabled students. These staff also affected many of the intergroup contact situations by providing reinforcement or modification of certain actions, by conveying role expectations, and by modeling certain behaviors.

Home Values and Experiences Participants (students and staff) identified home values and experiences as an important influence on the development of positive relations between disabled and nondisabled students. Examples set by parents who worked with disabled persons, contact with family members or kin who were disabled, and moral values taught in the home were among the influences identified in the present study. Several staff members observed that young people who had themselves experienced troubles could be expected to be more accepting of others' problems, thereby accounting for the disproportionate number of black youth from poor neighborhoods who were observed to engage in repeated interactions with the disabled students.

Peer Group I observed that existing relations among nondisabled peers also influenced the initiation and development of relations between disabled and nondisabled students. Regulars were likely to introduce their "buddies," best friends, fellow clique members, or boyfriends to the disabled students, thus widening the circle of students with whom the disabled students were acquainted and so influencing the development of intergroup relations.

While subcultural "rules" discouraged cross-ethnic association between nondisabled students, these were not seen to apply to associations between disabled and nondisabled students, perhaps because the special education teachers often employed cooperative intergroup activities involving disabled and nondisabled students of different racial and ethnic groups. Attention to the quality of contact situations had already been shown to promote such relations (cf. Allport, 1954; Johnson & Johnson, 1974, 1975; Johnson et al., 1979). However, subcultural rules discouraging cross-sex friendships *did* apply in this situation, at least insofar as governing a disabled student's inclusion in an existing same-sex friendship group.

Human Needs Universal human needs were widely mentioned by participants who described factors they perceived to influence intergroup relations. Students said that meeting challenges, having personal contact with others, feeling good about themselves, helping other people, having the freedom to move around, and learning about one's own strengths and weaknesses were reasons they enjoyed their relations with the disabled students.

The Regulars were apparently unable to meet their human needs in regular classes, but found an alternative source of social rewards in these contact situations. They and the special education students developed intergroup relations that challenged long-held cultural assumptions about social possibilities for persons with severe disabilities.

IMPLICATIONS FOR SPECIAL EDUCATION RESEARCH

The results of the present study support the arguments that special education efforts, to be effective, must address nonclassroom concerns. The integration program at Explorer was unusually far-reaching in that it had begun with the REACH project's systems-change efforts (Piuma et al., 1983), attitude-change presentations (Murray & Beckstead, 1983), social interaction curricula (Doering & Hunt, 1983), and parent/community participation (Halvorsen, 1983). While these intense efforts had for the most part been discontinued by the time of the present investigation (1984–1985), they had generated a broad acceptance of integration activities that proved invaluable. At the time of this study, the administrative support, community-based curricula, and activities designed to promote social interaction with peers that *were* still in operation had positive effects on the disabled and nondisabled students involved.

These data supported the hypothesized benefits of proximal, helping, and reciprocal interactions widely discussed in the special education literature (Brown et al., 1983; Hamre-Nietupski et al., 1978). A further beneficial category, "mediated interactions," was discovered in the present investigation, and the low incidence of negative interactions at Explorer was documented.

These findings also supported the benefits of cooperative activity structure on intergroup social relations (Johnson & Johnson, 1974, 1975; Johnson et al., 1979), in that the organized activities within the special education classrooms promoted a noncompetitive reward structure in which IWEs earned high grades for working cooperatively with disabled students.

In addition, the present study documented the fact that, at Explorer, nondisabled students gained personal benefits and social rewards through school integration that were observed by regular and special education staff, and that were validated in interviews with the students themselves.

However, the present findings open to further question the assumption that tutoring conducted by nondisabled students mitigates against the development of intergroup friendships (Meyer et al., 1985). At Explorer, students with severe disabilities gained access to a wide range of relations with nondisabled teenagers, whether or not peer tutoring was involved. These results are corroborated in an experimental study by Haring, Breen, Pitts-Conway, Lee, & Gaylord-Ross (1987) that compared the social behavior toward severely disabled students of "peer tutors," "special friends" (volunteers whose involvement was social rather than tutorial), and a control group of high school students. Similarly, these authors found no significant difference in the willingness of tutors or "special friends" to engage in social interactions, although both groups were significantly more responsive to contact than were the teenagers in the control group.

Finally, these data suggest that future special education research should examine more closely the *cultural-ecological context* of school reform. While district and site-level staff in San Francisco had achieved positive results by locating teenagers with severe disabilities in age-appropriate regular schools and by developing policies and procedures to support community-based curricula, these educators failed to recognize *the unexpected ways in which elements of the broader social ecology were affecting program outcomes.*

IMPLICATIONS FOR
SOCIOCULTURAL STUDIES OF SCHOOLING

Although the movement of young people with severe disabilities from segregated to regular public schools was viewed by special educators primarily as a challenge to teaching technology and administrative practices, this movement also could be conceptualized as a sociopolitical challenge to established ways of dealing with individual differences. From this perspective, disabled persons were seen as an "unexpected minority" that had long experienced unequal access to societal rewards, prejudice, and segregation (Gleidman & Roth, 1980), much as had the racial and ethnic minorities that frequently have been the subject of sociological or anthropological inquiry.

From this viewpoint, the schools were *the* major societal institution that could be used to begin the process of reforming society's response to disability. The joint education of disabled and nondisabled children would ensure movement toward equity (Gilhool & Stutman, 1978), change the attitudes toward disabled persons held by future physicians, secretaries, legislators, and parents (Brown et al., 1983), and in general lay the foundations for disabled persons' "absorption" into the community (Brown et al., 1976).

Sadly, the evidence from the present study contradicted special education's view of the school as an agent of societal change. Although concerted efforts at Explorer had successfully changed attitudes, helped to teach new social behaviors, and given young disabled people access to a normalized range of social relations, the disproportionate representation in these relations of nondisabled students belonging to devalued racial/ethnic groups or to whom undesirable roles and expectations were ascribed gave evidence of the ways in which school social systems resist change and reproduce existing social patterns (e.g., Bowles & Gintis, 1976; Sarason & Doris, 1979; Wolcott, 1975).

Cultural Ecology

From the cultural ecological perspective, the outcomes of this school integration movement could be understood in terms of *adaptation* in a changing environment that increasingly gave disabled individuals more access to integrated social and physical contexts. For example, the students and staff at Explorer developed new responses to individual differences as they adjusted to this novel form of intergroup contact. At the same time, institutions within the culture, as in this case the public schools and the state and federal governments, adapted and adjusted to the "integration imperative" that required them to respond to severely disabled individuals in a changed way.

The findings of the present study support propositions related to the importance of the "effective environment" (the social possibilities perceived by participants) described in cultural ecological research (Kaplan & Manners, 1972; Ogbu, 1974, 1978, 1981). For example, the contrast between the Regulars' poor performance in academic classes and their highly rated participation with disabled peers could be explained as an adaptive response, triggered by their perceptions of the effective environment. To the Regulars, the "rest of school" failed to provide reinforcement, both in terms of present satisfactions and promises of future rewards. In contrast, the Regulars perceived involvement with the special education classes (staff and students) to be rewarding in terms of both personal growth and preparation for work, meeting challenges, accepting human differences, and parenting in the future.

Economic factors that influence cultural change (one of the foci of cultural ecological theory) also were illustrated in the present study. For example, one proposition advanced in participant explanations for the disproportionately low involvement of Asian newcomers and other Honors Type students in intergroup relations was the proposition that these students were "too busy with academic work to do anything else." These "sharp kids" were likely to experience an "effective environment" characterized by perceived opportunities for upward mobility and well-paid employment dependent on high school success and university-granted credentials. They were, therefore, thought to be motivated to enroll in college prep classes at Explorer, and to work doubly hard to master the English language at the same time as their other subjects, postponing gratification in order to obtain future economic rewards. "Anything else" (i.e., peer relations) was apparently less important.

The Socialization Function of Schools The present findings support the proposition that young people learn social behavior in addition to academics through their school experiences (Hamilton, 1983; Henry, 1963; LeCompte, 1978). The curricular emphasis on learning social skills through peer relations was, in fact, an important way in which special and regular education classes differed at Explorer. Of particular importance were the data that demonstrated and socially validated the positive outcomes of program efforts designed to teach disabled and nondisabled students how to get along with each other.

The findings of the present study also support the proposition that the prominence of peer interactions among secondary school students was not solely determined by the students' characteristics, but was a response to the structure and climate of schools (Coleman, 1961; Cusick, 1973; Hamilton, 1983; Henry, 1963). At Explorer, participants explained the Regulars' social relations with the disabled students as a response to human needs unmet in the structure and climate of the school. The apparently contradictory fact of "bad kids" who acted responsibly and affectionately in their interactions with disabled students was explained not only in terms of their characteristics, but also in terms of opportunities that "bad kids" were particularly likely to lack in the "rest of school."

The present study also provides evidence of the existence of a school social system, structured by beliefs and practices of teachers and administrators, that affects "school climate" as well as student behavior and social relations (Hamilton, 1983; Harrington, 1973; Metz, 1978; Sieber, 1979). The differing experiences of Honors Types and Losers at Explorer could be understood in terms of staff norms and practices that established not only an overall school climate, but also (to borrow a term used in San Francisco, where adjoining neighborhoods get widely varied amounts of sunshine and fog) school "microclimates." The beliefs and practices of the guidance counselors, IWE director, and special education teachers provided an example of one part of the school's social system that clearly affected student behavior in that it worked to encourage *certain* nondisabled students to behave in positive ways toward students with severe disabilities.

Unequal Educational Opportunity As was discussed in Chapter 4, the literature on social relations in school reported that schools and teachers socialized students according to their presumed futures—preparing some students for middle-class responsibility and others for lower-class submission (Leacock, 1969; Rist, 1970; Wilcox, 1982). The present evidence of the guidance counselors' and IWE director's two-level informal selection process in which "sharp kids" were differentiated from "losers" gave partial support to this proposition. The staff's comments showed that the IWE jobs in the special education classrooms to which "losers" were assigned were perceived to have less status and to require less academic skill than jobs in the school's "front offices." This further suggests that, in fact, staff perceptions of students' social roles interacted with race and class to affect the *degree* of responsibility to which students were given access.

The present study adds further documentation in support of the proposition that "tracking" and guidance counseling could perpetuate social inequality (Erickson, 1976; Erickson & Schultz, 1982; Oakes, 1986a, 1986b; Ogbu, 1974). Counselors and the director of IWE at Explorer served as "gatekeepers," controlling student access to school resources. This affected students like the Regulars, who were guided into lower tracks and "easy" classes that would not prepare them for higher education (sometimes, as in Veronica's case, in spite of the student's expressed desires).

Furthermore, tracking worked against the sociopolitical goals of integration in that, as in a national study of this practice (Oakes, 1986a, 1986b), tracking served to stratify students socially as well as academically. Because special education teachers depended heavily on IWE as a means of promoting peer relations, their students had little contact with Honors Type students who used schooling to gain access to societal power. Hence, there was little chance that the physicians, politicans, and other future professionals targeted for attitude change by special education theorists (Brown et al., 1983) would develop the social relations with disabled individuals that were hoped for.

Finally, evidence from the present study supports the proposition that the schools' stratification of students by race and class is congruent with the stratification accomplished by other societal institutions (Hamilton, 1983; Hollingshead, 1949; Ogbu, 1974, 1978). The social system at Explorer mirrored the changing social hierarchy in the high school's environment.

In the Bay Area and in California at the time of this study, patterns of social stratification were changing as social institutions adjusted to the arrival of large numbers of immigrants from Asia and Latin America (Divoky, 1988; Olsen, 1988). Unlike in earlier times, when whites or "Anglos" were the most visible middle-to-upper class majorities and blacks the most visible middle-to-lower class minority, a social structure emerged that was described as "a multitiered society dominated by Anglos and Asians at the top and Hispanics and blacks at the bottom" (Reinhold, 1986, p. 1).

Among the new population groups, Asian newcomers were the most successful. In California in 1986, nearly 25% of the college undergraduates were Asian-Americans, although they constituted only 6% of the population, and this success was said to contradict the usually accepted correlation between socioeconomic class and educational achievement: "Asian students' good grades at six San Francisco-area high schools were unrelated to their parents' levels of education or economic status" ("Asian-Americans," 1986, p. 3). Newcomers (those from homes where little English was spoken) were said to be more motivated to do well in school than more established Asian-Americans ("Asian-Americans," 1986).

These patterns of achievement were duplicated in the staff-determined social system at Explorer. Staff evaluations of students revealed a vertical hierarchy in which status was decided by grades, "citizenship," and attendance. "Losers," at the bottom, were likely to be blacks. "Honors Types," at the top, were likely to be Asians. The "Newcomers" and "ESL kids" were said to "make the school" or, in other words, to give it whatever positive qualities it had. They were particularly valued by staff because of the way they applied themselves to academic tasks. In these ways, the stratification at Explorer mirrored patterns characteristic of the community and state (e.g., Talented Refugee Kids, 1985; Ogbu, 1982).

In summary, Explorer's integration program was surprisingly effective in terms of its stated goals of conveying information about, encouraging acceptance of, and increasing interactions between severely disabled students and their nondisabled peers. The program was perhaps not so successful as a *sociopolitical* effort with the ultimate goal of changing the social position of persons with severe disabilities. Indeed, the Explorer findings illustrate the ways in which a conservative cultural system could incorporate, adapt, and ultimately deflect an innovative effort aimed at social change.

chapter 13

How Can
We Promote
Community
Integration?

In this final chapter, I relate my findings to our daily practices. When I say "our" daily practices, I don't mean those of school staff only. From an ecological perspective, the success of any school-based reform (whether it is aimed at fighting drug abuse, reducing teenage pregnancies, or promoting social acceptance for disabled persons and other minority-group members) depends not only on teachers' and administrators' efforts, but on substantial *home and community support* for the goals of the program. Therefore, the suggestions made here are addressed to school staff, parents, church leaders, and community leaders, all of whom were identified by participants in this study as being important factors in the social ecology experienced by people with disabilities.

RECOMMENDATIONS

For Practitioners

What is the point of school integration? When I talk with parents, teenagers, or staff who have never participated in an integration program, I try to sum up this multidimensional effort by saying that our central goal is *to keep people with disabilities out of institutions.* Schools can do this in three ways: 1) by providing *community-based alternatives* to educational and habilitative services that formerly were available only in institutions, 2) by teaching *functional skills* that help our students be as independent as possible at home and in their neighborhoods, and 3) by providing a context in which disabled and nondisabled young people are encouraged to develop a range of positive *social relations* that will support community integration.

How can we best promote these important relations? The following recommendations come from the interviews I conducted with students and staff at Explorer, and from my own observations there and in the high school where I presently teach.

Staff Suggestions An integration program places demands on teaching and administrative staff that are different from those faced in special schools. At Explorer, as in segregated schools, the special education teachers were expected to train paraprofessional aides, assess their students, participate in the IEP process, teach classroom programs, and make sure that their students received needed therapeutic or medical services. But the integration program teachers also felt obliged to develop non-sheltered job training sites, supervise community-based instruction, provide opportunities for social interactions involving disabled and nondisabled teenagers, lecture about their students to regular education students and staff, and integrate *themselves* into the regular school's social system and power structure. The teachers at Explorer had taken on these extra responsibilities in order to make integration work at their school, and were fairly satisfied with the results of their efforts. In order to make such a program run even better, however, they compiled the following suggestions for other special education teachers:

1. At the beginning of any integration program, ask district special education administrators and building administrators to clarify insurance and liability issues. This would give teachers, paraprofessionals, and students a clear signal of support for community activities.
2. Make sure you schedule a regular time when you can meet casually with other teachers, guidance counselors, and administrators. This may be a planning period or simply a day when you plan to eat lunch in the teachers' room.
3. When disabled students are "mainstreamed," meet personally with the regular education teacher responsible for the class and give a clear idea of your goals for the student, the student's abilities, and his or her behavioral characteristics. Make sure that your need to promote positive student social relations though classroom cooperation is understood. Train a teacher aide or student assistant to help the disabled student participate, and monitor the situation through periodic visits to the class.

4. At the beginning of each semester, arrange to make informational presentations on disability issues and the goals of the integration program in regular classes (either those in which disabled students will be mainstreamed or in appropriate subject areas such as health, social studies, or biological science). Ask administrators to help you arrange for the supervision of your disabled students during the time you are making these presentations.

5. Seek opportunities for collegial contact with regular faculty by joining school committees, offering to cosponsor extracurricular activities, and attending faculty social activities.

Student Suggestions Nondisabled students involved in the integration program strongly supported the presence of students with severe disabilities in their high school. Although many reported that they had been intimidated by disabled students when they first met them, over time they came to feel more comfortable, and in some cases, they developed affectionate relations. They felt that, although disabled students were generally accepted by students at Explorer, the situation could be improved if the following things were done:

1. Dress the disabled students like other kids their age, and make sure that they look attractive and smell clean when they come to school.

2. Help kids who *are* afraid feel more comfortable with disabled students by talking with them and giving them a chance to ask questions.

3. Plan things disabled and nondisabled kids could do together *outside* school.

4. Let nondisabled kids assist disabled students with practical tasks that teach skills clearly related to their future needs.

5. Vary activities that disabled and nondisabled students do together, and don't require too much drill or repetition at one time.

Additional Suggestions The suggestions made by students and teachers included many valid ideas for improving integration at the school site, and often echoed recommendations made by nationally recognized experts in the special education field (e.g., Meyer, Eichinger, & Park-Lee, 1987; Wilcox & Bellamy, 1982). My further suggestions are guided by the assumptions characteristic of the ecological literature on education, especially those works that emphasize the importance of communication between different elements in the ecosystem (Bronfenbrenner, 1979) and argue for increasing minority-group access to political and economic power (Ogbu, 1974):

1. Re-evaluate departmental administrative structures that make "special" education separate—integration needs to be reinforced at faculty and

administrative levels. For example, teachers who work with students who have disabilities might be assigned to existing regular education departments (e.g., business), and special education administrators might also be given responsibility for school-wide concerns such as transportation or building maintenance.

2. Identify "gatekeepers" at school and in the community; cultivate informal, friendly relations with them through which information about disabled and nondisabled students can be shared.

3. Involve a broader range of student types—go beyond dependence on IWE programs for recruitment and reward. Get to know the students in your school by sponsoring an extracurricular club, by chaperoning dances, or by coaching a sport. Recruit "bus buddies" and other "special friends" through informational presentations in regular classes. Involve disabled students in school clubs that sponsor group activities.

4. Address problem or differential ethnic group involvement through collegial relations, informational presentations in ESL classes, and the use of community resources and parent contacts.

5. Recognize and use existing patterns of student social relations. Existing cliques or friendship groups can often expand to include a disabled friend. If cross-sex friendships are rare in your school, pair disabled students with same-sex peers for social activities.

6. Integrate school rituals (e.g., graduation and homecoming celebrations). Use school award ceremonies to honor kids' nonacademic achievements.

7. Work with college admissions offices and school guidance counselors to clarify the relevance of extracurricular activities such as peer tutoring and "special friends" experience to university entrance criteria. Write letters of recommendation (supporting university entrance or job applications) for nondisabled peers, stressing "character and decency" issues.

8. Continue efforts to develop opportunities for vocational training and job placement for students with disabilities. Coordinate these efforts with regular education "career education" and "outside work experience" programs.

9. Connect IWE experiences with outside employment opportunities; publicize the favorable future job market for special education staff, and work with guidance counselors to promote student enrollment in classes that will allow them to enter such employment.

10. Join a politically active disability rights organization. Educate yourself and your peers about current state and federal legislative changes related to education, employment, and community-living arrangements for people with disabilities. Remember that we are *all* either T.A.B. (temporarily able-bodied) or disabled, and act accordingly!

Further Research

Besides recommendations for practice, my investigation yielded findings that suggested the following areas of emphasis for future research:

1. Peer Relations One-third of the contact situations observed at Explorer involved students categorized as "Others." Their interactions with disabled peers varied widely in affect and activity, but included casual, friendly greetings that suggested aquaintanceship or previous positive interactions. Because the present study was designed to examine the social relations between students who were in regular, repeated association with each other in school, I learned little about the more serendipitous contact I observed between disabled students and Others. Nevertheless, this sort of contact represented a dimension of student social relations about which I would have liked to have learned more. Therefore, a future investigation might ask:

> What is the *full extent* of the peer relations experienced by an adolescent who is severely disabled? Who are *all* the persons involved with each disabled individual in the school, community, and the home neighborhood? What types of relations occur? What systemic linkages support these peer relations?

2. Generalization of Benefits The integration program was widely perceived to benefit nondisabled students at Explorer. Regulars reported a number of important personal gains, and both staff and students agreed that the contact situations provided an environment in which even "bad kids" could use abilities that were untapped in most other contexts. In particular, participants often described integration in terms of fairness and humanitarian values, echoing the "character and decency" issues discussed by Sizer (1984) and the concern with "moral education" currently so prevalent among U.S. educators (Benninga, 1988; Ryan, 1986). Therefore, a future investigation might ask:

> To what extent do the benefits reported in the present study obtain in other high schools? Do young people also experience *long-term benefits* from participation in a program such as Explorer's, affecting their future relations with disabled individuals and/or future employment? To what extent are individual abilities and strengths, such as were displayed by "Losers" in the present study, recognized in other schools? How could our schools (or other societal institutions) be restructured so as to capitalize upon rather than ignore these strengths? Does the integration of disabled students promote the goals of moral education by nurturing student character and decency? Could elements of the special education peer relations curriculum be usefully employed in regular classrooms to facilitate student socialization?

3. Generalization of Interaction Patterns Interaction between disabled and nondisabled students was quite varied; in particular, less "helping" and more "reciprocal" interactions occurred than might have been predicted, given the severity of individual student impairments and the expectations associated with the role of "peer tutor" or "teacher assistant." The types of social relations observed also ranged more widely than might have been predicted from the special education research literature. I observed that mediated interactions and peer influences have an unexpectedly positive effect in *promoting* (rather than discouraging) contact between disabled and nondisabled students. Therefore, a future investigation might ask:

> To what extent do these patterns occur in other schools? Do such patterns differ across age groups? What kinds of interactions and relations occur in nonschool environments (e.g., in integrated work places or in neighborhood peer groups)? What would a systematic comparison across settings reveal about influences on intergroup relations not identified in school-based studies? How could peer relations, first established in school, be encouraged to continue outside of school? What mesosystemic linkages might be created in support of relations that cross settings?

4. Certain Groups' Limited Participation Disproportionately low numbers of Honors Types, Newcomers, and Asian students were observed to be involved in positive contact with disabled fellow students at Explorer. Preliminary information from two other San Francisco high schools showed a similarly low incidence of involvement on the part of Asian students. The present study offered possible cultural, economic, and social-systemic explanations for this phenomenon. Further research might ask:

> To what extent does this pattern occur in other schools or in nonschool settings? What is the full extent of the economic factors that deter young people from involvement in integration efforts? What is the value system supporting college prep programs? How can humanitarian values be incorporated into student programs? What cultural explanations could be found, if such disproportionate involvement of ethnic/racial groups were more widely observed in the United States or other socieites? Would intervention be appropriate, and, if so, how could integration programs be adapted to suit diverse student ethnic and cultural groups? What personal, community, and institutional resources could be used to reinforce school-based integration efforts?

5. 'Ghettoization' A combination of formal and informal practices at Explorer worked to encourage association between two low-status groups in the staff-determined student hierarchy: the Regulars and the students with severe disabilities. I hypothesized that these two groups shared deviant social identities and therefore occupied a "social ghetto" within the school's social system. I further speculated that similar practices might be at work in other societal institutions. Therefore, a future study might ask:

> To what extent can "ghettoization" be observed in other schools and nonschool settings (e.g., in work places and recreational or residential settings)? Could deliberate efforts be made to promote mesosystems linking disabled and nondisabled individuals *throughout* hierarchical levels in stratified societies? Do regular educators perceive a stigma to be associated with employment in special education? If special education were perceived as a "stigmatized occupation,"

how would this affect professional relations in integrated schools? Would a study of "the sociology of disability workers" indicate influences on professionals that paralleled those identified as influencing Regulars in the present study? Can "ghettoization" be observed at the university level, operating informally to affect faculty relations and student participation in special education degree and credential programs? At the school-district level, are informal criteria differentially applied to applicants for special and regular education certification? If this phenomenon can be more widely documented, what are its implications for integration?

6. Participant Perspectives Participant perspectives are a focal point in ethnographic research, providing an alternative, "insider's" perspective as my interviews with the Regulars did in this study. However, one of the weaknesses of the present study was that I never succeeded in finding a way to obtain the perspective of the *disabled participants* at Explorer! I tried both informal and formal techniques in an attempt to get the more verbal members of the special education classes to confide *their* impressions of life in the integrated school, but had little success.

How can we help young people who have impaired communication skills express their opinions of school integration efforts and the social relations that result from them?

CONCLUDING THOUGHTS

At the end of the year, when I taped my final interviews with the Regulars, I asked them what kind of kids they thought would be good for the disabled students to get involved with. Tina and Andi, twin sisters quoted earlier, answered this question by describing their own relations with Lin (a teenager with Down syndrome to whom the reader was introduced in Chapter 3):

Andi:	. . . Somebody who's, like, CARING!
Tina:	Yeah, you know, who don't think of them like—you know . . .
Andi:	Who respects them like people, too, and not just . . .
Tina:	. . . ENJOY being with 'em, not somebody who like just gets in the class for an easy 'A' . . .
Andi:	Or just to run around. It's not LIKE that.
Carola:	Uh-huh.
Tina:	Just to get an easy 'A' or something! There's more than that to it, 'cause if you don't know how to TALK to the students, you know, and if you're AFRAID of 'em . . .
Andi:	You might not want to be in there.
Tina:	. . . If you boss 'em and say "Here, take this," and you . . .
Andi:	And they get mad and turn, you know, and you be SCARED, but it's not LIKE that! You just TALK to 'em!
Tina:	You most definitely can NOT treat 'em like babies!
Carola:	I know you guys DON'T!
Tina:	You gotta open-hearted—you know—just OPENLY talk to 'em, you know . . .

In the high school where I now teach, I have found young people like those I knew at Explorer, who also know how to "just openly talk to 'em." At the end of the school year, when preparing to move back to the States, one of my peer tutors sent this note to four of my students. The thoughts she expressed here, and in the notes that have followed, exemplify the best outcomes of school integration efforts:

THANK YOU for being my friends. I'll miss you, but I promise to write if you promise to keep in touch! For those of you who have doubts in yourself, remember this: Never give up! Work hard and you will always come out on top, I have faith in you, each and every one of you.

I love you all,

Juanita

appendix

Research
Methods
and Design

Methodology has been defined as the "logic-in-use" that structures the domain of research activities: the selection of phenomena of interest, modes of observation, propositions, and middle-range and general theory and models (Pelto & Pelto, 1970). The choice of methodology is integral to the theoretical system the researcher brings to the process of inquiry (Goetz & LeCompte, 1984). Therefore, a discussion of the methodology used in the present investigation begins with a description of the ecological theory that guided the present investigation.

ECOLOGICAL THEORY

In general, *ecology* deals with the interaction of life forms within a particular ecosystem (Kaplan & Manners, 1972). Historically, the ecological study of human behavior originated in research describing the spatial distribution of social phenomena (such as urban crime), and was further influenced by hypotheses tested in plant, animal, and geographic studies (Holman, 1971; Theodorson, 1961).

Ecological theory incorporates four assumptions that are relevant to the present study of intergroup social relations in school (Hamilton, 1983). These are:

1. Human behavior is a function of interaction between individuals and their environments (Barker, 1968; Lewin, 1935).·
2. This interaction is a multidirectional process of mutual accommodation in which the individual and elements of the environment continually affect and modify each other (Bronfenbrenner, 1979; Kaplan & Manners, 1972).
3. The environment with which an individual interacts is a broadly conceived "ecosystem" in which the physical and social elements of his or her immediate setting

161

are interconnected with elements of the larger social context that indirectly influence individual behavior (Bronfenbrenner, 1979; Ogbu, 1981).
4. An ecosystem includes not only objectively verifiable elements, but also the environment as perceived, described, and/or experienced by an individual (Bronfenbrenner, 1979; Lewin, 1917; Ogbu, 1981).

CULTURAL ECOLOGY

The present investigation drew on diverse sources of ecological theory (e.g., ecological psychology and the ecology of human development), but was strongly guided by a model developed in the field of anthropology: *cultural ecology* (Kaplan & Manners, 1972; Ogbu, 1981). This theoretical model focused on change involving *culture*—"the knowledge people use to generate and interpret social behavior" (Spradley & McCurdy, 1972, p. 8). Cultural ecology dealt with human adaptation to the changing ecosystem (including its sociocultural and physical elements), with the ways in which humans used culture to alter or manipulate that environment, and with the ways in which institutions within a given culture adapted and adjusted to one another. While cultural ecologists often emphasized the role played by technological and economic factors in the adaptation process, they also stressed the importance of the "effective environment"—the environment as perceived by participants in a social setting—in adaptive behavior (Kaplan & Manners, 1972).

Because cultural ecology dealt with environmental change and adaptation, it provided a theoretical framework suited to questions of individual and institutional response to changes in schooling. For example, Ogbu used this theoretical model in a participant-observation study of school performance among black and Hispanic young people in Stockton, California (1974), and later to make a cross-national comparative study of the same issue among other "caste-like" (nonimmigrant) minorities (1978). Ogbu's work has been cited as an example of ethnographic research outstanding for the way that it *explicitly* integrates theory throughout the entire research process (Goetz & LeCompte, 1984).

Ogbu's study began after the Civil Rights and school integration movements of the 1960s had made changes in the environment of the schools in Stockton. Black children, who had once been totally excluded, and then assigned to segregated settings, were officially integrated into the city's public schools. In spite of the improved educational opportunities assumed to accrue from this environmental change, certain minority group members still were overrepresented in menial jobs and unemployment statistics. Black and Hispanic students didn't appear to respond to these new educational opportunities. They cut classes, didn't do homework, and performed poorly on measures of school performance (Ogbu, 1974). Ogbu explained these facts in terms of differences between the effective (perceived) environment of poor minorities and middle-class whites.

Limited access to employment was one of the most powerful discriminatory practices recognized by parents and children. The perception of a negative correlation between school achievement and upward mobility by minority group individuals contributed to an "ethnoecology" of schooling (an element in the effective environment) that discouraged young people from taking school seriously. In the cultural-ecological sense, economic factors and social stratification influenced the development of a pattern of cultural responses in which poor school performance by members of "caste-like" minorities was actually an adaptive behavior—one that made sense in the light of limited future employment opportunities (Ogbu, 1979, 1981).

At the same time, institutions adapted to the changed environment. Although the public schools changed in that they admitted black and Hispanic students, administrative structures and staff practices functioned to minimize the effects of the change. Ogbu argued that many subtle mechanisms operated to maintain the inferior position of minority students. For example, observations demonstrated that teachers often failed to recognize competent student behavior when it occurred. Interviews demonstrated that teachers, administrators, and guidance counselors held low expectations for minority students and therefore tended to steer them into low academic tracks and "dead-end courses" in which they could not prepare for university education or competition in the job market (Ogbu, 1974).

Thus, cultural ecology provided a framework for the investigation of cultural change and individual adaptation. In this theoretical model, phenomena at the level of the individual and school were explained in terms of interactions between the individual and elements of the broad ecosystem; data on the effective environment, drawn from the participants' perspective, were central to the analysis.

The present investigation also was concerned with individual and institutional adaptation to environmental change where "caste-like" minorities were involved, although in this case the dependent variable was social relations rather than academic achievement. The general questions asked in the present investigation were: *What were the social relations between severely disabled and nondisabled adolescents in school?, How did participants understand these relations?,* and, *What elements of the environment appeared to affect the development of these relations?* In short, the investigator's overall goal was to understand the social outcomes of school integration, from both the participant and systems perspectives.

Consideration of this goal led directly back to the question of methodology. I had adopted a theoretical system that urged attention to the full range of environmental elements, including the effective environment perceived by participants, if one were to understand human behavior. In addition, two other considerations entered into the research design process: the current state of disability research, and the necessity of obtaining valid data on intergroup social relations.

THE STATE OF DISABILITY RESEARCH

The "state of development" of the phenomena studied also should contribute to decisions about methodology (Pohland, 1972). Situational understanding, obtained through observation and description of phenomena, promotes this state of development and thereby provides the basis for future experiment (Arkell, 1979).

The phenomenon of school integration for persons with severe disabilities was so novel that the social relations that occurred in integrated schools had only rarely been the subject of systematic observation or description. Because disabled individuals had historically been restricted in their access to the full range of environments available to nondisabled citizens (DeJong & Lifchez, 1983; Gleidman & Roth, 1980), disability research necessarily had been dominated by information about the functioning of people with disabilities in restrictive environments. Since the quality of intergroup social relations was assumed to be influenced by the context in which they occurred, and since school integration marked a significant context change, it was clear that the state of development of the phenomenon of interest was insufficiently advanced for experimental methods to yield meaningful information.

The research questions, the nature of the setting, the population, and the social phenomena of interest therefore demanded a "logic-in-use" that could accommodate nonexperimental observational and descriptive methods.

THE NEED FOR VALID DATA

In general, validity has to do with the accuracy of scientific observations in a specific setting. Obtrusive research methods threaten the validity of any study (Campbell & Stanley, 1963), and were a particular threat to the present investigation. For example, high school students in the role of research subjects would be susceptible to numerous influences: suspicion of the research goals, their relationship with the experimenter, and the desire for positive evaluation that might cause them to present their relations with disabled students in a false light (Rosenthal & Rosnow, 1969; Webb, Campbell, Schwartz, & Sechrest, 1966). Standardized test instruments also could cause reactions that could interfere with normal program functioning and distort research subjects' behavior (Shapiro, 1973). As Bronfenbrenner (1979) expressed it:

> Many of these experiments involve situations that are unfamiliar, artificial, and shortlived, and call for unusual behaviors that are difficult to generalize to other settings. From this perspective, it can be said that much of developmental psychology, as it now exists, is *the science of the strange behavior of children in strange situations with strange adults for the briefest possible periods of time.* (author's italics; pp. 18–19)

Because the present study focused on social relations that were hypothesized to be subject to strong societal sanctions, involving relations that crossed social boundaries (Berreman, 1981; Goffman, 1963), the use of unobtrusive measures was particularly necessary. While participant observation methods also could be obtrusive (a problem discussed later in this appendix), the long-term contact with subjects and the informal nature of participant observation techniques reduced distorting reactions to participation in a research study (Patton, 1980).

Social Validity

Social validity dealt with the social value perceived to accrue from research outcomes. In special education literature, social validity also referred to the ways in which consumers evaluated educational goals, procedures, and outcomes (Kazdin, 1977; Wolf, 1978). Because previous integration studies had emphasized researcher and/or adult perspectives over the viewpoints of those most directly involved in integration (that is, the students themselves), the social validity of these previous studies had been questioned. Therefore, the present investigation demanded a methodology that could accommodate multiple perspectives, and that incorporated research methods that could elicit participant perspectives.

In summary, the choice of methodology in the present study was based on theoretical and practical considerations. The lack of an informational data base in the research area reduced the efficacy of experimental methods. The recognition that the research area had been little explored indicated the necessity of generating theoretical propositions for future experimental evaluation. Furthermore, if the social relations between nondisabled and severely disabled high school students were to be observed as they naturally occurred, then they had to be investigated as unobtrusively as possible. In addition, the students' own perspective on these relations had to be incorporated into the study if socially valid data were to be obtained. Ethnographic methodology was known to be compatible with ecological theory, to value participant perspectives, and to offer observational techniques that were both unobtrusive and theory-generative. Therefore it was chosen for the present investigation (Erickson, 1979; Goetz & LeCompte, 1984; Murray et al., 1986).

ETHNOGRAPHY

Ethnographic research is characterized by a long period of field work (typically an initial investigation of 6–18 months), population and event sampling based on a preliminary comprehensive site inventory, and the collection and analysis of multiple types of data with the objective of creating a valid description of a cultural scene (Goetz & LeCompte, 1984). Frequently such studies report repeated research visits to the field over a period of years. For example, Edgerton accumulated data over a 20-year period in his participant observation study of the community adjustment of persons who experience mental retardation (Edgerton, 1967; Edgerton, 1984; Edgerton & Bercovici, 1976; Edgerton, Bollinger, & Herr, 1984).

Ethnographers aim to reconstruct systematically the culture of a group of people, and to create a "holistic depiction of uncontrived group interaction over a period of time, faithfully representing participant views and meanings" (Goetz & LeCompte, 1984, p. 51). Although the techniques employed in this task originated with anthropologists who studied exotic cultures, the same theoretical assumptions and research techniques are equally applicable to the task of describing the culture of subgroups nearer home.

For example, in educational ethnographies in modern societies, the school is treated as a societal subgroup with distinctive cultural features hypothesized to shape the process and outcomes of education. A classroom study might therefore describe communication conventions (e.g., Heath, 1982), use of space (e.g., Johnson, 1980), school rituals (e.g., Schwartz & Merten, 1974), or social organization (including tracking, peer relations, and social stratification), and would analyze the possible effects of these cultural features on educational outcomes.

Because of ethnography's emphasis on the need to "understand another way of life from the native point of view" (Spradley, 1980, p. 3), researchers combine participation *in* and observation *of* a cultural scene, in their effort to make the native view intelligible to cultural outsiders. Hence, the term *participant observation* has been used as a general descriptor for this methodology. As Kluckholm (1940) said, participant observation requires:

conscious and systematic sharing, insofar as circumstances permit, in the life activities and, on occasion, in the interests and affects of a group of persons. Its purpose is to obtain data about behavior through direct contact and in terms of specific situations in which the distortion that results from the investigator's being an outside agent is reduced to a minimum. (p. 331)

Researcher Roles in Ethnographic Studies

The social role(s) adopted by the researcher conducting a participant observation study can be best described in terms of a continuum of participation (Spradley, 1980). The degree to which the researcher can be involved with the people studied and the extent of participation in their activities depends on the role the researcher adopts. Researcher roles are determined not only by choice, but by the goals of the research and by circumstances of the study setting.

A typology devised by Junker (cited in Patton, 1980) describes four possible researcher roles in participant observation field work. At one end of the continuum, the researcher acts as a complete participant. Similar, but requiring less extreme involvement, is the role of participant-as-observer. Next is the role of observer-as-participant, which is more formal. Finally, at the other end of the continuum, is the role of complete observer. These roles will be summarized so as to clarify the researcher's role in the present study, which was that of participant-as-observer.

Complete Participant   Role pretense characterizes the activities of the complete participant. The researcher conceals the purpose of the activity and is accepted as a member of the group being studied. Although this role allows the researcher access to information that might otherwise be kept secret, this type of participation limits the researcher's ability to observe outside the "in-group," or to observe the relations between the research setting and the larger social context.

Participant-as-Observer   In this role, the identity of the researcher as an observer is not concealed, but the purposes of the research are kept under wraps to some extent, and the researcher's participant activities give the people in the situation a basis for understanding the researcher's role. Although this role may limit one's access to "secret" or sensitive information, it offers the advantage of allowing the researcher to observe formally—for example, during informant interviews—as well as informally.

Observer-as-Participant   The role of *observer-as-participant* emphasizes formal observation. The researcher is publicly accepted as an observer by the people in the social setting, and the purposes of the research are intentionally revealed in order to achieve the maximum freedom to gather information. Participation is often limited to a single interview. Although this role improves access to certain sorts of information (particularly official documents), the reactive effects of the observer's presence are more likely to be felt than when other roles are adopted, and the brevity of contact may lead to misunderstandings between researcher and informants.

Complete Observer   As a *complete observer*, the researcher observes in an inconspicuous manner that involves no participation in the research setting. While adopting this role may keep the observer's presence from "contaminating" the behavior under study, the investigator is constrained from directly questioning the participants about their behavior. A special problem with the complete observer role is the increased possibility of ethnocentric bias, which occurs when a researcher inappropriately applies his or her own cultural understandings to the behavior of another (Arkell, 1979).

The participant-as-observer role was employed in the present study.

PROCEDURES FOR THE PRESENT STUDY

Research Stages

The present study was conducted in four stages, the first of which was a pilot study conducted about 18 months before the actual investigation. Briefly, the stages were as follows:

Stage I   The pilot study
Stage II   Legitimizing the research study and negotiating entry into the field setting
Stage III   Observing and interviewing students, staff, and administrators while simultaneously analyzing preliminary data
Stage IV   Further data analysis and theory generation

Figure A.1 illustrates the timing of the four study phases.

Stage I The pilot study was designed to elicit students' views about interaction with severely disabled peers in an integrated middle school ("middle schools" in this city serve students approximately 12–14 years of age). The school was located in a middle-class neighborhood of San Francisco, and served about 600 students, 18 of whom were classified by the school district as "severely handicapped." Nine of these disabled students later participated in the present investigation, as they had by then graduated from middle school to high school.

My role was determined by the fact that I had worked for 2 years in the pilot study school as a "site coordinator" whose role was to support the special education

March 1983 --- October 1986

Stage I
Pilot Study
3/83–9/83

   Stage II
   Legitimization and
   Field Entry
   6/84–10/84

      Stage III
      Data Collection
      10/84–6/85

         Stage IV
         Data Analysis and
         Reporting
         8/85–10/86

March 1983 --- October 1986

Figure A.1.   Timing of study stages.

staff's efforts to promote integration of their students (cf. Murray & Beckstead, 1983). As such, I was well-known to the students as an "integration advocate," as I had helped to teach nondisabled students how to conduct "disability awareness activities" for their homeroom classes, and had led a drama workshop in which disabled and nondisabled students improvised short presentations satirizing prejudices commonly displayed toward persons with disabilities.

This pilot study was based on a review of the special education integration literature (Anderson, Beckstead, Halvorsen, Murray, & Piuma, 1983) and on a review of the literature on children's friendships (Murray, 1983). The study involved videotaped ethnographic interviews (Spradley, 1979) with 13 children who previously had been observed to interact with severely disabled schoolmates. These videotapes were then reviewed by both the classroom teacher and myself, and were analyzed to yield data about students' motivations to interact, initial reactions, beliefs about severe disability, and assessments of their relationships with their disabled schoolmates (Murray, 1984). Many of the research strategies used in the present investigation were retained from (or refined as a result of) the pilot study. For example, in the present study, I was careful *not* to become identified as an integration advocate, and so, for instance, avoided any direct involvement in the disability awareness activities conducted at the high school.

Stage II During this stage, I worked to legitimize the research study and to negotiate entry into the field setting. Specifically, this work involved 14 steps:

1. Locating potential school sites.
2. Conducting preliminary meetings with administrators from two local districts
3. Conducting preliminary meetings with classroom teachers from both districts
4. Observing classes at both potential school sites
5. Arranging funding
6. Securing approval from the Committees for the Protection of Human Subjects at San Francisco State University and the University of California at Berkeley
7. Meeting with the director of research of the chosen school district to negotiate activities and reporting obligations
8. Meeting with school administrators and staff to explain the goals of the study and to negotiate the role of the researcher
9. Completing a physical examination and a tuberculosis test required for entry into the school milieux
10. Obtaining insurance coverage by enrolling in the School Volunteers program
11. Obtaining parents' permission for student participation in the study
12. Collecting and analyzing documents related to the history of the school's programs
13. Gathering police statistics and census data on the community setting
14. Developing spatial and temporal maps of the school and community settings

Only after steps 1–11 had been completed was I granted "researcher status" by the school district and allowed to begin observing students. The end of Stage II was marked in two ways. First, a vice-principal invited me to attend a school dance, and second, my name was entered in the staff sign-in book, which I was instructed to initial each time I entered the building.

Stage III   During Stage III, most of the data were collected (except for that collected in steps 12–14 above), and simultaneously subjected to preliminary analysis in the cyclical pattern characteristic of ethnographic research. Specifically, this involved:

1. Conducting preliminary document analysis to determine the nature of individual disabled students' behavioral and medical characteristics and the types of medical and instructional interventions being used with each
2. Conducting "grand tour" observations (Spradley, 1980) of the three classes of severely disabled students in order to learn where and when interactions with nondisabled students were most likely to occur
3. Participating in and observing activities in which nondisabled students were involved with the classes through the school's Internal Work Experience (IWE) program
4. "Hanging out" in and around the school in areas identified during the preliminary grand tour observations as likely spots for observing intergroup interactions
5. Observing four randomly selected students with severe disabilities throughout their school days
6. Observing randomly selected nondisabled students (selected from among those previously observed to interact with severely disabled schoolmates) throughout their school days
7. Conducting interviews with students and school staff
8. Working with students both with and without disabilities to prepare a slide show
9. Collecting and analyzing classroom documents, student essays, and other artifacts
10. Entering observation and interview data into a personal computer in order to use those data to refine later participant observation activities.

Stage III ended on the last day of the school year, and was marked by the high school's graduation ceremonies.

Stage IV   The final stage of the study involved data analysis and subsequent generation of theory. Grand tour observations followed by a theoretical sampling strategy facilitated the systematic data collection. Data analysis based on inductive logic revealed patterns of participant behaviors and thought that, when compared with program goals, led to the development of an ecological theory of social relations between adolescents with severe disabilities and their nondisabled schoolmates.

Research Decisions

Ethnographers recognize four major decision areas that affect research design and therefore the validity and reliability of the final study. The quality of an individual ethnography is evaluated, in part, by the clarity with which the researcher's decisions regarding these design areas are described (Dobbert, 1982; Goetz & LeCompte, 1984). In brief, these are: 1) selecting a study setting and populations to sample within it, 2) gaining entry to the site and access to information sources within it, 3) researcher role-structuring, and 4) choosing data collection strategies and adapting them to suit various populations.

Setting Selection and Population Sampling The field setting for the present study, a high school that had a low academic standing in its district and which served a multiethnic population of approximately 2,100 students from predominantly low-income families, was chosen by means of a criterion-based selection process that employed both theoretical and practical criteria (Goetz & LeCompte, 1984).

Theoretical criteria were drawn from the special education literature on integration. One consideration was the severity of disabilities experienced by students attending the school. The disabled students had to be considered "severely handicapped" as defined by their educational service needs (Sailor & Guess, 1983; Sailor & Haring, 1977). Another factor was the program model used in the special education classrooms. "Integration" programs are typified by: 1) the presence of same-age peers on site, 2) planned opportunities for interaction between disabled and nondisabled peers, and 3) similar school-day schedules for both groups of students (Wilcox & Bellamy, 1982).

Two practical criteria were included. One was the length of time that the special education teachers and their classes had been established in the integrated setting. Teachers newly assigned to a school need time to set up programs and establish classroom routines before they can conceivably welcome collaboration with a researcher. A second criterion was funding restrictions. The available funds were only sufficient for a single-site study.

The criteria used to determine the initial study population were broadly inclusive, and reflected the theoretical assumptions of the study in that the sample included not only students, but also those persons in the school environment whom ecological theory suggested might influence the formation of student social relations. The study population therefore included three groups of subjects: 1) nondisabled students, 2) severely disabled students, and 3) school staff. Nondisabled students included all those who voluntarily and regularly associated themselves with members of the classes for severely disabled students. Severely disabled students included all members of the three "severely handicapped classes." School staff included all members of the school professional staff who were directly and regularly involved with the students with severe disabilities or with those nondisabled students belonging to Group 1.

Access and Entry To gain access to the broadest range of information sources within the high school, I had to approach the field setting through multiple channels at three status levels. Approach through both formal and informal channels facilitates entry to hierarchically segmented organizations (like school districts); approaching individuals at different status levels mediates against the likelihood that, for example, lower status school staff might identify the researcher too closely with superordinant personnel and therefore be afraid to provide some forms of information (Goetz & LeCompte, 1984). In negotiating field entry, I was careful to follow Goetz and LeCompte's guidelines (1984, pp. 87, 89). As I met with each new person, I briefly outlined the goals and ethical principles of the study, asked what I could do in return for their cooperation, and deliberately assumed the role of "apprentice" advocated in participant-observation literature—asking each person I met whom he or she would suggest I meet with next in order to "learn more about how the disabled and nondisabled students get along together." In this way, I was able to negotiate the steps listed on p. 168 as Stage II.

Individuals at three status levels were approached using a variety of formal and informal tactics to gain entry. First, meetings with top-level district administrators were entry activities necessitated by the organizational structure of the school district research site. These formal contacts, initiated by letters and telephone calls to the appropriate offices, were facilitated by the fact that university personnel had already established a positive working relationship with this level of district personnel.

Second, I had personal connections within the district that led to informal contacts. In 1980, San Francisco State University and the San Francisco Unified School District (SFUSD) had received one of the first federal grants designed to support the development of a model service delivery system for the integration of the city's severely disabled students. As a site coordinator for this project from 1980 to 1983, I had assisted in establishing integration programs in five city schools, including the high school where the present study took place, and therefore had previously developed a working relationship with one of the school's present vice-principals and three regular education teachers. I also had previously worked with two of the three teachers of severely disabled students when they had been student teachers in the classrooms where the Stage I pilot study had been conducted, so it was easy to meet informally with all three teachers to enlist their help and obtain their guidance. These teachers identified key site-level administrators whose approval I would have to obtain, and later collaborated extensively in the study.

Third, I employed my status with the university to obtain appointments with those key members of the school's administrative staff identified by the teachers. Interviews were conducted with the principal, three vice-principals, the guidance counselor in charge of Internal Work Experience (IWE), and the department head in special education. Since I had both the approval of the top level of district administrators and the teachers' support, these interviews went smoothly, and one administrator initiated the researcher's interaction with students by inviting me to attend a dance in the school's gymnasium.

Once these negotiations were completed with the district level administrators, site-level administrators, and classroom teachers, I was able to enter the high school site freely, and was given official access to staff and student information sources. This access to information was constrained by district research guidelines and university standards designed to protect the privacy of human subjects. Naturally, access was also governed by the extent to which I was able to gain the confidence of the individual informants whom I got to know over the course of the study.

Researcher Role I worked to adopt a role that would allow maximum possible access to information while still respecting ethical and practical constraints on research activities. In terms of the continuum of participant observer roles described earlier in this chapter, I adopted the role of participant-as-observer, in that, although I identified myself as an observer, the purposes of the research were kept somewhat vague. The ways in which I negotiated my role as participant-as-observer are discussed in more detail in Chapter 2 (pp. 7–9).

Data Collection Techniques The most common techniques used by ethnographers to collect data are *observation, interviewing, researcher-designed instruments,* and *content analysis of artifacts* (Goetz & LeCompte, 1984). In general, the credibility of such studies increases when multiple techniques are used to collect as wide a variety of data as possible (Stainback & Stainback, 1984; Wolcott, 1975). The present study combined all four techniques.

Direct observation was a key technique. For example, when individuals cannot provide information (as was the case with the mentally retarded participants in the present study), or are discouraged by powerful social sanctions from reporting truthfully on sensitive topics (such as the topic of social relations with disabled persons), then direct observation becomes an indispensible technique.

Three types of direct observations were made in the present study: grand tour observations, focused observations, and selective observations (Spradley, 1980). Grand tour observations (similar to "ecological inventory" tactics used in special education) provided broadly descriptive information about where, when, and with whom intergroup interactions were likely to take place. Focused observations provided more detailed information about the various categories of interactions—for example, those that occurred during scheduled class periods and involved IWE volunteers, and those that occurred more casually and involved serendipitous contacts that occurred, for example, during hall passing or at lunch time.

Selective observations were planned in order to allow me to contrast the categories of interaction and the types of social relations that occurred within these categories. Although all three types of observations took place throughout the study, the emphasis shifted over time. At the beginning of Stage III, grand tour observations were most important; focused observations were emphasized during the middle months of field study, and selective observation occurred most frequently toward the end of Stage III.

Observational information was recorded in field notes. These notes contained two types of information (Dobbert, 1982; Patton, 1980): 1) a factual description of events recorded with minimum interpretation and maximum inclusion of actual participant dialogue, and 2) summary observations and interpretations that recorded my inferences and tentative interpretations of the events observed. These notes also included maps of the physical setting. The Type 1 field notes were recorded by hand, either during the ongoing event or immediately afterward, and at the end of the day I reviewed them and filled in Type 2 comments.

The openness of my notetaking depended on the formal or informal nature of the activity observed and on my relationship to the participants. For example, I openly took notes while a nondisabled peer tutor showed me how she taught a disabled student to clean cafeteria tables. However, when I was "messing around" with the same nondisabled student and two other student volunteers who had been left behind while one of the special education classes went to a baseball game, I memorized their comments about the special education program and then reconstructed the conversation after the students left for their next class.

Interview techniques supplemented direct observation. Two general types of interviews, *informant* and *respondent,* were used in the present study. These interviews were conducted in two ways: as *unstructured* interviews in which questions were spontaneous and prompted by ongoing incidents and current conversational topics, and as *semi-structured* interviews that were cast in a conversational mode but supported by a predetermined structure (Goetz & LeCompte, 1984). These semi-structured interviews were tape-recorded and transcribed verbatim. Informant interviewing was used when I required information about events that took place before I entered the field, about events that occurred infrequently, or about those that could not be directly observed for some other reason (Pelto & Pelto, 1978). In those situations, I interviewed "key informants" who had witnessed these events. This approach proved especially useful when the informants were giving information on concrete subjects (i.e., When did the special education class first move to this building?) or procedures with which they were very familiar (i.e., What steps does a student have to go through to enroll in Internal Work Experience?), and when the researcher was able to compare the interviews of several informants speaking about the same event (e.g., an administrator, a teacher, and a student).

Respondent interviewing was used when I was concerned less with information about external or past events than with the personal feelings, motivations, and perceptions of the interviewee (Arkell, 1979). Both types of interviews proved most effective when used with direct observation. For example, unstructured respondent interviews coupled with direct observation yielded verbatim records of conversations that provided evidence for the cognitive categories (i.e., terms such as "teacher assistant," "tutor," or "buddy") that respondents (high school students and staff) used to understand their own behavior and the behavior of others towards severely disabled students (cf. Spradley, 1979). These cognitive categories were then compared with the observed behavior patterns of respondents for consistency or contradictions, and these contradictions then provided the basis for further semi-structured interviews.

After spending 6 months gathering material through observing and interviewing, I created a "participant construct instrument" (Goetz & LeCompte, 1984, p. 122). This interview instrument employed photographic slides to elicit statements about the feelings students had and the linguistic categories they used to categorize each other. I had taken the photographs in the field setting after several months of developing rapport with the participants, in accordance with Collier's guidelines for visual research methods (1967).

In the context of helping the researcher prepare a slide show that would later be viewed at a special education parent meeting, the participants met in small groups and were interviewed while viewing photographs of interactions between disabled and nondisabled students. Their comments were tape-recorded. The researcher asked general questions such as, "Tell me what's going on here," "Who's that?," and "What are you doing there?" These comments were later transcribed and compared with data obtained through participation, observation, and interviews in order to make possible further analysis of participant constructs related to their social relations.

Content analysis of artifacts complemented the data collected through observation and interview. These "paper traces that are the spoor of contemporary organizations" (Patton, 1980, p. 154) included demographic and census data, attendance and academic records, administrative directives, bulletin board notices, curricular materials (task analyses, data sheets, and IEP goals), school publications, student essays, and other tangible objects related to the phenomena of interest. Content analysis of these artifacts yielded information on the history of the school and its integration program, as well as information on the administrative and legislative strictures affecting the special education program. This analysis also suggested inconsistencies between program goals and actual practices that served as the bases for interview questions.

DATA ANALYSIS

Ethnographic methodology differs from better-known experimental methodologies in that analytic processes, instead of being postponed until after data collection is complete, occur throughout the study, *both during and after* the data collection period (Goetz & LeCompte, 1984; Spradley, 1980). In this way, feedback from the field experience allows researchers to redefine research questions as their understanding of the culture increases, and thereby to generate theoretical propositions explaining what they have observed.

For example, in the present investigation, when a comparison between the demographic characteristics of the nondisabled students in the study sample and the demographic characteristics of the student body as a whole showed disproportionate numbers of black students interacting with their disabled schoolmates (although 14% of the school's population was black, 50% of the study sample was black), I interviewed staff and students to learn more about social and structural factors influencing black students at Explorer, and eventually broadened my definition of the term "school structures" as employed in the research question, "How do school structures affect intergroup involvement?"

Although ethnography is, as described earlier, most appropriately applied in situations requiring a theory-*generative,* inductive approach, the ethnographer's mind is not a blank slate when he or she enters the field. Like all researchers, ethnographers bring theoretical systems to the research process that define, for example, the specific phenomena attended to, as well as the *unit of analysis* employed.

As previously discussed in this chapter, the ecological theoretical framework judged to be best suited to the present investigation dictated my attention to phenomena that included both individual behavior and environmental characteristics. In addition, research design required that intergroup contact situations be the study's unit of analysis. Therefore, I chose a compatible conceptual model to guide the research process: Bronfenbrenner's model of the ecology of human development (1979).

Elements of the Ecological System

Bronfenbrenner's model conceptualizes the environment as a collection of structures that have been nested "like a set of Russian dolls" (Bronfenbrenner, 1979, p. 3). The individual and his or her immediate setting form the central structure or "microsystem," surrounded by successively more distant meso-, exo-, and macrosystems (see Figure 12.1, p. 144). A description of these structures in reverse order (from the outside moving inward) follows.

The Macrosystem   This structure can be understood in terms of broad, culturally differentiated patterns of societal organization. Bronfenbrenner defines the macrosystem as:

consistencies, in the form and content of lower order systems (micro-, meso-, and exo-) that exist, or could exist, at the level of the subculture or the culture as a whole, along with any belief systems or ideology underlying such consistencies (1979, p. 26).

As Bronfenbrenner explains it, macrosystem patterns are responsible for the fact that, within a given society such as France, one day care center, classroom, or grocery store looks and functions much like another, but they all *differ in a consistent way* from their counterparts in another society, such as the United States. There are variations within such settings in each society, of course. For example, in both France and the United States, a classroom serving children from high-status families is not the same as one serving children from low-status families. But the "blueprints" by which different cultures structure such intrasocietal contrasts also represent macrosystem phenomena—allocating differential status to various religious, ethnic, or other subcultural groups, for example.

In terms of the present investigation, cultural responses to severe disability (e.g., stigmatization and segregation), societal patterns of race/class stratification, and the culture of U.S. public schools were identified as macrosystem elements that, as potential independent variables, might influence the social outcomes of the integration program at Explorer High School.

The Exosystem   This ecological structure can be understood in more concrete terms. Bronfenbrenner defines the exosystem as:

one or more settings that do not involve the developing person as an active participant, but in which events occur that affect, or are affected by, what happens in the setting containing the developing person. (1979, p. 25)

Bronfenbrenner presents the example of a young child, whose exosystem might include the parent's work place, a class attended by an older sibling, or the activities of the local school board.

In the present investigation, federal and state legislative settings, the San Francisco Unified School District's school board and special education offices, and the REACH project at San Francisco State University were identified as potential independent variables at the exosystem level that might interact with settings and individual behavior in the high school setting.

The Mesosystem   The mesosystem is made up of interconnected microsystems. As defined by Bronfenbrenner,

A mesosystem comprises the interrelations among two or more settings in which the developing person actively participates (such as, for a child, the relations among home, school, and neighborhood peer group; for an adult, among family, work, and social life). (1979, p. 25)

The individual's active participation is said to be the primary link between microsystems, but interrelations can take additional forms: "indirect linkages" in which a third party serves as a link between persons in two settings, "intersetting communications" based on messages that pass from one setting to another, and/or "intersetting knowledge," that is, attitudes, information, and perceptions existing in one setting about the other.

The present investigation focused on mesosystems that included students with severe disabilities. Settings within Explorer High School (e.g. the counseling and guidance office, special education classrooms, regular education classrooms, the cafeteria, hallways, and the assembly hall) and in the school's community ("hangout" areas, bus stops, nearby stores) were identified as potential independent variables at the mesosystem level in the present investigation. I hypothesized that interrelations might occur through active participation in multiple settings by disabled students, by nondisabled students who might serve as "indirect linkages," or through communication and information-sharing organized by special education teachers.

The Microsystem   The microsystem is central to the ecological system. Bronfenbrenner defines the microsystem as "a pattern of activities, roles, and interpersonal relations experienced by the developing person in a given setting with particular physical and material characteristics" (1979, p. 11).

The term, "experienced," as used in this definition, emphasizes a basic assumption of ecological theory: that both the objective *observer's* viewpoint and the phenomenological *participant's* viewpoint are important determinants of any ecological structure.

Activities   Bronfenbrenner defines activities as "the tasks or operations in which a person sees himself or others as engaging" (1979, p. 25). A *role* is "a set of activities and relations expected of a person occupying a particular position in society and of others in relation to that person" (p. 85). *Interpersonal relations* are defined as "the perceived interconnections between the people in the setting" (p. 25). Finally, a *setting* is defined as a "place where people can readily engage in face-to-face interaction" (p. 11).

Throughout the present investigation, I collected and analyzed observational data in terms of these systemic structures and their elements as defined here. Activities (and their duration), student roles, and settings were all hypothesized to be potential independent variables in the investigation of intergroup social relations.

Interpersonal Relations   In Bronfenbrenner's ecological model of human development, interpersonal relations are viewed as highly important influences on human learning. Such relations occur whenever "one person in a setting pays attention to or participates in the activities of another" (1979, p. 56). Interpersonal relations are said to encourage development to the extent to which they are characterized by three properties: *high reciprocity, flexible balance of power,* and *positive affect.*

Reciprocity refers to *mutual adaptation* and/or coordination of activity by members of a dyad, together with mutual feedback, and is said to "generate a momentum of its own that motivates the participants not only to persevere but to engage in progressively more complex patterns of interaction" (p. 57). High levels of reciprocity therefore characterize the most valued dyadic relations.

Balance of Power refers to *control* of the joint activity, or the "extent to which, in a dyadic relation, A dominates B" (p. 57). Situations in which the balance of power "gradually shifts in favor of the developing person, in other words, when the latter is given increasing opportunity to exercise control over the situation" (p. 58), are said to be optimal learning situations.

Affect refers to the participants' *feelings* about one another. These may be "mutually positive, negative, ambivalent, or asymmetrical . . . but to the extent that they are positive and reciprocal to begin with and become more so as interaction proceeds" (p. 58), they enhance development and learning.

During the present study, indicators of these three concepts were noted during direct observation, and served to guide the data analysis conducted during field work. When I had left the field, a typology of social relations was redefined, based on a content analysis of my field notes and the transcripts of my interviews with students and staff.

Computer Applications

I conducted the analytic process in the present investigation by scanning my field notes and marking situations in which disabled and nondisabled students were both present. A well-known participant observation text had identified the three primary elements in any social situation as *setting, activity,* and *actors* (Spradley, 1980). As these three elements reflected the emphasis of the special education efforts to promote integration (described in Chapter 1), and as they were also compatible with Bronfenbrenner's (1979) definitions of microsystem elements, I operationalized the basic unit of analysis as follows: A *contact situation* is a pattern of setting, activity, and persons in which a nondisabled adolescent and an adolescent with severe disabilities are involved in a relation.

Bronfenbrenner's definitions of "setting," "activity," and "interpersonal relation" were applied here. I assumed *discrete* contact situations to be bounded by these three primary elements. A new pattern, and therefore a new contact situation, was assumed to occur whenever one or more of the three primary elements changed in a *major* way. For example, if Fifi (nondisabled) was playing cards with Juan (severely disabled), and then Preston joined the game, that was counted as a new contact situation (change of persons). If the teacher later asked Fifi and Juan to leave the card game and take the attendance slip to the office, another new contact situation was counted (change of persons, setting, and activity).

In contrast, when Candi (nondisabled) was monitoring the progress of Phuc Sanh and Belinda as they used a computer program for a drill on numeral recognition, and then they changed to a letter recognition program, this was *not* considered to be a "major" change of activity (they were still practicing academic skills), and therefore a new contact situation was not counted.

I then returned to the field notes, bracketed each discrete contact situation, and assigned each a number. In the end, 311 contact situations were thus identified. The three elements within each contact situation were identified, and my theoretical framework indicated further elements of interest, which were noted.

Computer Data Base The data base function of Appleworks software and an Apple IIc computer (with 128K) were used to categorize and organize these data. Each of the 311 contact situations was set up as a separate "record," numbered consecutively to correspond with the bracketed field notes. Thirteen categories, originating in the special education literature and theoretical framework described here, were entered into each record:

1. Severely disabled student(s) present
2. Nondisabled student(s) present
3. Staff present
4. Setting

5. Activity
6. Duration
7. Activity goal
8. Objects used
9. Role(s)
10. Affect (feelings verbalized by participants and/or perceived and noted during participation by the researcher)
11. Balance of power
12. Interaction category (proximal, helping, reciprocal, mediated, or negative)
13. Other (an open category for noting subjective impressions or thoughts)

I then examined the field notes describing each contact situation, analyzed each of the contact situations according to the 13 categories, and entered these data into each of the 311 records. The Appleworks data base is not very powerful when used on a computer with only 128K, allowing only one 80-character line of text per category. I abbreviated descriptors where necessary, however, and found the program sufficient for my purposes.

Although one could also have accomplished the same task using file cards, the advantages of using the computer became apparent once the data were entered into the data base. A single category could be compared across all records, or multiple associated categories could be located with just the push of a key. For example, one could easily identify all contact situations in which a particular student was present, scan them to look for behavior patterns, and then quickly re-order the same data to compare observations when staff members were or were not present, to see if his or her behavior changed.

The computer was similarly used to categorize and analyze interview transcripts and demographic data on the socioeconomic and racial/ethnic characteristics of the high school's students. At this point, I was ready to prepare the written report of the investigation.

References

Abramson, M., Ash, M., & Nash, W. (1979). Handicapped adolescents—a time for reflection. *Adolescence, 14* (5), 557–565.

Agar, M.H. (1980). *The professional stranger: An informal introduction to ethnography.* New York: Academic Press.

Alioto, R.F. (1985, April). *California Assessment Program: Preliminary comparisons in percent correct.* Unpublished memorandum, San Francisco Unified School District.

Allen, K., Hart, B., Buell, J., Harris, F., & Wolf, M. (1964). Effects of social reinforcement on isolate behavior of a nursery school child. *Child Development, 35,* 511–518.

Allport, G. (1954). *The nature of prejudice.* Cambridge, MA: Addison-Wesley.

Amir, Y. (1969). The contact hypotheses of ethnic relations. *Psychological Bulletin, 71,* 319–343.

Amir, Y. (1976). The role of intergroup contact in the change of prejudice and ethnic relations. In P. Katz (Ed.), *Towards the elimination of racism.* New York: Pergamon Press.

Anderson, J., Beckstead, S.P., Halvorsen, A., Murray, C., & Piuma, C. (1983). *Review of the literature: Integration of students with severe disabilities into the least restrictive environment.* San Francisco: San Francisco State University, California Research Institute on the Integration of Students with Severe Disabilities.

Apolloni, T., Cooke, S., & Cooke, T. (1977). Establishing a normal peer as a behavioral model for developmentally delayed children. *Perceptual and Motor Skills, 44,* 231–241.

Arkell, C.G. (1979). *A study of the interpersonal behavior of the profoundly mentally retarded in a small residential facility.* Unpublished doctoral dissertation, University of New Mexico, Albuquerque.

Asian-Americans heed opportunity's knock. (1986, August 11). *International Herald Tribune,* p. 3.

Asian-Americans lead the way in educational attainment. *Phi Delta Kappan, 68*(3), 546.

Avgar, A., Bronfenbrenner, U., & Henderson, C.R. (1977). Socialization practices of parents, teachers, and peers in Israel: Kibbutz, moshav, and city. *Child Development, 48*, 1219–1227.

Barker, R.G. (1968). *Ecological psychology*. Stanford, CA: Stanford University Press.

Bates, P., Morrow, S.A., Pancsofar, E., & Sedlak, R. (1984). The effect of functional vs. non-functional activities on attitudes/expectations of non-handicapped college students: What they see is what we get. *The Journal of The Association for Persons With Severe Handicaps, 9*(2), 73–79.

Bateson, M.C. (1984). *With a daughter's eye: A memoir of Margaret Mead and Gregory Bateson*. New York: Morrow.

Bell, R.R. (1981). *Worlds of friendship*. Beverly Hills: Sage.

Benham Tye, B. (1987). The deep structure of schooling. *Phi Delta Kappan, 69*(4), 281–283.

Benninga, J. (1988). An emerging synthesis in moral education. *Phi Delta Kappan, 69*(6), 415–418.

Berreman, G.D. (1981). Social inequality: A cross cultural analysis. In G.D. Berreman (Ed.), *Social inequality: Comparative and developmental perspectives* (pp. 3–39). New York: Academic Press.

Bigelow, B., & LaGaipa, J. (1980). The development of friendship values and choice. In H. Foot, A. Chapman, and J. Smith (Eds.), *Friendship and social relations in children* (pp. 15–44). New York: John Wiley & Sons.

Bolton, C. (1980). *San Francisco Youth Needs Assessment*. San Francisco: San Francisco Delinquency Prevention Commission Coordination Council.

Bowe, F. (1978). *Handicapping America*. New York: Harper & Row.

Bowles, S., & Gintis, H. (1976). *Schooling in capitalist America: Educational reform and the contradictions of economic life*. New York: Basic Books.

Breen, C., Haring, T., Pitts-Conway, V., & Gaylord-Ross, R. (1985). The training and generalization of social interaction during breaktime at two job sites in the natural environment. *The Journal of the Association for Persons with Severe Handicaps, 10*, 41–50.

Bricker, D.D. (1978). A rationale for the integration of handicapped and nonhandicapped preschool children. In M.J. Guralnick (Ed.), *Early intervention and the integration of handicapped and nonhandicapped children* (pp. 3–26). Baltimore: University Park Press.

Brinker, R. (1982, October). *The rate and quality of social behavior of severely handicapped students in integrated and nonintegrated settings*. Paper presented at the Integration Evaluation Advisory Committee Conference, Educational Testing Service, Princeton, N.J.

Brinker, R. (1985). Interactions between severely mentally retarded students and others students in integrated and segregated public school settings. *American Journal of Mental Deficiency, 89*(6), 587–594.

Bronfenbrenner, U. (1970). *Two worlds of childhood: U.S. and U.S.S.R.* New York: Russell Sage Foundation.

Bronfenbrenner, U. (1979). *The ecology of human development: Experiments by nature and design*. Cambridge, MA: Harvard University Press.

Bronfenbrenner, U. (1986). Alienation and the four worlds of childhood. *Phi Delta Kappan, 67*(6), 430–436.

Brown v. Board of Education, 347 U.S. 483 (1954).

Brown, L., Ford, A., Nisbet, J., Sweet, M., Donnellan, A., & Gruenewald, L. (1983). Opportunities available when severely handicapped students attend chronological age appropriate regular schools. *TASH Journal, 8*, 16–24.

Brown, L., Nietupski, J., & Hamre-Nietupski, S. (1976). The criterion of ultimate functioning and public school services for severely handicapped students. In M. Thomas (Ed.), *Hey, don't forget about me: New directions for serving the severely handicapped* (pp. 2–13). Reston, VA: Council for Exceptional Children.

Bruininks, R., Rynders, J., & Gross, J. (1974). Social acceptance of mildly retarded pupils in resource rooms and regular classes. *American Journal of Mental Deficiency, 78*(4), 377–383.

Bureau of the Census, U.S. Department of Commerce. (1983). *County and city data book 1983*. Washington, DC: Government Printing Office.

Campbell, D., & Stanley, J. (1963). *Experimental designs and quasi-experimental designs for research*. Skokie, IL: Rand McNally.

Certo, N., Haring, N., & York, R. (1984). (Eds.). *Public school integration of severely handicapped students: Rational issues and progressive alternatives*. Baltimore: Paul H. Brookes Publishing Co.

Coleman, J.S. (1961). *The adolescent society*. New York: The Free Press.

Collier, J., (1967). *Visual anthropology: Photography as a research method*. New York: Holt, Rinehart, & Winston.

Cowardin, N. (1986). Adolescent characteristics associated with acceptance of handicapped peers. *Adolescence, 21*(84), 931–940.

Crime in the Mission (1985, April 11). *The North Mission News*, p. 3.

Criner, J. (1981, February). *Official special education enrollment counts for the 1980–81 school year.* Unpublished memorandum, San Francisco Unified School District, Special Education Office of Budget, Attendance, and Management.

Cusick, P. (1973). *Inside high school*. New York: Holt, Rinehart & Winston.

DeJong, G., & Lifchez, R. (1983). Physical disability and public policy. *Scientific American, 248*(6), 40–49.

Delehanty, R. (1980). *Walks and tours in the Golden Gate City*. New York: Dial.

Divoky, D. (1988). The model minority goes to school. *Phi Delta Kappan, 70*(3), 219–222.

Dobbert, M.L. (1982). *Ethnographic research: Theory and application for modern schools and societies*. New York: Praeger.

Doering, K.F., & Hunt, P.C. (1983). Inventory Process for Social Interaction (IPSI). San Francisco: San Francisco State University, San Francisco Unified School District. (ERIC Document Reproduction Service No. ED242181).

Donaldson, J. (1980). Changing attitudes toward handicapped persons: A review and analysis of research. *Exceptional Children, 46*, 504–514.

Douvan, E., & Adelson, J. (1966). *The adolescent experience*. New York: John Wiley & Sons.

Dunn, L.M. (1968). Special education for the mildly retarded—Is much of it justifiable? *Exceptional Children, 35*, 5–22.

Dusek, J.B., & Flaherty, J. (1981). The development of the self-concept during the adolescent years. *Monographs of the Society for Research in Child Development, 46*, 1–61.

Dybwad, G. (1968). Treatment of the mentally retarded: A cross-national view. In

H.C. Haywood (Ed.), *Social-cultural aspects of mental retardation* (pp. 560–586). New York: Appleton-Century-Crofts.

Edgerton, R.B. (1967). *The cloak of competence.* Berkeley: University of California Press.

Edgerton, R.B. (Ed.). (1984a). Lives in process: Mildly retarded adults in a large city. *Monographs of the American Association on Mental Deficiency, 6.* Washington: AAMD Press.

Edgerton, R.B. (1984b). The participant observer approach to research in mental retardation. *American Journal of Mental Deficiency, 88*(5), 498–505.

Edgerton, R.B., & Bercovici, S. (1976). The cloak of competence: Years later. *American Journal of Mental Deficiency, 80,* 345–351.

Edgerton, R.B., Bollinger, M., & Herr, B. (1984). The cloak of competence: After two decades. *American Journal of Mental Deficiency, 88,* 345–351.

Erickson, F. (1976). Gatekeeping interaction: A social selection process. In P.R. Sanday (Ed.), *Anthropology and the public interest: Fieldwork and theory* (pp. 111–145). New York: Academic Press.

Erickson, F. (1979, March). *On standards of descriptive validity in studies of classroom activity.* Paper presented at the annual meeting of the American Educational Research Association, Toronto.

Erickson, F., & Schultz, J. (1982). *The counselor as gatekeeper: Social interaction in interviews.* New York: Academic Press.

Erikson, E. (1950). *Childhood and society.* New York: Norton.

Filler, J., Goetz, L., & Sailor, W. (1986). *Factors which predict opportunities for interaction between students with severe disabilities and their nondisabled peers.* San Francisco: California Research Institute on Integration.

Fine, G.A. (1980). The natural history of preadolescent friendship groups. In H.C. Foot, A.J. Chapman, & J.R. Smith (Eds.), *Friendship and social relations in children.* Chichester, England: John Wiley & Sons.

FitzGerald, F. (1986, July 21). A reporter at large: San Francisco Part 1. *The New Yorker,* pp. 34–70.

Fredericks, H., Baldwin, V., Grove, D., Moore, W., Riggs, C., & Lyons, B. (1978). Integrating the moderately and severely handicapped preschool child into a normal day care setting. In M. Guralnick (Ed.), *Early intervention and the integration of handicapped and nonhandicapped children* (pp. 191–206). Baltimore: University Park Press.

Freud, A. (1969). Adolescence as a developmental disturbance. In G. Kaplan & S. Lebovici (Eds.), *Adolescence: Psychological perspectives.* New York: Basic Books.

Frey, W. (1984). Introduction. In R. Habeck, D. Galvin, W. Frey, L. Chadderton, & D. Tate (Eds.), *Economics and equity in employment of people with disabilities* (pp. ix–xiii). Lansing: University Center for International Rehabilitation, Michigan State University.

Gartner, A., & Lipsky, D. (1987). Beyond special education: Toward a quality system for all students. *Harvard Educational Review, 57*(4), 367–395.

Gaylord-Ross, R. (1981). *Task analysis and the severely handicapped.* Unpublished manuscript, San Francisco State University.

Gaylord-Ross, R., Haring, T., Breen, C., & Pitts-Conway, V. (1984). The training and generalization of social interaction skills with autistic youth. *Journal of Applied*

Behavior Analysis, 17, 229–247.

Gilhool, T., & Stutman, E. (1978). Integration of severely handicapped students: Toward criteria for implementing and enforcing the integration imperative of P.L. 94-142 and Section 504. In *LRE: Developing criteria for the evaluation of the least restrictive environment provision.* Philadelphia: Research for Better Schools.

Gleidman, J., & Roth, W. (1980). *The unexpected minority: Handicapped children in America.* New York: Harcourt Brace Jovanovich.

Goetz, J.P., & LeCompte, M. (1984). *Ethnography and qualitative design in educational research.* Orlando, FL: Academic Press.

Goetz, L., Piuma, C., Gaylord-Ross, R., Halvorsen, A.T., & Birns, P. (1983). Effects of integrated services: Evaluating attitude change in regular education students. Unpublished manuscript, San Francisco State University, California Research Institute on Integration.

Goffman, E. (1963). *Stigma.* Englewood Cliffs, NJ: Prentice-Hall.

Grossman, H.J. (Ed.). (1973). Manual on terminology and classification in mental retardation. *American Journal of Mental Deficiency Special Publication,* Series No. 2.

Guralnick, M. (1980). Social interactions among preschool children. *Exceptional Children, 46,* 248–253.

Hallinan, M.T. (1980). Patterns of cliquing among youth. In H.C. Foot, A.J. Chapman, & J.R. Smith (Eds.), *Friendship and social relations in children* (pp. 321–342). Chichester, England: John Wiley & Sons.

Halvorsen, A.T. (1983). *Parents and Community Together (PACT).* San Francisco: San Francisco State University; San Francisco Unified School District. (ERIC Document Reproduction Service No. ED 242 183.)

Hamilton, S. (1983). The social side of schooling: Ecological studies of classrooms and schools. *The Elementary School Journal, 83*(4).

Hamre-Nietupski, S., Branston, M., Ford, A., Stoll, A., Sweet, M., Gruenewald, L., & Brown, L. (1978). A delineation of four types of interactions that can occur between severely handicapped students and nonhandicapped students in school, home/neighborhood, and community environments. In L. Brown, S. Hamre-Nietupski, S. Lyon, M. Branston, M. Falvey, & L. Gruenewald (Eds.), *Curricular strategies for developing longitudinal interactions between severely handicapped students and others and curricular strategies for teaching severely handicapped students to acquire and perform skills in response to naturally occurring cues and correction procedures* (Vol. 8, Part 1, pp. 39–49). Madison, WI: Madison Metropolitan School District.

Hamre-Nietupski, S., & Nietupski, J. (1981). Integral involvement of severely handicapped students within regular schools. *Journal of the Association for the Severely Handicapped, 6,* 30–39.

Hanline, M.F., & Murray, C. (1984). Integrating severely handicapped children into regular public schools. *Phi Delta Kappan, 66*(4), 273–277.

Haring, T., Breen, C., Pitts-Conway, V., Lee, M., & Gaylord-Ross, R. (1987). Adolescent peer tutoring and special friends experiences. *Journal of the Association for Persons with Severe Handicaps, 12*(4), 280–286.

Harrington, C. (1973). Pupils, peers, and politics. In S.T. Kimball & J.H. Burnett (Eds.), *Learning and culture.* Seattle: University of Washington Press.

Hartup, W.W. (1978). Children and their friends. In H. McGurk (Ed.), *Issues in child-*

hood social development. London: Methuen.

Heath, S.B. (1982). Communication conventions in classroom behavior. In G. Spindler (Ed.), *Doing the ethnography of schooling: Educational anthropology in action.* New York: Holt, Rinehart, & Winston.

Henry, J. (1963). *Culture against man.* New York: Random House.

High School. (1975). [Accreditation application]. Unpublished document.

High School. (1982). [Accreditation application]. Unpublished document.

High School. (1984). *Profile.* (Photocopied pamphlet available to school visitors)

High School (1985). *High School Honor Roll Spring 1985.* (Pupil Personnel Bulletin No. 15). San Francisco: Author.

Hollingshead, A.B. (1949). *Elmtown's youth.* New York: John Wiley & Sons.

Holman, J. (1971). The moral risk and high cost of ecological concern in applied behavior analysis. In A. Rogers-Warren & S.F. Warren (Eds.), *Ecological perspectives in behavior analysis* (pp. 63–99). Baltimore: University Park Press.

Jackson, P. (1968). *Life in classrooms.* New York: Holt, Rinehart, & Winston.

Johnson, D.W., & Johnson, R.T. (1974). Instructional structure: Cooperative, competitive, or individualistic? *Review of Educational Research, 44*(2), 213–240.

Johnson, D.W., & Johnson, R.T. (1975). *Learning together and alone: Cooperation, competition, and individualization.* Englewood Cliffs, NJ: Prentice-Hall.

Johnson, D.W., & Johnson, R.T. (1980). Integrating handicapped students into the mainstream. *Exceptional Children, 47*(2), 90–98.

Johnson, N.B. (1980). The material culture of public school classrooms: The symbolic integration of local schools and national culture. *Anthropology and Education Quarterly, 11,* 173–191.

Johnson, R.T., Rynders, J., Johnson, D.W., Schmidt, B., & Haider, S. (1979). Interaction between handicapped and nonhandicapped teenagers as a function of situational goal structuring: Implications for mainstreaming. *American Education Research Journal, 16*(2), 161–167.

Johnson v. San Francisco Unified School District, 339. F. Supp. 1315 (N.D. Cal. 1971).

Jones, R.L. (1984). *Attitudes and attitude change in special education: Theory and practice.* Reston, VA: Council for Exceptional Children.

Kaplan, D., & Manners, R.A. (1972). *Culture theory.* Englewood Cliffs, NJ: Prentice-Hall.

Karweit, N., & Hansell, S. (1983). School organization and friendship selection. In J. Epstein & N. Karweit (Eds.), *Friends in school: Patterns of selection and influence in secondary schools.* New York: Academic Press.

Kaufman, S.Z. (1988). *Retarded isn't stupid, Mom!* Baltimore: Paul H. Brookes Publishing Co.

Kazdin, A. (1977). Assessing the clinical or applied importance of behavior change through social validation. *Behavior Modification, 1,* 427–452.

Kirp, D.L. (1982). *Just schools: The idea of racial equality in American education.* Berkeley: University of California Press.

Kluckholm, F. (1940, November). The participant-observer technique in small communities. *American Journal of Sociology, 46.*

Kohlberg, L. (1969). Stage and sequence: The cognitive developmental approach to socialization. In D.A. Goslin (Ed.), *Handbook of socialization theory and research* (pp. 347–380). Chicago: Rand McNally.

Kuhn, T. (1962). *The structure of scientific revolutions*. Chicago: University of Chicago Press.

Landis, P.H. (1980). *Sociology* (3rd ed.). Lexington, MA: Ginn.

Larry P. v. Riles, 495 F. Supp., 926 (N.D. Cal. 1979).

Leacock, E. (1969). *Teaching and learning in city schools*. New York: Basic Books.

LeCompte, M. (1978). Learning to work: The hidden curriculum of the classroom. *Anthropology and Education Quarterly, 9*, 22–37.

Levy, M.J. (1975). *Evaluation of elementary school desegregation: Resegregating tendencies in special programs*. (Report No. 2). San Francisco: Integration Department, San Francisco Unified School District.

Lewin, K. (1917). Kriegslandschaft. *Zeitschrift fur Angewandte Psychologie, 12*, 440–447.

Lewin, K. (1935). *A dynamic theory of personality*. New York: McGraw-Hill.

Lewis, M., & Rosenblum, L. (Eds.). (1975). *Friendship and peer relations*. New York: John Wiley & Sons.

Lightfoot, S.L. (1983). *The good high school: Portraits of character and culture*. New York: Basic Books.

May, E. (1964). *The Progressive Era*. New York: Time, Inc.

Mead, M. (1928). *Coming of age in Samoa: A psychological study of primitive youth for Western civilization*. New York: Morrow.

Metz, M.H. (1978). *Classrooms and corridors: The crisis of authority in desegregated secondary schools*. Berkeley: University of California Press.

Meyer, L., Eichinger, J., & Park-Lee, S. (1987). A validation of program quality indicators in educational services for students with severe disabilities. *The Journal of The Association for Persons with Severe Handicaps, 12*(4), 251–263.

Meyer, L., Kennedy, M., Kishi, G., Pitts-Conway, V., & Sasso, G. (1985, December). *Why nonhandicapped children should be friends rather than peer tutors*. Panel presented at the annual meeting of The Association for Persons With Severe Handicaps, Boston.

Mills v. Board of Education of the District of Columbia, 348, F. Supp. 866 (D.D.C. 1972).

Murray, C. (1983). *On the possibility of friendship between able-bodied and disabled children*. (Unpublished manuscript, Project REACH, San Francisco State University).

Murray, C. (1984). [*Individualized Education Program*]. Unpublished raw data.

Murray, C., Anderson, J., Bersani, H., & Mesaros, R. (1986). Alternative research methods in special education: Ethnography, microethnography, and ethology. *Journal of Special Education Technology, 7*(3), 15–31.

Murray, C., & Beckstead, S.P. (1983). *Awareness and Inservice Manual (AIM)*. San Francisco: San Francisco State University; San Francisco Unified School District. (ERIC Document Reproduction Service No. ED 242 182)

Nirje, B. (1969). The normalization principle and its human management implications. In R. Kugel & W. Wolfensberger (Eds.), *Changing patterns in residential services for the mentally retarded* (pp. 179–195). Washington: Government Printing Office.

Nirje, B. (1988, August). *Reflections on normalization*. Paper presented at the First International Conference on Family Support and Disability, Stiftelsen Institutet för Integration, Stockholm, Sweden.

Oakes, J. (1986a). Keeping track, part 1: The policy and practice of curriculum inequality. *Phi Delta Kappan, 68*(1), 12–17.

Oakes, J. (1986b). Keeping track, part 2: Curriculum inequality and school reform. *Phi Delta Kappan, 68*(2), 148–154.

Offer, D., Marcus, D., & Offer, J. (1970). A longitudinal study of normal adolescent boys. *American Journal of Psychiatry, 126*, 917–924.

Ogbu, J.U. (1974). *The next generation: An ethnography of education in an urban neighborhood.* New York: Academic Press.

Ogbu, J.U. (1979). Social stratification and the socialization of competence. *Anthropology and Education Quarterly, 10*(1), 3–20.

Ogbu, J.U. (1981). School ethnography: A multilevel approach. *Anthropology and Education Quarterly, 10*(1), 3–29.

Ogbu, J.U. (1982). Equalization of educational opportunity and racial/ethnic inequality. In P.G. Altbach, R.F. Arnove, & F.P. Kelly (Eds.), *Comparative education* (pp. 269–289). New York: Macmillan.

Olsen, L. (1988). Crossing the schoolhouse border: Immigrant children in California. *Phi Delta Kappan, 70*(3), 211–218.

Patton, M.Q. (1980). *Qualitative evaluation methods.* Beverly Hills, CA: Sage.

Pelto, P.J., & Pelto, G.H. (1978). *Anthropological research: The structure of inquiry* (2nd ed.). Cambridge, England: Cambridge University Press.

Pennsylvania Association for Retarded Children v. Commonwealth of Pennsylvania, 343 F. Supp. 279 (E.D. Pa. 1972).

Pettigrew, T., Useem, E., Normand, C., & Smith, M. (1973, Winter). Busing: A review of the evidence. *Public Interest*, 88–118.

Piaget, J. (1932). *The moral judgment of the child.* London: Routledge & Kegan Paul.

Piuma, C., Halvorsen, A., Beckstead, S., Murray, C., & Sailor, W. (1983). *Project REACH Administrator's Manual (PRAM).* San Francisco: San Francisco State University; San Francisco Unified School District, (ERIC Document Reproduction Service No. ED 242 181).

Platt, M. (1984). *Displaying competence: Peer interaction in a group home for retarded adults* (Working Paper No. 29). Los Angeles: Socio-Behavioral Group, Mental Retardation Research Center, University of California-Los Angeles.

Pohland, P.A. (1972). Participant observation as a research methodology. *Studies in Art Education, 13*(3), 4–28.

Porter, R.H., Ramsey, B., Tremblay, A., Iaccobo, M., & Crawley, S. (1978). Social interactions in heterogenous groups of retarded and normally developing children: An observational study. In G.P. Sackett (Ed.), *Observing behavior* (Vol. 1; pp. 311–328). Baltimore: University Park Press.

Ragland, E., Kerr, M., Strain, P., (1978). Behavior of withdrawn autistic children. *Behavior Modification, 2*(4), 565–579.

REACH. (1981). *Languages spoken in the San Francisco Unified School District.* Unpublished memorandum.

REACH. (1983, June 15). [Parents' meeting on school site selection, Presidio Middle School, San Francisco]. Unpublished cassette recording.

Reinhold, R. (1986, July 1). New migrants, new debate. *International Herald Tribune*, p. 1.

Rist, R. (1970). Student social class and teacher expectations: The self-fulfilling prophecy in ghetto education. *Harvard Education Review 46*, 411–451.

Rosenbaum, J. (1976). *Making inequality: The hidden curriculum of high school tracking*. New York: John Wiley & Sons.

Rosenthal, R., & Rosnow, R. (1969). *Artifact in behavioral research*. New York: Academic Press.

Rubin, Z. (1980). *Children's friendships*. Cambridge, MA: Harvard University Press.

Ryan, K. (1986). The new moral education. *Phi Delta Kappan, 68*(4), 228–233.

Rynders, J.E., Johnson, J.T., Johnson, J.W., & Schmidt, B. (1980). Producing positive interaction among Down syndrome and nonhandicapped teenagers through cooperative goal structuring. *American Journal of Mental Deficiency, 85*(3), 268–273.

Sabsay, S., & Platt, M. (1985). *Weaving the cloak of competence* (Working Paper No. 32). Unpublished manuscript, Socio-Behavioral Group, Mental Retardation Research Center, School of Medicine, University of California-Los Angeles.

Sailor, W., & Guess, D. (1983). *Severely handicapped students: An instructional design*. Boston: Houghton Mifflin.

Sailor, W., Halvorsen, A., Anderson, J., Goetz, L., Gee, K., Doering, K., & Hunt, P. (1986). Community intensive instruction. In R.H. Horner, L.H. Meyer, & H.D.B. Fredericks (Eds.), *Education of learners with severe handicaps: Exemplary service strategies* (pp. 251–288). Baltimore: Paul H. Brookes Publishing Co.

Sailor, W., & Haring, N. (1977). Some current directions in education of the severely/multiply handicapped. *AAESPH Review, 2*, 3–23.

Sailor, W., Wilcox, B., & Brown, L. (1980). *Methods of instruction for severely handicapped students*. Baltimore: Paul H. Brookes Publishing Co.

Sarason, S., & Doris, J. (1979). *Educational handicap, public policy, and social history*. New York: Free Press.

Savin-Williams, R.C. (1980). Social interactions of adolescent females in natural groups. In H.C. Foot, A.J. Chapman, & J.R. Smith (Eds.), *Friendship and social relations in children* (pp. 343–364). London: John Wiley & Sons.

Scheerenberger, R.C. (1983). *A history of mental retardation*. Baltimore: Paul H. Brookes Publishing Co.

Schofield, J.W. (1982). *Black and white in school: Trust, tension, or tolerance?* New York: Praeger.

Schofield, J.W., & Sagar, A. (1979). The social context of learning in an interracial school. In R. Rist (Ed.), *Desegregated schools: Appraisals of an American experiment*. New York: Academic Press.

Schuler, L., & Goetz, L. (1981). The assessment of severe language disabilities: Communicative and cognitive considerations. *Analysis and Intervention in Developmental Disabilities, 1*, 333–346.

Schutz, R.P., Williams, W., Iverson, G.S., & Duncan, D. (1984). Social integration of severely handicapped students. In N. Certo, N. Haring, & R. York (Eds.), *Public school integration of severely handicapped students: Rational issues and progressive alternatives* (pp. 15–42). Baltimore: Paul H. Brookes Publishing Co.

Schwartz, G., & Merten, C. (1974). Social identity and expressive symbols: The meaning of an initiation ritual. In G. Spindler (Ed.), *Education and cultural process: Toward an anthropology of education*. New York: Holt, Rinehart, & Winston.

Selman, R., & Selman, A. (1979, October). Children's ideas about friendship: A new theory. *Psychology Today*.

SFUSD. (1981, May). *Local Plan for The California Master Plan For Special Education*. San Francisco: Author.

SFUSD. (1981, September). *Job Description for Teachers of the Severely Handicapped Involved in Project REACH*. Unpublished memorandum.

SFUSD. (1984). [Research authorization guidelines]. Unpublished document.

SFUSD Attendance Office. (1985). [Computerized daily attendance statistics]. Unpublished data.

SFUSD. (1985, January). *Excellence and equity: Creating opportunities in San Francisco high schools*. Unpublished memorandum.

Shapiro, E. (1973, November). Educational evaluation: Rethinking the criteria of competence. *School Review*, 523–549.

Sherif, M., Harvey, O.J., White, B.J., Hood, W.R., & Sherif, C.W. (1961). *Intergroup conflict and cooperation: The Robber's Cave experiment*. Norman: Institute of Group Relations, University of Oklahoma.

Shimara, N.K. (1983). Polarized socialization in an urban high school. *Anthropology & Education Quarterly, 14*, 109–130.

Sieber, T. (1979). Classmates as workmates: Informal peer activity in the elementary school. *Anthropology and Education Quarterly, 10*(4), 207–235.

Sizer, T.R. (1984). *Horace's compromise: The dilemma of the American high school*. Boston: Houghton Mifflin.

Snell, M.E. (1978). *Systematic instruction of the moderately and severely handicapped*. Columbus, OH: Charles E. Merrill.

Snyder, L., Apolloni, T., & Cooke, T.P. (1977). Integrated settings at the early childhood level: The role of nonretarded peers. *Exceptional Children, 43*, 262–266.

Sontag, E., Smith, J., & Certo, N. (Eds.). (1977). *Educational programming for the severely and profoundly handicapped*. Reston, VA: Council for Exceptional Children.

Spradley, J. (1979). *The ethnographic interview*. New York: Holt, Rinehart, & Winston.

Spradley, J. (1980). *Participant observation*. New York: Holt, Rinehart, & Winston.

Spradley, J., & Mann, B. (1975). *The cocktail waitress: Women's work in a male world*. New York: John Wiley & Sons.

Spradley, J., & McCurdy, D.W. (1972). *The cultural experience: Ethnography in a complex society*. Chicago: Science Research Associates.

Stainback, S., & Stainback, W. (1984). Broadening the research perspective in special education. *Exceptional Children, 50*(5), 400–488.

Stainback, S., & Stainback, W. (1985). *Integration of students with severe handicaps into regular schools*. Reston, VA: Council for Exceptional Children.

Stainback, W., & Stainback, S. (1981). A review of research on interaction between severely handicapped and nonhandicapped students. *The Journal of The Association for the Severely Handicapped, 6*(3), 23–29.

Stainback, W., & Stainback, S. (1982). The need for research on training nonhandicapped students to interact with severely retarded students. *Education and Training of the Mentally Retarded, 17*(1).

Strain, P. (1981). Foreword. *Exceptional Education Quarterly, 1*(4).

Strain, P., & Fox, J. (1981). Peer social initiations and the modification of social withdrawal: A review and future perspective. *Journal of Pediatric Psychology, 6,* 417–433.

Talented Refugee Kids of S.F.'s Tenderloin. (1985, May 27). *San Francisco Chronicle,* pp. 1, 14.

Theodorson, G.A. (1961). *Studies in Human Ecology.* Evanston, IL: Row, Peterson.

Thomas, D. (1982). *The Experience of handicap.* London: Methuen.

Thomason, J., & Arkell, C. (1980). Educating the severely and profoundly handicapped in the public schools: A side by side approach. *Exceptional Children, 47,* 114–122.

Trip downhill! (1985, April). *The West Wing,* p. 3.

United Nations. (1971). *Declaration of general and special rights of the mentally retarded.* New York: Author.

U.S. Department of Education (1980). *Summary of existing legislation relating to the handicapped.* Washington: Government Printing Office.

Voeltz, L.M. (1980). Children's attitudes toward handicapped peers. *American Journal of Mental Deficiency, 84*(3), 455–464.

Voeltz, L.M. (1981). Effects of structured interaction with severely handicapped peers on children's attitudes. *American Journal of Mental Deficiency, 86*(4), 380–390.

Voeltz, L.M., & Brennan, J. (1983). Analysis of interactions between nonhandicapped and severely handicapped peers using multiple measures. In J.M. Berg (Ed.), *Perspectives and progress in mental retardation, Vol. 1: Social, psychological and educational aspects.* Baltimore: University Park Press.

Voeltz, L.M., Hemphill, N.J., Brown, S., Kishi, G., Klein, R., Fruehling, R., Collie, J., Levy, G., & Kube, C. (1983). *The Special Friends Program: A trainer's manual for integrated school settings* (rev. ed.). Honolulu: University of Hawaii Department of Special Education.

Webb, E.J., Campbell, D.T., Schwartz, R., & Sechrest, L. (1966). *Unobtrusive measures: Nonreactive research in the social sciences.* Chicago: Rand McNally.

White, K.M., & Spiesman, J.C. (1968). *Adolescence.* Monterey, CA: Brooks/Cole.

Wilcox, B., & Bellamy, T. (1982). *Design of high school programs for severely handicapped students.* Baltimore: Paul H. Brookes Publishing Co.

Wilcox, K. (1982). Differential socialization in the classroom: Implications for equal opportunity. In G. Spindler (Ed.), *Doing the ethnography of schooling: Educational anthropology in action.* New York: Holt, Rinehart, & Winston.

Wolcott, H. (1975). Criteria for an ethnographic approach to research in schools. *Human Organization, 34,* 111–128.

Wolf, M. (1978). Social validity: The case for subjective measurement, or how applied behavior analysis is finding its heart. *Journal of Applied Behavior Analysis, 11,* 203–214.

Wolfensberger, W. (1972). *The principle of normalization in human services.* Toronto: National Institute on Mental Retardation.

Wolfensberger, W. (1985, October). *Normalization in the USA and Canada.* Paper presented at the First European Congress of the International League of Societies for Persons with Mental Handicaps, Hamburg, Federal Republic of Germany.

Yearbook Staff. (1985). *The Looks of Today.* San Francisco: Author.

Zetlin, A. (1986). *The learning status of mildly learning handicapped high school adults*

(Working Paper No. 34). Unpublished manuscript, Socio-Behavioral Group, Mental Retardation Research Center, School of Medicine, University of California-Los Angeles.

Zetlin, A., & Turner, J. (1985). Transition from adolescence to adulthood: Perspectives of mentally retarded individuals and their families. *American Journal of Mental Deficiency, 89*(6), 570–579.

A

Activities involving disabled and
nondisabled students
nature of, 141–142
types of, 75–80
classroom chores, 79
communication, 75
functional academics, 80–81
independent living, 75–76
leisure, 74–75
mobility, 76
school meals, 77–78
special events, 78
vocational training, 79–80
Administrators, *see* School staff
Affect, definition of, 176
Age-appropriateness
of interactions, 68
of social skills, 28–29
ARC-US, 17
Asian students, underinvolvement
in interactions of, 129–131,
158
Association for Retarded Citizens
of the United States
(ARC-US), 17
Attitudes
changing, 30–32

behavior change and, 31
components of, 30
effectiveness of, 32
negative, 39

B

Balance of power, definition of, 176
Bank-Mikkelson, N.E., 20
Best Friends, definition of, 70, 72
Blacks, disproportionate involve-
ment in interactions of,
127–129
Brown v. Board of Education, 21

C

California Master Plan for Special
Education, 2, 49
California Research Institute on the
Integration of Students with
Severe Disabilities, 7
Chapter I eligibility, 3
"Cholos," definition of, 69–70
Civil rights, 18, 21–22
Cliques
racial/ethnic, 38–39
same-sex, 39